Send My Roots Rain

�֍

Also by Megan McKenna

Not Counting Women and Children: Neglected Stories
from the Bible (Orbis)

Leave Her Alone

Blessings and Woes: The Beatitudes and the Sermon on the
Plain in the Gospel of Luke

Lent: The Daily Readings

Dancing with Angels: Selected Poems (Continuum)

Rites of Justice: The Sacraments and Liturgy as Ethical
Imperatives

Keepers of the Story: Oral Traditions in Religion

Parables: The Arrows of God

Angels Unawares

Mary: Shadow of Grace

Lent: The Sunday Readings

Advent, Christmas, and Epiphany

Mary, Mother of All Nations

Prophets: Words of Fire

Marrow of Mystery: Selected Poems (Sheed & Ward)

Justice Charity Community: Our Trinity on Earth
(Audio Cassette)

Advent, Christmas, and Epiphany: The Sunday Readings

Send My Roots Rain

A Spirituality of Justice and Mercy

Megan McKenna

DOUBLEDAY

New York   London   Toronto   Sydney   Auckland

Published by Doubleday
a division of Random House, Inc.
1540 Broadway, New York, New York 10036

Doubleday, and the portrayal of an anchor with a dolphin are
trademarks of Doubleday, a division of Random House, Inc.

Send My Roots Rain contains previously published selections
from works by Megan McKenna published by Orbis Books, and
Sheed & Ward & Continuum (Poems) Maryknoll, NY 10545-
0308. See final page for a complete list of credits.

Library of Congress Cataloging-in-Publication Data

McKenna, Megan.
  Send my roots rain : a spirituality of justice and mercy /
Megan McKenna.—1st ed.
    p. cm.
  1. Christianity and justice—Catholic Church. 2. Mercy.
3. Christian life—Catholic authors. I. Title.

BX1795.J87 M35 2003
242—dc21

                                              2002073816

ISBN 0-385-50237-0

Book design by Donna Sinisgalli

PRINTED IN THE UNITED STATES OF AMERICA

First Edition

1   3   5   7   9   10   8   6   4   2

For

Noel Woods, Glasgow

and

Mark O'Toole, London
Mary Mullins, Dublin
Dan O'Connell, Dublin
Bob Whiteside, Dublin

who make sure that my roots
get soaked with rain every spring

Contents

✢

Introduction

The underlying foundation of many of the selections in this book is buried deep in the concepts of justice and mercy. For many human beings these two concepts are difficult to hold together. We tend to think of them as opposing forces and actions. But the tradition of the Judeo-Christian world is that somehow mysteriously the Holy One holds them bound together, like intertwined roots of a great tree. And we who ascribe to the beliefs and practices of the writings of the Hebrew and Christian Scriptures of the Bible are called to spend our lives learning to integrate these powerful concepts within our own lives and in our relationships with one another. This is the wisdom that the prophet Jeremiah speaks about when he says:

> This is what Yahweh says: ". . . Blessed is the man [one] who puts his [their] trust in Yahweh and whose confidence is in him! . . . He [They] are like a tree planted by the water sending out its roots towards the stream. He [They] have no fear when the heat comes, his [their] leaves are always green; the year of drought is not problem and he [they] can always bear fruit."

(JER. 17:5, 7–8)*

*Quotes from the Bible come from both the New American Bible and from the Community Christian Bible.

Roots: the roots of the soul's vibrant inner life, the roots of thought, expression, and action in the life of a disciple, the roots of remembrance of a community—all these roots are found in the Word of God, the Scriptures of the New and Earlier Testaments of the Bible. The Scriptures are a root system for all those seeking to manifest and show forth the presence of the Holy One in the world. We literally die without being connected to this Word. Bernard of Clairvaux in ages past penned this reflection (The 4th Homily in Praise of the Blessed Virgin Mary, from *Bernard of Clairvaux* [Ramsey, N.J.: Paulist Press, 1997], p. 85):

> *Washed in the Word*
> *Only say the Word and receive the Word:*
> *Give Yours and receive God's.*
> *Breathe one fleeting word and*
> *embrace the everlasting Word.*

It is as though there is a breathing back and forth between the Word and those who hear, the One who whispers and cries out and the one whose ears and heart are open to living this interpenetrating life.

In the paradoxical richness of meaning found in such symbols, this Word is both written and oral, and in the history of the prophets, the promises, and the psalms it becomes a Person, the Messiah, and for Christians, the person of Jesus the Holy One of God. The church year begins with the Advent readings that herald whom we have long awaited and who continues to come into our world to dwell among us until the end of time. Isaiah's songs and dreams cry out to a weary world:

> *From the stump of Jesse a shoot will come forth:*
> *From his roots a branch will grow and bear fruit.*
> *The Spirit of the Lord will rest upon him—*
> *a Spirit of wisdom and understanding,*
> *a Spirit of counsel and power,*
> *a Spirit of knowledge and fear of the Lord . . .*

Not by appearances will he judge
nor by what is said must he decide,
but with justice he will judge the poor
and with righteousness decide for the meek.

(ISA. 11:1–4)

And the result of his coming will be a remarkable shift in the very consciousness of the earth and the way all things dwell together! This reading and what follows are saturated with justice and what flows forth
inevitably from its practice. The one line sings out: "The wolf will dwell
with the lamb" (Isa. 11:6). These words sear souls and reveal shining
truth. This person, this child who grows to be a human being among us,
brings knowledge of God and dwells with us. "The dream of the wolf and
the lamb as guests, the vicious and the tamed together, the child that
guides them, the food they share, and no harm anywhere seeps again into
a violent, wearying world. We need to remember that this dreaming
shapes our lives! The dream of no hurt, no harm, and security for all.
Food and no hunger, and a universal peace with justice, are a necessity
of life in this millennium, not an option" (excerpted from Megan
McKenna, "Who Will Summon the Dawn?" Pax Christi Advent Booklet,
2001). Word, Presence of God, and Person—all are the Root of justice
and mercy come to earth.

And those who are born of this Root, the incarnation of God as a human being, they too are called to live in the power of this Spirit, this
abundant water and moisture that is amazingly dew on the earth, underground well, torrents of rain, soft mist, and fountain in the desert. The
missionary Paul writes to his community in Rome: "When the first fruits
are consecrated to God, the whole is consecrated. If the roots are holy,
so will be the branches" (Rom. 11:16). One of the earliest prayers of the
church was based on this mystery and reality:

And now I kneel in the presence of the Father from whom every
family in heaven and on earth has received its name. May he

strengthen in you the inner self through his Spirit, according to the riches of his glory; may Christ dwell in your hearts through faith; may you be rooted and founded in love.

All of this so that you may understand with all the holy ones the width, the length, the height and the depth—in a word, that you may know the love of Christ which surpasses all knowledge, that you may be filled and reach the fullness of God.

Glory to God who shows his power in us and can do more than we could ask or imagine; glory to him in the Church and in Christ Jesus through all generations for ever and ever. Amen.

(EPH. 3:14–21)

These are the roots of our tradition, the Root of Jesse, the Son of Justice, the dawn of the Day Star named Jesus, who will be raised from the dead, who judges with justice and metes out mercy, as though the two hands danced together from one heart, one mind and spirit. And we who come after, who are rooted in Christ, have always found that our roots inevitably seek nourishment, encouragement, strengthening, and even pruning from the Word made flesh, the Scriptures, and the presence of God among us so that justice and mercy characterize our own lives and repair our worlds and remake our history in the image of the God of Just Mercy.

The title of this book is cut from a branch of the rich tradition of the poetry of Gerard Manley Hopkins, S.J., from his poem "Thou art indeed just, Lord, if I contend" (in *Poetry and Prose, Gerard Manley Hopkins,* ed. Walford Davies, Everyman [Rutland, Vt.: Charles E. Tuttle, 1998]). The entire last line, the prayer of a thirsty, desirous, and longing Christian, reads desperately, hopefully, passionately, "Mine, O thou Lord of life, send my roots rain." May all these gathered pieces of writing on the Word of God, on the spirituality and practice of justice and mercy, be borne like leaves from a tree on the wind of grace and bring small showers of fresh water to those who wait for the Rain of God and the Word of God to come true in the world.

Megan McKenna

PART I

Justice

※

Introduction

Let the heavens send righteousness like dew
and the clouds rain it down.
Let the earth open and salvation blossom,
so that justice also may sprout;
I, Yahweh, have created it.

—ISA. 45:8

There is a true, thought-provoking, and even shocking story about a man named Tom Wilson. The shock is a shock of grace. He lived in Terre Haute, Indiana, an ordinary man with a wife and children. And one day he was arrested for breaking and entering, burglary. He was identified in a police lineup, went to court, and in spite of pleas of innocence, was sentenced to jail for two to five years. He served more than two years of his sentence. He lost his house, job, reputation, and savings, and his family was devastated.

And then someone came forward and confessed to the crime that he had been prosecuted and punished for. Tom Wilson showed up at the sentencing hearing of the man now being judged. As the judge was about to rule on punishment, Wilson asked to speak to the court. Permission given, he told the courtroom that this man who stood before them in the docket wasn't the same man who robbed the house that night. He had traveled a road few take, to confession, repentance, and atonement—

restitution for his actions. He had come forward despite knowing that someone was serving time for his crime and that he did not have to worry about being found out.

What Wilson said next, no one was expecting. "Judge," he said, "I have already served more than two years, almost three, for this crime. Justice has been served in my time in jail. I ask the court to not punish this man in the name of the law, for what I have already done restitution for." The courtroom was stunned, as was the judge. And the judge ruled that Tom Wilson's words be applied as the court's ruling, letting the man go free, only asking that some atonement be made on behalf of society. When praised for his mercy, he responded that NO!, this wasn't mercy. This was justice, under the law.

Justice. The word has many meanings. In a court of law in the United States it is freely used as "equal opportunity under the existing law, specifically in the areas of jobs, housing, education, etc." For many people, justice is whatever they personally consider fair—it can be as arbitrary and changeable as stock market value, at the whim of circumstances and history, worth one thing one day and altogether another the next day. For others, it can be explained by such catchphrases as "an eye for an eye and a tooth for a tooth." And it all too easily can slide into vengeance, self-righteous demands, racism, or revenge and retaliation on an emotional level. But religiously in the Judeo-Christian tradition, justice always looks more like mercy than anything we would label justice.

The ancient prophets continually cried out for justice from God because their experience and the experience of the poor were sadly bereft of it. Jeremiah the prophet cried out:

> Yahweh, you are always right
> when I complain to you;
> nevertheless, where is your justice?
> Why do the wicked prosper?
> And why do traitors live in peace?
> You plant them and they take root;

they grow and are fruitful;
they honor you with words
but their heart is far from you.

(JER. 12:1–2)

In fact, this prayer from centuries before the coming of Jesus is the basis for Gerard Manley Hopkins' first verse of his poem "Thou art indeed just, Lord, if I contend." His prayer reads:

Thou art indeed just, Lord, if I contend
With thee; but sir, so what I plead is just.
Why do sinners' ways prosper? And why must
Disappointment all I endeavor end?

It seems this question is a perennial one, torn out of experience and the injustice of the earth, and every age demands an answer once again, hoping that God will intervene and bring true justice to bear on history's violence. Isaiah, the prophet of justice, builds the bridge between justice and mercy. The bridge is peace.

> When at last the spirit is poured on us from on high, then will the desert become a garden, and this garden will be free as a fallow land.
> Justice will dwell in the wilderness; and in the fertile land, righteousness. Justice will bring about peace; justice will produce calm and security forever.

(ISA. 32:15–17)

What makes for peace is rooted in justice. Contemporary popes have written short, pithy lines such as "If you want peace, work for justice" (Paul VI) and "If you want peace, go to the poor" (John Paul II). Justice, peace, and the poor are the strands of a single braid that ties all together in the world and ties us in turn to God. The definition of justice I most often use is this: justice is love expressed in terms of sheer human need: food, water, clothing, shelter, medicine and health care, education, human rights and freedom, hope for a future for one's children, freedom from fear and violence, the dignity of work, and participation in society and history. Our lives are made of justice. Our moral and ethical choices are first of all about justice. Our relationships must be steeped in justice, or terror and violence begin to reign on earth and destruction inevitably follows.

Jesus' prayer the Our Father prays about justice in imperative, demanding terms that reveal right relationships between God and us and one another. It says, "Forgive us our debts as we forgive those who are in debt to us"—a simple demand that posits everlasting judgment as a result of what is practiced here and now. There are two words for "debt" in Aramaic (the language of Jesus) and in Hebrew. Both are found in this line of the prayer. The first is a debt that is unimaginable, unforgivable, because of the magnitude, depth, and offense against the one who has power and goodness. The second word is the debt that is minuscule, minor, and in terms of actual monetary worth, nickel-and-dime. This is the primary relationship of justice: our debt to God is indescribable and unforgivable, yet it is freely written off, and our debts to one another in light of our indebtedness to God are nothing at all. More to the point is the root of Jesus' prayer: God forgives us as we forgive all others. That is justice, according to God the Father, Son, and Spirit, the Trinity.

We as Christians are called to be the children of justice. And it is Isaiah once again who is clearest in the demands of those who claim to live in covenant with God. As with all the other prophets, the coming of the kingdom of justice and peace, the care of the poor, and the true honor and worship of God are a three-pronged arrow. It is all of a piece. Listen!

See the fast that pleases me:
breaking the fetters of injustice

and unfastening the thongs of the yoke,
setting the oppressed free
and breaking every yoke.
Fast by sharing your food with the hungry,
bring to your house the homeless,
clothe the man you see naked
and do not turn away from your own kin.

Then will your light break forth as the dawn
and your healing come in a flash.
Your righteousness will be your vanguard,
the Glory of Yahweh your rearguard.
Then you will call and Yahweh will answer,
you will cry and he will say, I am here.

(ISA. 58:6–9)

This is the heart line of our religion, the rope that pulls us to safety and security, the lifeline of the community that is described in the early church as "see as those Christians love one another, there are no poor among them!" *(Didache)*. The Psalms echo what we are to know even here on earth in our lives and what the dream of the God who has made all things is for creation.

Love and faithfulness have met;
righteousness and peace have embraced.
Faithfulness will reach up from the earth
while justice bends down from heaven.
The Lord will give what is good,
and our land will yield its fruit.
Justice will go before him,
and peace will follow along his path.

(PS. 85:11–14)

In the older translations, the second line of this passage is even more shocking and intimate: justice and peace have kissed! This is the way things were created to be, in the beginning. God kissed Adam into existence, pouring Spirit into his mouth, and all the children of God learned to kiss back in the life, death, and resurrection of Jesus, the beloved child of God. We are all, in the words of the Irish and other Europeans, "kissing cousins." Without this foundation of justice, mercy remains illusive, ethereal, and a naive concept that is hard to experience personally and as a people. Mercy only makes sense if one knows what justice is and what it demands and how it frees for limitless possibilities for all. The prayer for justice unites us to the Son/Sun of Justice, Jesus the Lord.

From Parables: The Arrows of God

Introduction

For many of us, the most familiar parts of Scripture are the parables that Jesus used in his teaching. To Jesus' audiences, the parables covered common ground; the people knew about sheep and shepherds, lost coins, vineyards, unjust judges, wayward children. The parables were easy for his hearers to relate to, because they dealt with practical, down-to-earth matters.

The parables are easy for us too, at least on the surface. We've heard them for years. Given the title of one of the parables, most of us can tell the story. We know the tale of the prodigal son, the one lost sheep, the seed that fell on good ground, and all the rest. But we may need to hear these meaning-filled and provocative stories again and again. When we open our ears and our hearts, we may indeed end up acknowledging that for all our familiarity with the parables, we have never taken them into our hearts.

The fact is that these seemingly simple stories are multifaceted views into inner truth and reality. They provoke basic questions: What is our treasure? What kind of ground do we provide for the seed? What price are we willing to pay for the kingdom? Often they turn on a phrase, one pivotal point. And they seldom end as we would expect—or in ways that allow us to be comfortable with ourselves.

We need to keep the reality reflected in the parables before us. And we don't have to get too psychological, spiritual, personal—or even theological—to understand the reality of these stories. We do need open ears and open minds and open hearts. For the parables don't simply recount a clever tale. They start out that way, grounded in the most commonplace experiences and locations, but then they jerk the rug from under us, turning our world upside down and challenging some of our most basic assumptions about ourselves, our neighbors, our world, our God. They grab our hearts and minds and twist them into a new position, a fresh awareness. And ultimately, of course, the insights and enlightenment they provide encourage us—drive us!—to change our way of being human, of being Christian.

The parables are all about justice and mercy. The two are entwined in Jesus' revelation of the kingdom of his Father. They reveal the truth of the heavenly reign and challenge us to live in the now of that kingdom, the now we know in one special way in the least of our brothers and sisters. Jesus is adamant on the Father's option for the poor. The parables are prophetic and demanding. They call us to conversion and humility—and acknowledgment that we are given much and must return much, that our lives belong to the kingdom and to God, practiced in our sharing with others.

Parables draw us in, softly and with subtlety. Then they hit us with the sledgehammer of revelation. They are revolutionary, subverting reality and undermining the existing structures and systems and relationships and attitudes—all the trappings of the status quo that keep the least among us in slavery and without hope while we look the other way, choosing to be oblivious to their claim upon us. "Listen, you who have ears to hear."

Parables point to the kingdom. They are, indeed, the "arrows of God." They pierce us and make us painfully aware of our need to change the way we relate to ourselves, others, and God. We look—we see. This is how we must live in God's kingdom. We are called, and we know ourselves called.

What kind of parable are we? What can we become? Perhaps the answer is in a story.

✳ *Once upon a time there was a king who ruled a small kingdom. It wasn't great, and it wasn't really known for its resources or people. But the king did have a diamond, a great perfect diamond that had been in his family for generations. He kept it on display for all to see and appreciate. People came from all over the country to admire and gaze at it. Word of it spread to neighboring countries, and more people came to look at it. Soon the people felt the diamond was theirs; it gave them a sense of pride, of dignity, of worth.*

One day a soldier came to the king with the news that, although no one had touched the diamond, for it was guarded night and day, the diamond was cracked. The king ran to see, and sure enough there was a crack right through the middle of the diamond.

Immediately the king summoned all the jewelers of the land and had them look at the diamond. One after another they examined it and gave the bad news to the king: the diamond was irredeemably flawed. The king was crushed, as were the people. Somehow they felt they had lost everything.

Then out of nowhere came an old man who claimed to be a jeweler. He asked to see the diamond. After examining it, he looked up and confidently told the king, "I can fix it. In fact, I can make it better than it was before." The king was shocked and a bit leery. But the old man said, "Give me the jewel, and in a week I'll bring it back fixed."

Now, the king was not about to let the stone out of his sight, even if it was ruined, so he gave the old man a room, all the tools and food and drink he needed, and he waited. The whole kingdom waited. It was a long week.

At the end of the week the old man appeared with the stone in his hand and gave it to the king. The king couldn't believe his eyes. It was magnificent. The old man had fixed it, and he had made it even better than it was before! He had used the crack that ran through the middle of the stone as a stem and carved an intricate, full-blown rose, leaves, and thorns into the diamond. It was exquisite.

The king was overjoyed and offered the old man half of his kingdom. He had taken something beautiful and once perfect and improved upon it! But the old man refused in front of everyone, saying, "I didn't do that at all. What I did was to take something flawed and cracked at its heart and turn it into something beautiful."

That is, of course, the only thing any of us can ever hope to do: take something that is cracked and flawed at its heart and turn it into a diamond rose for God. But we must remember that someone else carves us and that we are meant to do the same for strangers, neighbors, and friends so that there will be a bouquet of roses at the end of time.

The Compassionate One

Who are our neighbors? Our neighbors are those in need of compassion. Our neighbors are those who are the victims of injustice, violence, robbery, who are placed or find themselves in life-threatening positions, stripped of dignity. Our neighbors are those who need ongoing commitments from us and others to get them back on the way, back to normal lives. Our neighbors are those who reveal God: outsiders, "ditch folk," "Samaritans," enemies, other races, heretics, criminals. Our neighbors are those who befriend the poor, speak out against injustice, do mercy, critique the system, and, inevitably, join the victims in the ditch. Our neighbors are those who do not validate our behaviors and choices and reasoning but challenge us to change, to look again, and not to use our religion to manipulate our reality into a better position or place with God. Our neighbors are those who remind us forcibly that society's givens do not help those most in need and sometimes create the environment that produces as many victims as there are those who can take advantage of the system. Our neighbors are the painful, frightening presences who remind us of the violence, lawlessness, and hate in our society and who afford us the chance to bring hope into those situations.

Commitment to the poor and contemplation lies in a gradual discovery that no matter how many times we get into the ditch, no matter how many singular acts of mercy we do, it is the system and the structures that perpetuate the misery and contribute to the violence. Society keeps adding to the victims, stripping people of self-worth and value by laws and attitudes, robbing, beating, and leaving many half-dead in the ditch. Structural injustice and violence are the root causes of individual problems. This is the dark night of the senses and purgation, which results in a lifestyle and spirituality that is made up of the acts of mercy, asceticism sharing the suffering, the pain, and the disease of others. It means reaching out to touch the other person; it means forgetting self and consciously separating ourselves from the structures that cause so much inhumanity to others.

This awareness of the enormity of evil, of sin and its structural as well as individual character, leads to another kind of anger and rage: the prophet's rage. And it leads into the dark night of the soul: the recognition of the nearness of evil, the enormity of the struggle, and the terrible price of dignity, liberation, and salvation.

Yet this is also illumination and the choice to accompany, the choice to get into the ditch and stay with the victims. It is the time to push our own privilege, as Mary did, and speak the truth on behalf of those who have no voice and walk with and break bread with them. It is the choice to sit at the feet of the poor, with Jesus. This is the better part: to become a disciple with Jesus, who will be left to die as a criminal on a hill outside the city.

This choice makes one a prophet publicly or privately, seeing and knowing sin and yet seeing at the same time that it is the victims of evil who will save us all. They are more capable than we are of standing in opposition to evil and sin because they have experienced its power in their own flesh and lives. This choice begins a deep conversion to humility, a call to serve others in body and soul with our own weaknesses, lacks, and failures, our own poverty. It is a choice to stand outside, against oppression, and begin to bear the cross within our own flesh on behalf of and with others who have no choice. It is an enduring way, a commitment to the way of the cross, a faithful acceptance of the ditch, and an awareness that God lies in the ditch with the victims.

Resurrection life is a pledge of life as an act of hope that makes us one both with God and with our neighbors. This is the way the kingdom comes: in mercy, in compassion and love, in siding with the ditch folk, with Jesus, with the Scriptures that call us to obey the presence of God in our midst. If we do this, then we will know resurrection life, the eternal life, even now.

This is the way of hospitality, of making space for God and others in our lives, of making the world and the earth a more habitable place to live. It is the way of putting ourselves out so that others may enter into the kingdom.

A story reminds us of the depth and extent to which Jesus practiced compassion himself and calls us to practice it with him. It is a story from the Hindu tradition, and it is called "The Guru and the Mantra of Life and Death."

※　*Once upon a time there was a teacher, a guru who had many followers. They came from all over to listen, to learn wisdom and enlightenment, and to be liberated from their desires and needs. There were classes and one-on-one apprenticeships. At the end of the students' teaching the master would send them into the world to share their learning and knowledge with others as masters in their own right. And just before they left, he would give them a gift: the mantra of life and death. Phrase by phrase he would teach them until they had learned it by heart. Then he would tell them that as long as they said this mantra faithfully, they would be* blessed: that its power would give them insight and clarity and allow them to discern the truth when all around them were lies and shadows; that its power would keep them from despair and give them hope in the midst of misery and hopelessness; that its power would strengthen their faith and one day save their souls and give them everlasting life. The disciples were grateful and humbled by the gift. Then he warned them never to teach anyone else the mantra; it was for them alone, those who had been enlightened.

And so for years students finished their studies, were given the mantra, and went out into the world to share their wisdom and pray their mantra in secret.

One day a young man came to the master, ready to go into the world. He too was taught the mantra and humbled by the enormity of the gift he was given. However, when the master warned him not to share the mantra with anyone, he asked why. The master looked long and hard at him: "If you share this with others, then what it was to do for you will be handed over to them. And you will live in darkness even when the light is all around you. You will know only despair and misery of body and soul all your life. You will stumble over the truth and be confused endlessly. Worst of all, you will lose your faith, and you will lose your soul. You will be damned forever."

The disciple turned white and shook visibly and nodded and left the master's presence. He was troubled in spirit. Finally he decided what he had to do. He went to the nearest large city and gathered the multitudes about him, teaching and enthralling them with his stories and wisdom. Then he taught them the mantra, line by line, phrase by phrase, just as his master had taught him. There was a hush, and people left whispering the mantra to themselves.

A number of the master's disciples were in the crowd, and they were horrified at the man's actions. He had disobeyed the master. He had betrayed his community. He had given away the wisdom and the gift to the ignorant and the unenlightened. They immediately went back to the master and told him what had happened.

They asked him, "Master, are you going to punish him for what he has done?"

The master looked at them sadly and said, "I do not have to. He will be punished terribly. He knew what his fate would be if he shared the mantra of life with those who were not enlightened. For him it has become the mantra of death. He will live in darkness and despair, without hope or knowledge of the truth. He will live isolated, alone, without comfort or faith, and he will die terribly and lose even his own soul. How could I possibly punish him? He knew what he was choosing."

And with those words, the old master rose and gathered his few belongings and began to walk away.

"Master," one disciple asked, "where are you going?"

And the master looked at all of them sadly and spoke, "I am going to that man who gave away my gift of the mantra of life and death."

"Why?" they chorused.

"Because," he said, "out of all my students, he alone learned wisdom and compassion. Now that man is my master."

And he left them to follow the man who walked now in darkness and despair, who had chosen compassion over wisdom and knowledge.

Our God broke all the laws, shattered all the boundaries, and turned over all the understandings of religion, of obedience, and of love in sending us the Compassionate One, Jesus of Nazareth, the Crucified One who is the mantra of life and death. This choice of compassion and pity is what opens the door to resurrection and hope. It is the better part. And nothing can take it away from those who have been touched by the mercy of God.

The First and the Last

Jesus' parables affected those who heard them, and they are supposed to affect us. They are intended to stun us into reevaluating our positions, our enemies, our love and practice of justice.

So what is the criterion for justice in the Christian Scriptures? All the parables seek to answer that question. What is it to be among the children of God, the brothers and sisters of Jesus, the Christians? Does our God deal with us justly or mercifully? If we were all to die today in an earthquake or nuclear disaster, and we all came before the Son of Man and were seen clearly and truthfully for who we are, would we want this Son of Man to deal with us justly or mercifully? This question works its way throughout all the parables.

Do we want God to deal with us mercifully if it means being merciful to others in our lifetime? Or would we rather God deal with us justly, as justly as we deal with others in our lifetime? Mercy goes beyond justice. Although we want God to deal with us mercifully, we usually seek justice for all other people. We begin with justice and hope our way toward mercy. But we *will* be judged as we judge and do justice to others.

For the prophets, justice is one thing; justice in love, reconciliation, and the cross is another matter. This latter form of justice is developing in liberation theologies throughout the universal church as its members are faced with persecution and struggle.

So what is justice in Christian terms? Let's look at one of Matthew's parables, the parable of the laborers in the vineyard, for a look at relationships in the kingdom. We need to remember that for Jesus relationships were important—blood relationships and, more so, relationships created by the waters of baptism and belief. When Jesus was approached and told that his mother and brothers and sisters were outside waiting for him, he responded by looking around at his disciples and asking, "Who is my mother? Who are my brothers and sisters?" Then he pointed to his disciples and said, "Look! Here are my mother, my brothers and my sisters. Whoever does the will of my Father in Heaven is my brother, my sister, and my mother" (Matt. 12:48–50; Mark 3:31–35; Luke 8:19–21).

The kingdom is relational, binding beyond ancestry and family, binding in obedience and response to the word of God and the blood of the cross and Eucharist. Intimacy in the kingdom of God comes from hearing and obeying the will of God and making it come true, incarnating it in history now. Mary is holy, a disciple, not only or primarily because she is the mother of God but because she has heard the word of God, believed in it, and put it into practice, incarnating in her very flesh and blood. That is why in the Eastern churches she is called Theotokos, the God-bearer. She brings the Word and she bears the presence of God in Jesus to the earth, and we are called to follow in her footsteps of belief and discipleship. We are to bear God to one another; this is what informs the society that Jesus announces and describes in the parables.

A landowner went out early to hire workers for his vineyard. The workers accepted the salary offered, a piece of silver for the day, and he sent them to his vineyard.

He went out again at about nine in the morning, and as he saw men idle in the square, he said to them: "You too, go to my vineyard and I will pay you what is just." So they went.

The owner went out at mid-day and again at three in the afternoon, and he did the same. Finally he went out at the last working hour and he saw others standing there. So he said to them: "Why do you stay idle the whole day?" They answered: "Because no one has hired us." The master said: "Go and work in my vineyard."

When evening came the owner of the vineyard said to his manager: "Call the workers and pay them their wage, beginning with the last and ending with the first." Those who had come to work at the last hour turned up and were given a denarius each (a silver coin). When it was the turn of the first, they thought they would receive more. But they, too, received a denarius each. So, on receiving it, they began to grumble against the landowner.

They said: "These last hardly worked an hour, yet you have treated them as us who have endured the day's burden and heat." The owner said to them: "Friend, I have not been unjust with you. Did we not agree on a denarius a day? So take what is yours and go. I want to give to the last the same as I give to you. Do I not have the right to do as I please with my money? Why are you all so envious when I am kind?"

So will it be: the last will be first, the first will be last.

(MATT. 20:1–16)

This parable of the vineyard owner and his workers and foreman centers on the description of the reign of God. Any reign is about power, including God's reign. The reign of the United States has to do with power, with violence, with stating who we are unequivocally for others' benefit and with authority. What is the reign of the United States like? I studied this parable with a group of international students only days after the United States sent a retaliatory force against Iraq. This was a show of force, intended to teach a lesson and to assert indignation; but it was also a warning of what could come upon them. But God's reign is about power, authority, and an absolute *abhorrence* of violence in history; it is about how those who submit to God's reign practice peace and justice.

The reign of England, from the royal family and the court down through the lords and ladies and the people of the realm, is about class and hierarchy, behavior and place. The reign of God is about hierarchy too, about structure and class, but the structure is upside down, with the masses of people, the sparrows, the poor, the lilies of the field, holding the power. The power base is in the lowly ones. The more power one has in this reign, this realm, the more one is required to become a servant to others. It is a class of downward mobility in imitation of Jesus, who came down from heaven to become human and dwell among us in the small ones.

Those of us submitting to the reign of God are called to reflect the values and morality of that kingdom. In a reign everything is political. And this is no different in the kingdom of heaven. Liturgy, spirituality, ministry, catechetics, religious community, the structures of the church—all are political and reveal how power operates among those in the community of God, the Body of Christ. That is why the prophet Amos critiques all the countries around Israel, ripping them to shreds and saving the best until last: Israel. The kingdom is about authority and discipline, learned from others and sensed inwardly as the core of belief and practice. There is a story about this concept of kingdom:

Once upon a time there was a boy who loved horses. He got a job working with horses at a stable, and he spent his time grooming them, exercising them, and riding them. It was fantastic, like being in heaven, for him.

One day he was sitting on the fence watching a trainer with one of the thoroughbreds on the track. The owner of the stables and track was standing beside him watching the trainer put the horse through his paces. First he'd let the reins out, and the horse would bolt, running like the wind. Then he would pull the reins as tight as he could, and the horse would almost stop in its tracks. Then he would ease up and let the horse run free, and again pull the reins back hard. He did this again and again until the horse was dancing, prancing, and lathered in a thick sweat.

The boy watched the horse and trainer, watched the reins, the bridle, and the bit, and became more and more angry. Finally he turned to the owner and said, "That man is abusing that horse. He is not thinking about the horse and its possibilities and capabilities but only about his own power and how far he can push that horse,

*how much control he has over that animal. He's not thinking
about the horse and its limitations."*

*The owner did not say anything for a moment, and then he
looked at the young man and said, "It's obvious that you know
nothing about horses or, for that matter, about discipline."*

The boy did a double take. "What do you mean?" he said.

*The owner replied, "A good horse, like that thoroughbred,
runs at even the intimation of a command. The difference between
a horse and a thoroughbred like this one is the trainer, who triggers
the internal authority of the horse. The horse does not run to win
or even in obedience to the trainer. The horse knows the trainer,
and the trainer knows that the horse runs because it is a horse. It's
obvious that you know very little about horses, about discipline or
obedience. What a pity."*

*And with that, the owner left the boy on the fence, watching
the horse from a distance.*

Our reactions to the parable and to the story are usually negative.
The reign of God is about authority, about discipline, about commands
and obedience. Do we run at the very shadow of authority, at the intimation of a command? If so, whose? Do we respond like this? Do we
obey anyone? Daniel Berrigan says, "I have spent my whole life looking
for someone to obey." He also says, "If you are going to be a Christian,
you'd better look good on wood." These two statements are intimately
connected. Our reactions to the parable and to the words of Daniel
Berrigan are similar. We want the kingdom to come, and we want to be
a part of it, but we could do without the discipline, the authority, and the
obedience. But the reign of God does have to do with reins, checks, and
holds that trigger our internal discipline, that touch the essence of who
we are and why we run, because we are human.

John the Baptist

Listen to me, O islands,
pay attention, peoples from distant lands.
Yahweh called me from my mother's womb;
he pronounced my name before I was born.
He made my mouth like a sharpened sword.
He hid me in the shadow of his hand.
He made me into a polished arrow
set apart in his quiver.

(ISA. 49:1–2)

Isaiah speaks of one who is the servant of Yahweh, one who will gather the remnant of the people. This description can be either of Jesus the Suffering Servant or of John the Baptizer, the cousin and forerunner of Jesus the prophet. It is often used for the feast of John, June 24.

In Mark's Gospel we see this prophet-preacher who makes his appearance in the desert, warning the people and announcing the necessity of a baptism of repentance for the forgiveness of sins. He is the messenger of advent, of the long-awaited one hidden in the midst of the people, hidden in God's quiver. John, the first arrow, is out and on his way, straight to the heart of the people of Israel and all peoples who wait for hope, for transformation, and for the good news of God baptizing us with the Spirit, with fire and truth. And people come from the country of Judea and even from the city of Jerusalem to confess their sins in the river Jordan. But even as John baptizes them, he is clear: "After me there will come one who is mightier than I am; as for me I am not worthy to bend down and untie his sandals. I have baptized you with water, but he will baptize you in the Holy Spirit." (Mark 1:7–8).

This is John, and Isaiah's reading can be called John's Magnificat, the praise of God through John's life, just as Mary's Magnificat is praise of God through her life. Isaiah begins with a lengthy description of John and how God sees him—as a polished arrow. The immediacy, once loosed and set free, cannot be retrieved, brought back. John points, even when not in motion. Look! He points to another. To Jesus, the Lamb of God, and he sends his own disciples away, after the one he points out (John 1). Until the moment John appears, he has been hidden in the quiver of God, in the desert, but perhaps more hidden in the heart of God. God uses John the way an archer uses an arrow, to pierce the hearts of the hunted. God hunts his people Israel with the force and directedness of John, with an arrow sent straight to the heart of people, to call them to repentance. A sharp sword or arrow, when honed, will go straight through to the bone with no pain until afterward. It reveals, opens up. John will be that laying bare for Israel. His words and his actions will cut straight through flesh and bone with clarity and sureness, and only afterward will the pain of that revelation be felt.

Yet the power of John is nothing in comparison to the one to come: Jesus, his cousin. John is born of an old barren woman in the usual human ways, but Jesus is born of a young virgin without sexual intervention. This is the way prepared for the new creation, where nothing will be impossible. It prepares us to believe in the resurrection of this child, once destroyed by others. These others, those who do not believe in dreams and portents, seek from the very beginning to kill both children. Eventually they succeed, only to be tripped up by God.

John teaches us the art of faith-dancing. We first meet him in an announcement: "And you, my child, shall be called prophet of the Most High, for you shall go before the Lord and prepare the way for him" (Luke 1:76). He dances before God, as David danced before the Ark of the Covenant in worship and delight at the presence of the Lord hidden in the midst of the people; for when Mary with Jesus in her womb comes to visit John's mother, Elizabeth, John stirs. This is the one he points to, and he kicks and leaps in recognition and begins the dance of the new kingdom of the meek and the humble and the poor. The dance begins with an old woman, a young girl, and two yet-to-be-born children on a hill outside Jerusalem. As John grows up, he dances off to the desert to live hidden in the hand of God, hidden in God's quiver. When John makes his appearance and preaches a new way of living—the turn-around dance step—he lures others into the waters of the Jordan, into the waters of baptism. He dances the prophet's and leader's dance much as many folk dance down aisles in church to come to the altar and commit themselves to hope, to a fresh start, to a new life of grace and freedom with others.

John is the first parable, the first surprise, the first and the greatest in the old ways and the least in the new paths to peace and justice. In this kingdom whose king John is not worthy to bend before and offer homage to or even untie his sandals, the greatest is the least, the poor, the sheep, the lost child and coin, the widow's mite, the old woman mother, the lowly virgin, the dangerous children. These are the prophets of the testament of Jesus, the words of hope, the flesh and blood of justice. Even John's work and world are turned upside down and inside out. In prison, this parable of freedom from sin and evil learns what liberation will be. The arrow is no longer needed, for the archer, the one who wields the double-edged sword of tender regard and justice, is no longer hidden in the quiver of God but present in the people's midst. Hope has come, and the intimations of incarnation, of life's strength in the face of murder and unnecessary death and resurrection, are here. These are Jesus' words to John; they comfort him in prison. The new steps in the dance are being tried out in the cities and towns of Judea.

And so John's life ends with a dance, one of the old dances of power and intrigue and dishonesty and rage, and John loses his head. Another dances for the old regime of kings and queens and politics and sex for power, and John, the dancer, is dead. This parable, this first twist of the new times asks us if we dance for the kingdom. Do we dance for preparation, for justice and hope, for Jesus and the Spirit, or do we dance for another in power?

John is the least in the kingdom of Jesus, because he recognizes Jesus but does not know him. He sends others to Jesus to ask if he is the one. John must change his mind about Jesus and trust in him, believing that he is the one long awaited. John dies, with his death forcing Jesus' hand and moving him into the forefront. John lives and dies passionately devoted to only one thing: being the polished arrow, the sharpened sword of the Lord held in his hand, used to change the direction of history, to focus attention on another, and to stir all fears attached to power and might. John lives to bring change, altercations, and to rekindle a hope that had died into ashes.

I once watched in fascination, awe and near terror as a friend, a Native American, took down a deer with one arrow. It thrust through skin, flesh, sinew and bone. The arrow had been polished until it was razor sharp. Suddenly I knew John the Baptist—his power, his meaning, his utter singularity and singleheartedness, the very strength of God gathered, loosed, unleashed into the world and set at us. We, the people of God, were and are the target, targeted for repentance, for justice, for the maturation of the Spirit, for hope.

John, the arrow, the first parable of Jesus' reign, asks, "At whom are we aimed? To whose heart are we sent? Who is aiming at ours? What are we meant to be? For whom are we kept by God? When is our time to be launched into history and the hope of the poor? Where are the arrows concealed and hidden now?" John, this arrow, was hidden in the mind of God for generations, then in his old mother's womb for nine months, then in the desert of Israel and lastly in a jail cell. This arrow, this man, was named by God before birth, wrested away from kin, family, blood ties, belonging only to earth, to history and the fullness of time, born only to turn and face the Christ, even in his womb, recognizing him and rising up and dancing.

Nietzsche once said, "Only those who can contain within themselves the pressure and the chaos of tension can give birth to a dancing star." John the Baptist teaches us all to live with that pressure and chaos and give birth to the light of the world. John, the arrow, the dancer, the child who goes before the Lord with words of repentance and forgiveness and wild fire, the prophet of hope and what is to come, is the parable of preparation. Nothing is as it appears to be, and nothing will ever be the same. John is a practice parable to get us used to the stories that Jesus will tell.

Come now, it's time to practice being taken off guard, questioned, being taught new dance steps, and falling finally into the outstretched arms of God.

The Lost Sheep and the Shepherd

"What did you think of this? "If a man has a hundred sheep and one of them strays, will he not leave the ninety-nine on the hills and go and look for the stray one?" (Matt. 18:12). No way! Leave ninety-nine sheep to marauders, thieves, wolves? No way! We might notice the one and curse silently about the stupidity of the dumb sheep, but we are not about to go traipsing off and leave the others all alone. But Jesus does go off, leaving all the others, and eventually does find the one that led him on a wandering chase through briars and brambles, ravines and rocks. And he rejoices more over this dumb sheep than all the others he left behind! The world does not operate like this! It operates in the exact opposite way! That is the heart of the issue. Jesus and Jesus' God are shepherds of whole peoples in history. They shepherd all the masses of people in the world's nations with the Spirit to find the wandering and lost and those who don't stay with the ones in the structures. Just as one sparrow's loss does not go unnoticed, no straying sheep is abandoned, and not one of these least among the earth's peoples is forgotten or uncared for. God rejoices over these little ones, these lost ones, these least and forgotten more than all the others who, left to themselves, took care of themselves.

Do we want God to deal with us justly or mercifully? When God looks at us and thinks about justice and mercy, what is God thinking about? What does the justice of God look like when God looks at us, and what does the mercy of God look like when God looks at us? What is the difference?

Justice in the Jewish community is strong and encompasses relations and actions among themselves as light to the nations. In the Christian community, in the "good news," this justice is fulfilled, completed, expanded to encompass all nations, all peoples, even and especially our enemies and those who have done us harm. It becomes deeper and broader, more involving and intense. Mercy also evolves. Justice in the early Jewish law was "an eye for an eye and a tooth for a tooth," which at least limited what could be done in response or retaliation to wrong. It put limits on reactions. But justice is much more than that: "You are to love the Lord your God with all your heart and all your strength and all your soul and all your mind and you are to love your neighbor as yourself." (Mark 12:33) Justice includes the worship and honor of God and its parallel behavior toward others. Jesus extends justice among his community members to the right treatment of all. Matthew, in Jesus' Sermon on the Mount, states it most clearly:

> You have heard that it was said: *Love your neighbor and hate your enemy.* But this I tell you: Love your enemies, and pray for those who persecute you, so that you may be children of your Father in Heaven. For he makes his sun rise on both the wicked and the good, and he gives rain to both the just and the unjust.
>
> If you love those who do love you, what is special about that? Do not even tax collectors do as much? And if you are friendly only to your friends, what is so exceptional about that? Do not even the pagans do as much? For your part you shall be righteous and perfect in the way your heavenly Father is righteous and perfect.
>
> (MATT. 5:43–48)

Justice tells us how to deal with evil as well as how to respond to the good or the innocent or the least among us.

And mercy in the earlier tradition? God says, You are my chosen people. I will make a covenant with you and I will be faithful and keep you in my heart and I will come after you again and again, leading you back to my heart and teaching you faithfulness through the law and the prophets and my choosing you always. Mercy in the Christian Scriptures says, Now *all* are chosen, the least among us, the poor, the widow, the orphan, the illegal alien, the outcast, the slave, the servant, the undesirables, the untouchables, the enemy. All these reveal the extent and depth of God's mercy, given to them first. Mercy will be extended to us by how we treat these least among us. Mercy assumes that justice has been done. The practice of justice is a response to the experience of God's mercy in our lives. We begin to live and to hunger and thirst for justice for all when we experience the reality that God has never dealt with us primarily in the form of justice but has been merciful to us from the very beginning—thank God!

If we have ever known the mercy of God, if we have ever realized that we didn't get the punishment we deserved from God, then the only response to this experience of God's mercy is to act justly and begin to walk humbly with our God. And yet we are not a people known for the justice we extend to others, let alone mercy. The practice and exercise of justice is the religious response to having experienced the mercy of God in our lives. If we have ever been forgiven, let off the hook, given another chance, then the only response to that gift is to live justly, to give to others what is demanded in justice because they are all human beings and because when God could have dealt with us justly, he didn't. Instead, he gave us another chance to repent and be converted to the justice of Jesus. We are always forgiven. But if we are going to accept this forgiveness and be reconciled to God and to the community, then we must do justice; we must make restitution and restore the balance and mend the wounds caused by our sin, evil, and injustice individually and collectively. Reconciliation means "to walk together again with God and one another," and the way to do that is to practice justice.

The Talents

Jesus was now near Jerusalem and the people with him thought that God's reign was about to appear. So as they were listening to him, Jesus went on to tell them a parable. He said, "A man of noble birth went to a distant place to have himself appointed king of his own people, after which he would return. Before he left, he summoned ten of his servants and gave them ten pounds [talents]. He said: 'Put this money to work until I get back' [invest it]. But his compatriots who disliked [hated] him sent a delegation after him with this message: 'We do not want this man to be our king.'

"He returned, however, appointed as king. At once he sent for his servants to whom he had given the money, to find out what profit each had made. The first came in and reported: 'Sir, your ten pounds have earned ten more.'

"The master replied: 'Well done, my good servant. Since you have proved yourself capable in this small matter, I can trust you to take care of ten cities.' The second reported: 'Sir, your investment earned five more pounds.' The master replied: 'All right, take charge of five cities.'

"The third came in and said: 'Sir, here is your money which I hid for safekeeping. I was afraid of you, for you are an exacting [hard] person; you take up what you did not lay down and you reap what you did not sow.'

"The master replied: 'You worthless servant, I will judge you by your own words. So you knew I was an exacting person, taking up what I did not lay down and reaping what I did not sow! Why, then, did you not put my money on loan so that when I got back I could have collected it with interest?'

"Then the master said to those standing by: 'Take from him what I have given and give it to the one with ten pounds.' They objected: 'But, sir, he already has ten!'

" 'I tell you: everyone who has will be given more: but from him who has not, even what he has will be taken away. As for my enemies who did not want me to be king, bring them in and execute them here in my presence.' "

(LUKE 19:11–27)

The story starts ordinarily enough. Someone in the government gives ten servants one pound each and tells them to invest it while he goes off to get himself crowned king in a foreign country. When he returns as king, he calls in his servants for an accounting. Simple enough. Ten servants, the same amount of money. Two of them really work at investing the money and come up with lots more—the first earns ten pounds more, the second earns five pounds more. Both are praised by the master and receive a reward for their stewardship—they get to take over ten and five cities respectively. The third one buries the money in the ground because he is afraid of the king—with good reason considering what follows. But what happened to the other seven servants?

A parable begins as an ordinary event, in circumstances based on life experience that all share: a man becomes king, even though a good number of his fellow citizens despise him and make very clear publicly that they do not want him to be king over them. A typical case of political intrigue. But then the story turns ugly. The king turns on the third man and judges him on his own words, his own character assessment. He takes the pound from him and gives it to the one with ten already. Even the king's servants (those who are standing by) are appalled and object, but he is clear about his actions: the rich get richer and the poor lose what little they have and are excluded from the system. And then, his last act of judgment: all those who stood against him, opposed his kingship conferred on him by another country, are executed right there, without trial, without justice—an act of terrorism to wipe out any opposition and anyone who disagrees with him. Still, what about the other seven? Did they just disappear into the cities with the money or refuse to play according to his rules?

Jesus tells his disciples this story because they are close to Jerusalem, and they think the kingdom of heaven is about to make its appearance. They are keyed up, hopeful, expectant; they are not looking at reality, the reality of what is going to happen in Jerusalem. Jesus is telling his disciples to remember how the world operates. Those who don't play the games of power, politics, intrigue, and injustice are going to get killed. Those who play the game but are afraid will lose what little they have been given by the powers-that-be and the system. But those who play the game will end up just like those who are in power, to varying degrees. Incidentally the next line of the Gospel is: "So Jesus spoke, and he went on ahead of them, on his way to Jerusalem" (v. 28). Jesus is going to be killed by such a king, Herod, who went off to Rome to get himself crowned by the occupying army and nation, who was detested and hated by his own people both for collaboration with Rome and for his brutality and lack of respect for the Jewish faith and people, his own people.

What does all this say theologically about us, about the way the kingdom comes into the world, about the world of politics and economics and governments everywhere in relation to the kingdom and the gospel of Jesus? If we are going to lead a true Christian life in this world, we will be persecuted! If we follow the masters who rule in the world, we will end up just like them in values, actions and relationships and priorities, in money and power. But if we follow our master Jesus, we will end up in Jerusalem at the cross. We can't be both; we must choose. And the seven? Perhaps Jesus is saying that most of them will die eventually, along with him. The gospel is about risking crucifixion and believing in resurrection. It is about risking telling the truth, so that the kingdom of heaven might enter into this world through us. The world is based on power, violence, investments, interest (usury), exploitation, dominance, occupied territories, nationalism, arrogance, terrorism, slaying enemies without justice or recourse. It is about the rich getting richer and the poor becoming destitute and miserable by decisions made by those in power.

How did we get so off base in our individualistic interpretations of this parable, stripping it of its basic elements of economics, money, and power in politics and nations? Why do we make God a harsh vindictive despot, who slays his enemies and takes from those who live in fear of injustice and arbitrary power? Why do we insist on interpreting the parables and the stories so that they confirm existing conditions, endorse dominant cultural values, rather than convincing us of injustice, sin, evil, or the need to be converted to the cross and community? The interpretation just presented is a radically different alternative to existing conditions, and some would say a subversive description of society. It affirms boldly that the kingdom of peace and justice, of dignity for all, of good news for the poor, comes in very different ways than the world says it does—and from the way many believers in Jesus think it does. The kingdom comes in conflict, in struggle, in the cross and suffering with others and, of course, resurrection. God stands behind Jesus and his disciples with power, but not the power of money, arrogance, dishonesty, hatred, violence, and cold-blooded heartlessness.

The parables are about how the kingdom comes in the context of violence, fear, injustice, amid nations and states, war and terror, and how it comes communally though based on personal choices. Our past readings of this parable reveal us to be so steeped in our own culture that, at best, we are first citizens and only then, perhaps, Christians, followers of Jesus. We are dominated by our lifestyles, individuality, nationalism, capitalism, personal incentive, and the need for security, profit, greed. We tolerate injustice and violence, and we rationalize it all, even using the gospel to further our culture's influence on us and others. But the parable tells us that the kingdom comes most clearly and powerfully in the death of anyone who stands against injustice and the kingdoms of this world that refuse to hear the good news of God. The parable asks us who and what we resist and where we are headed. What is really going on as the kingdom seeks to enter the world through believers? Whom do we travel with? Do we have a community that carries us as Jesus carried his disciples into Jerusalem and as Jesus carried his cross on behalf of others?

From Advent, Christmas, and Epiphany: The Sunday Readings

Introduction

The ancient greeting of the Kalahari Bushmen: "I saw you loom-ing up afar, and I am dying of hunger. Now that you have come, my hunger is gone."

The Response: "Good day! I have been dead, but now that you are come, I live again!"

An East African story begins: "Once upon a time there was a man who couldn't find God." And it continues:

✼ *All the people lived on the plains and they were like people everywhere, some bad and some good. A man named John Shayo lived in the valley. He was a faithful Christian and participated in his small Amani Christian community, helping the poor and needy, especially the lepers that lived on the slope. But in the val-ley itself there was discord, thieves and tricksters walked about openly. There was fighting, witchcraft, and lying. Finally John de-cided to move, saying to himself, "God isn't here. God is the Un-surpassed Great Spirit who doesn't like fighting and discord. He wants peace and harmonious relationships in his human family."*

John saw a mountain in the distance and thought, "Ah, God our Great Ancestor must live up there in the quiet and peace. I will go and find God."

It took a long time, days and days, until he reached the mountain, and then he undertook the arduous climb in the burning equatorial sun. Late one day, he rested by the side of the footpath. He was startled to see a bearded stranger with a staff making his way down the mountain! "Jambo!" they greeted each other. "What is the news?"

John told him he was on his way up the mountain to see God the Creator and Source. The traveler said he was on his way down the mountain to live with all the people below. They talked as was the custom and parted with the greeting, "Goodbye until we meet again."

As he continued his climb, John thought of the man and admired him. He spoke well. John wondered why he was going down to the valley.

As John climbed the air thinned and John moved more slowly. It was quite and still, with the only noise coming from the birds. He thought, "Ah, now I will find God here." He looked around but there was no one there. Then he cried out, "Is God home? Where is God?"

Suddenly a gaunt old man appeared and greeted John, "Welcome. Rest after your journey and climb."

John told him of the journey and how he sought the All Peaceful One. The old man listened and then answered, "I'm sorry, but God doesn't live here. I live alone. But, surely, you met God on the path. He was going down to live with the people there."

John was astonished. "Are you sure? I thought he'd be up here. Why would he want to live down there among the fighting, jealousies, and anger of people?"

The old man answered, "God knows the weaknesses of his people. There is an African fable about an African hunter who was an-

*gry with God. He shot an arrow into the clouds. So God with drew
into the high heavens to getaway from the angry human beings.
But God the Great Elder loved his human family and wanted to
give them tender care. So God our Great Ancestor sent his Son to
pitch his tent among us, to live with us, to share our joys and sorrows, successes and failures in order to save us. This is Christmas."*

*John was moved and listened to the old man (the mzee, the
wise one) speak. "This Jesus, Emmanuel, is a mystery who prefers
the company of the poor, the lowly, the simple, and the needy."*

*John knew he had learned the wisdom of the mountain top,
but now it was time to go* down *to the valley where God was. He
told the old one, "I need to live with the people as God lives."*

*The old one reached out and touched John's head. John turned
slowly and the valley stretched out before him. He began his climb
down. Now he knew where to find God. (Adapted from "The Man
Who Couldn't Find God," in* What Language Does God Speak?
African Stories about Christmas and Easter, *ed. Joseph G. Healy,
M.M. [Nairobi: St. Paul Publications] date TK, 17.)*

God came down. This is core of the seasons of Advent, Christmas,
and Epiphany. God prefers to live with us in spite of our anger, our violence, and our lack of love for one another. We find God here on earth.

One of the Hebrew liturgical psalms sings out: "Gates, lift up your
heads! Stand erect, ancient door, and let in the King of glory." (Psalms
24:7) This announcement invites us into the season of Advent, the season of comings. There are so many comings: of Christ in glory at the end
of time, of God as human in the birth of Jesus-Emanuel, of the world
made flesh entering our hearts, and of peace with justice on earth. Along
with the season of Christmas, the celebration of the coming of God
among us as a human being in the mystery of the incarnation, Advent
reminds us of the coming of God as King of glory and Judge of the universe.

The readings for these seasons are rich and layered. They compress past, present, and future into the single moment of now! Now decides what comes first. The first Advent was incarnation, Christmas, and Epiphany; the second Advent will be the coming of Christ in glory to fulfill the kingdom brought to earth in the person of Jesus. This second Advent is "simply the longing and waiting of the church for the return of the Lord Jesus, the King of glory."

At every liturgy we proclaim, "Christ will come again!" For Christians, this is as sure as the first coming in the incarnation, and its completeness is already set in motion by the coming of Christ in our hearts in the Word of the Lord and in hope born of the cross and resurrection. We live between the two advents. They are our meaning and source, our horizon and shadow. The first advent turns our eyes and hearts toward the mystery of God's presence among us. As the story above reminds us, the first Advent turns us toward the valley, the vale of tears where people dwell in joy and tears, in mildness and violence, in justice and injustice. This is where we find God.

The second Advent commands us to turn our eyes and hearts toward the Word of God that reveals the mystery of God's plan for the world, its freedom and liberation, its transformation, and its holiness, as it was meant to be in the beginning.

Advent, Christmas, and Epiphany are about God being here, God who has come and will return. God does return as we let God in—into our political and economic systems, our relationships, and all the places that are in sore need of redemption. The child-king rules within Mary's womb, and the child and the woman are both in the womb of God's world the universe that was created to be a blessing and a dwelling place secure for all men and women. This is God in lowliness. Then, it will be God in glory.

We wait, as the remnant of Israel waited, as the prophets and people in exile waited, as Mary and Joseph waited, as all those who are poor, imprisoned, oppressed, and in darkness wait for the light to dawn and God to save. Once upon a time, when God came, a seed was planted in the world, and now all creation groans until it springs forth and life blooms for all again. Then when God comes, the blossom will declare a new springtime, an everlasting spring of everlasting life. In the meantime, we wait, we sing, we decide aright for the land's afflicted, and we go where God first came—among the people. And we take the light of incarnation, of the Word made flesh, of God-with-us always and forever, out into the ends of the earth and tell the good news that God is in our land.

First Sunday of Advent, Cycle A

Readings: Isaiah 2:1–5

Romans 13:11–14

Matthew 24:37–44

Stay awake! This is the moment when it begins, when the world begins to turn toward home and everything we know changes. God is coming and he's creeping up on us like a thief breaking into our house and into our world. Advent is a guard dog barking loudly and rousing us from a sound sleep. There is an intruder in the house, in the world. Are we awake? Today we are warned: throw open the door! Rouse everyone in the house! Roll out the red carpet. Get busy with preparations. Sweep the house and be on your toes. God is so close!

Isaiah's vision is centered on the Lord's mountain, Jerusalem, but this involves more than a geographical location: it is a place of light and truth, of justice and judgment, where God's supreme power and authority are honored and enacted. It is a vision place, a place of no more war. Isaiah's words have over the centuries been used by poets, musicians, preachers, and common folk alike to dream aloud of what is possible for human beings here on earth. But they are words of prophets too: words of warning of the dire consequences that will follow upon those who refuse to heed the words that outlaw war, violence, and the destruction of the earth and its kind. To stop training for war and to unlearn violence and these things abhorrent to the Holy One are the beginning of in-struction in the Lord's ways. We begin way back at the beginning—at the first lesson—and turn again into the path of God.

Welcome to Advent! This is our wake-up call. Time to shake off sleep, lethargy, and old ways and habits. It is meant to be a rude awakening, like a trumpet blast that signals hope, glory, and worldwide judgment. What are we concerned about? Do our day-to-day lives reveal that we have "put on the Lord Jesus Christ"? The event itself will be momentous. Do we wear the livery of the Son of Man? Do we live proclaiming that we belong to the light? Or do we carouse in drunkenness, in greed, in piling up material possessions? Do we live excessively, emotionally, sexually, with revenge and quarrels, dissension and jealousy? Do we participate in war, train for war, and live off the spoils of war, or do we dismantle weapons and till the earth for food and a harvest of justice?

This first Sunday of the season looks at universal issues: time and eternity, our lives against that backdrop, war and peace, salvation and death. It is about the connections between the poor and the push to kill through weapons of mass misery, arms sales, land mines, and the manufacture of ever-new forms of destruction. It is about hard questions like this one asked by Korean theologian Chung Ryan Kyung: "Your economy is based on inflicting pain in other persons' lives. So, I ask, where is God in your country?" (from Maryknoll's film *Arms for the Poor*).

The voices of the prophets and the poor stir our consciences, awaken and nudge our hearts, oppose our politics and our prayers. We in the United States are the leaders by a wide margin in arms sales around the world: $11.3 billion in 1996 alone (with England and Russia far behind us). The warning of President Eisenhower in 1953 still rings true today: "Every gun that is made, every warship launched, every rocket fired signifies, in the final sense, a theft from those who hunger and are not fed, those who are cold and are not clothed." Advent begins with the lesson that if we are followers of the child who was threatened by Herod's sword, then we must convert the weapons of mass destruction into technology and resources for food and the future of children of the earth.

The imagery of this reading often disconcerts people, even disorients: that of thieves and God as a thief in the night, breaking into our house. But it is a familiar image, for one of the readings for the previous Sunday (the last Sunday of the church's year of readings) concerns the thieves on either side of Jesus at the crucifixion. One thief acknowledges Jesus, even in pain, and is taken into paradise. The other cannot see, curses, and joins those who mock and scorn and is lost to hope. Now the image overlaps and continues in this reading of the first Sunday of the church year. Our text from Matthew's Gospel refers first to Noah, who beckoned to others to join him. They refused, and the flood came and destroyed them even while they were "eating and drinking and marrying." The text says it will be the same when the Son of Man comes: "Two men will be out in the field; one will be taken and one will be left. Two women will be grinding meal; one will be taken and one will be left." So stay awake! Live like you expect to be broken into! Visited by a thief! Robbed while you sleep! What provisions are you making, taking? For the Son of Man is coming when we least expect him to appear. But this coming is not so much about our individual deaths or the end of our lives. It is more plural, communal. This is about universal judgment.

Matthew's call is to look, to see. It is connected to Isaiah's vision, and it is focused in a single point: the presence and overwhelming image of the Son of Man. This image of God is not one that we often look to, contemplate, or pray to, for it's frightening, often confusing. The best description of the Son of Man comes in the visions of Daniel the prophet. They are terrifying, involving the judging of nations, yet they bring hope to those oppressed and long burdened with others' rage and hate. Daniel writes:

> As the visions during the night continued, I saw One like a son
> of man coming, on the clouds of heaven; when he reached the
> Ancient One and was presented before him, he received do-
> minion, glory, kingship; nations and peoples of every language

serve him. His dominion is an everlasting dominion that shall not be taken away, his kingship shall not be destroyed.

(DAN. 7:13–14)

This person is dazzling, coming on the clouds of heaven, accompanied by angels, coming to judge the nations with justice. He is human, yet full of power, glory, and light. It is an odd mixture of a king robed in majesty and holiness, splendor and strength (Ps. 93:1–2, 5), and the Lamb of God from the book of Revelation and from ancient descriptions of the paschal lamb of sacrifice, slaughtered so that the people might escape from death. This one is innocent, going freely to death to save others, a ransom for the many and the only one worthy to open the scroll of revelation and judge the living and the dead, all the nations, with justice, because he himself has suffered unjustly at the hands of all peoples. This Son of Man is described in Revelation as

Jesus Christ the faithful witness, the first born from the dead and ruler of kings of earth. To him who loves us and freed us from our sins by his own blood, who has made us a royal nation of priests in the service of his God and Father—to him be glory and power forever and ever! Amen.

See, he comes amid the clouds! Every eye shall see him. . . .

All the peoples of the earth shall lament him bitterly. So it is to be! Amen!

The Lord God says, "I am the Alpha and the Omega, the One who is and who was and who is to come, the Almighty!"

(REV. 1:5–8)

This Son of Man is Christ the King, crucified on the cross, standing with all those who die unjustly, innocently before their time, unnecessarily, followers of the Lamb who are slaughtered in war or for profit. To stand before this one is to stand before the God of peace, justice, mercy, and hope for the lost and downtrodden of the earth. It is to know that this is a day of vindication by our God. It is like standing before a towering icon of Christ, first born of the dead, the presence of life torn to death and now bursting out of all bounds.

And we are told to stand there together, prepared, awake, living out the vision in today's world that Isaiah promised in hope to all the people mourning and waiting on God. We have been instructed in the Lord's ways; now it is time to walk in them and take the Word of the Lord forth into the world, to impose terms on people: the terms of care for the poor; the terms of peace; the terms of unity and enduring justice for all, especially those most in need of restitution and hope.

The image of God as a thief. Have you ever been robbed? Has your home ever been broken into? How does the image of God as a thief strike you? Do you have a lot to steal? Would he find you vigilant? Ready for him? Waiting?

God is a thief, intent on stealing our sins, our evil and vengeance, our violence, and all that clutters and stands in the way of hope, of salvation, and of unity among us all. Our God is a thief, and Advent is the beginning of the adventure, the time when God breaks into our house, our world, and steals us blind, shifting all of history and saving the lost. It is a story worth telling over and over, a story within a story within a story! It is God's story, the earth's story, and our story today, singularly and as a nation. Advent is about dreams and visions, old ones from the prophets (primarily, in this cycle of readings, from Isaiah), and how the dreams come true in flesh and blood, in a child born to us, Jesus, human and Son of Man, Son of Justice, Son of God, son of Mary and Joseph.

It is a time of patient endurance and waiting, hoping outrageously for peace now, for passionate repentance, for justice to come among us. It is a time for clothing ourselves again in the garments of light we were given at our baptisms, of putting on glory, of putting on the Lord Jesus, of wearing those garments publicly, proudly, boldly, as once Noah built an ark. And if we do that, people will stream toward the Word of the Lord heard in our midst once again, seen in our lives this year of the Lord. Advent is about judgment and standing in the presence of the thief, the Son of Man, not flinching, looking God straight in the eye, and rejoicing that our God is on the side of the poor, the immigrant, the family struggling in the system and falling through the cracks and being blamed for that and a host of other social ills. God is against the arms buildup, the war machine, the threats and hard lines, the uncapped spending on military endeavors, and anything that does not make for peace for all and the restoration of human dignity and life on earth for those who come after us. It is a time of hope, fiery change, and light, a time for seekers of vision and hope-bringers. The kingdom is come and dwells among us—where? The Son of Man is coming at the time we least expect!

Our response to this pronouncement is that of the psalmist: "I rejoiced when I heard them say: 'Let us go to the house of the Lord.' . . . I will say: 'Peace be within you!' Because of the house of the Lord, our God, I will pray for your good" (Ps. 122:1, 8b–9).

Thursday of the Third Week of Advent

Isaiah 54:1–10
Psalm 30:2–6, 11–13
Luke 7:24–30

The readings for this day present extremes. On the one end is wild hope in the wonders of God; at the other end are those who "defeat God's plan in their regard." This is a day of jubilant song and tragedy, and it is up to us to decide which group we are a part of. We must choose, and we must see our choices in the perspective of God's long-standing plan for us: wanting only to love us, to never leave us, and to have the covenant of peace established with us last forever, extending until all the world knows the mercy of God.

Isaiah begins with a command issued to those who have absolutely nothing to rejoice over: the barren woman, the deserted wife, the poor, the forsaken, and those grieved in spirit. Things are going to change drastically because of God's intervention in the world. God will not allow earth to remain abandoned or at a distance from his presence and intimacy. We are to sing in expectation. Remember, this third week of Advent was formerly called gaudate: Rejoice!

> *Raise a glad cry, you barren one who did not bear,*
> *break forth in jubilant song, you who are not in labor,*
> *For more numerous are the children of the deserted wife*
> *than the children of her who has a husband, says the Lord.*
> *Enlarge the space for your tent,*
> *spread out your tent clothes unsparingly;*
> *lengthen your ropes and make firm your stakes.*
> *For you shall spread abroad to the right and to the left;*
> *your descendants shall dispossess the nations*
> *and shall people the desolate cities.*

The people of Israel are broken and oppressed and a long way from home. Isaiah is intent on turning their despair and grief into rejoicing and faithfulness. Isaiah is eloquent in his descriptions of what God will do for them. His prophesies are couched in the familiar language of reversals: those without will be given so much they can't imagine it—stretching the limits of their tents, their place in society, and even their place in time through their descendants. Though they have known God's displeasure, even anger, they will once again know intimacy, freedom, and great tenderness. God will be for them husband, maker, redeemer, and Lord, as well as the Lord of hosts and the Holy One of Israel. They will know God again. Isaiah tells them to cling to these words and images, these promises of what is to come:

> *For a brief moment I abandoned you,*
> *but with great tenderness I will take you back.*
> *In an outburst of wrath, for a moment*
> *I hid my face from you;*

But with enduring love I take pity on you,
says the Lord, your redeemer.

God refers back to the days of Noah, swearing not to be angry or re-
buke the Israelites again, just as Yahweh once promised never again to
"deluge the earth with water." Isaiah ends with words of endearment:
"Though the mountains leave their place and the hills be shaken, my love
shall never leave you nor my covenant of peace be shaken, says the Lord,
who has mercy on you." God is faithful, always coming to us, seeking our
presence, our worship, our mutual love, and our devotion. With steadfast
reliance on God's word and deed, we are to respond: "I will praise you,
Lord, for you have rescued me."

This entire segment of Isaiah is addressed to the people as a whole,
and each person responds individually. But when we respond, we sing
the praises of God together with one heart and voice. Throughout all of
history and throughout our individual lives God has been near. We are
alive, and in spite of whatever has befallen us or what we have brought
upon ourselves because of our sin and infidelities, God is always close to
us. Our lives depend solely on God in all times and circumstances. This
is faith. It is fraught with joy even in the midst of great suffering.

Rabbi Nachman, a descendant of the Ba'al Shem Tov and a famous
storyteller and preacher among the Jewish communities of Eastern Europe in the 1800s, sought to teach his followers about sadness and joy.
Nachman writes in *The Empty Chair*:

He [i.e., Rabbi Nachman] was shattered, empty. His infant son
had just died. His closest followers came to console him but
they couldn't bear to witness his torment and ran from the
room. When they returned the next day, the Rebbe said to them,
"Had you not run out, I would have told you something beautiful." He then taught them a lesson entitled the Garden of the
Souls, explaining how we can extract meaning from even our
greatest suffering. This is what we must do if we are to leave

sadness and find hope and joy. He said to them: "Always remember: Joy is not merely incidental to your spiritual quest. It
is vital."

(LM 1:24)

We are to be joyful, an undeniable sign of God's presence and of our
faith, no matter what transpires as we wait for our God to make his glory
visible and to show forth goodness and mercy. Remembrance of the past
and what God has always done helps us to sustain joy. The Psalm gives
us words of remembrance:

*I will extol you, O Lord, for you drew me clear
and did not let my enemies rejoice over me . . .*

*O Lord, you brought me from among those going down into
        The pit.
Sing praise to the Lord you his faithful ones,
and give thanks to his holy name.
For his anger last but a moment;
a lifetime, his good will.
At nightfall, weeping enters in,
but with the dawn, rejoicing . . .*

*Hear, O Lord, and have pity on me;
O Lord be my helper.
You changed my mourning into dancing . . .*

O Lord, my God, forever will I give you thanks.

This Psalm is for the in-between times, between the sorrow and the
joy. It is a psalm for faith, for enduring gracefully, and for professing with
our prayer and our daily lives that we believe in God and God's words and
that God waits for us. Part of preparing the way for the Lord's coming

among us is to remain joyful, faithful, and attentive for any sign of his approach.

The Gospel continues the account of the previous day's Gospel reading. The messengers from John go back with Jesus' answer based on Isaiah's prophesies. Jesus turns to the crowd to talk about John and what they think of him. Jesus questions them on why they went out into the desert: "What did you go out to see—a reed swayed by the wind? What, really, did you go out to see—someone dressed luxuriously? Remember, those who dress in luxury and eat in splendor are to be found in royal palaces. Then what did you go out to see—a prophet? He is that, I assure you, and something more." Jesus is attesting to John's being a true prophet, faithful and enduring in the face of evil, rejection, the harshness of the desert, and the materialism and hedonism of the people who have turned from God.

As the reading continues, there is rejoicing: "the entire populace, even the tax collectors, gave praise to God, for they had received from John the baptismal bath he administered." They are the new children of God, the lowly who are in the company of John and considered to be great in the eyes of God. This is Luke's gospel. These persons who once were lowly and are now great are many—the true followers of Jesus, like Mary and Elizabeth, the shepherds, the old faithful ones like Anna and Simeon, and the masses of those who are poor and lost without a shepherd, caught in the politics of Herod and Rome and in the institutions of religion. They are cared for only by God and by God's messengers, the prophets and the followers of Jesus. Again, there is rejoicing. This is a season that springs from one joy to another, to deeper levels of joy, and a pervasive sense of the power of God in the world.

Yet the Gospel reading ends on a harsh, truth-telling note. Luke adds the fact that "the Pharisees and the lawyers, on the other hand, by failing to receive his baptism defeated God's plan in their regard." The leaders of the people forgot what God had done for them, forgot the promises, and did not believe in God's power made manifest in John. Because they refused baptism and repentance, there was to be no forgiveness of sins for them yet. But Jesus will offer the opportunity to them again and again, even though they continuously strive to thwart God's plans. Lest we be too hard on the Pharisees and the lawyers, we should remember that most of us would find ourselves more in their company than that of the crowds, the tax collectors, the lepers, the deaf, the blind, and the poor who rejoiced in the coming of Jesus' life-giving presence.

We have heard John's words. We have heard Isaiah's words. We have heard the Word of God. Have we repented? We have been baptized both in water and in the fire of the Spirit. Have we lived remembering the goodness of God shown to us by sharing that kindness, mercy, and re-membrance with others caught in pain and trouble? The Communion antiphon tells us again: "Let our lives be honest and holy in this present age, as we wait for the happiness to come and when our great God re-veals himself in glory." How are we waiting? Does the world know that we hang on God's word, that we are intent on preparing the way of the Lord by walking the highway of holiness?

Harold Kushner, in his book *To Life!*, writes, "Judaism is less about believing and more about belonging. It is less about what we owe God and more about what we owe each other, because we believe God cares more about how we treat each other than He does about our theology." We must put our waiting into practice and our joy into the lives of oth-ers. Our prayer must be contagious, and our kindness must stretch to the ends of our domains. Simone Weil said, "The feeling of those that are hungry is a form of contemplation." We wait. We rejoice. And we live so as to give others cause to rejoice.

Christmas Mass During the Day: Cycles A, B, C

Isaiah 52:7–10

Psalms 98:1–6

Hebrews 1:1–6

John 1:1–18

Today is the birth of the Son of God; the earth, all the creatures on it, and we human beings begin to come back together again. Even the angels gather near to us, sing to us, worship with us this presence of God in the world in a way not even the angels imagined. This is God's design: Father and Son together breathing, knowing, and creating, which is Spirit. Today God speaks a new language: a person, a body, a human being, a baby, mortal flesh that is divine. Until forever we will be learning this language, its music, its cadences, its silences and pauses, its power and expressions. It is at root, at heart, the language of love.

We hear the long form of the Gospel (always better, more whole and complete, easier to understand). It takes practice to read. It is poetry. It begins to sing to you, not so much from understanding as from being spoken aloud and revealing itself as you speak publicly. As C. S. Lewis once said: "Some things are far too precise for mere human speech and words." It is the sound as well as the meaning of the words that carries the communication. Images and feelings are evoked and stirred that can transform human life and relationships, knowledge and love. This is the beginning of the new language, the language of Jesus' flesh and spirit, the language of glad tidings.

John is interested in taking us way back, before creation, before time, into God as God is and then leading us forward as God comes toward us and then into us and as one of us. This is John's view, as if from the great eye of a soaring eagle. He gives us a prologue and perspective of all that is to come. It is God's time now seeping through history, rewording all things with the truth. It is about words, about the Word, wisdom, a person, the face and form of God in our faces and forms. This is God's long-loving look at reality, even the reality that is hard to look at because of what we have refused to see and believe.

This is glory intimately connected to the cross, to suffering and death, to the destruction of God's flesh, to the silencing of the Word. This is new gift, new covenant, new blood, new love that is enduring, revealing. In the older Testament a person who saw God died. Now we see God and we die, but we are returned to life in God through Jesus. This

Word, this sound, this flesh, dwells and stays with us, endures faithfully, and is literally and physically, in every sense of the term, "God-with-us." We should remember that the Word comes with a warning, a memory of what happened in history and what so often still happens today, that his own did not accept him, did not know him, and refused to speak this language and instead sought to destroy him.

Again, this presence, this glory, is hard to speak about or to express, and yet it is the source, the wellspring, of our belief, our life, our hope, and our destiny. All the readings of this day are referred to in the Russian Orthodox Church as "a splendid three-day Pascha, a winter Pascha, the Pascha of the coming, the Pascha of the incarnation." Resurrection will begin here in incarnation, but all the shadows and intimations of crucifixion and death are here too. This day is victory over sin and evil and death. This is new birth in the Spirit of God, the Word of God. It is we who are given birth to on this day. It is not nativity that we celebrate, but incarnation, God putting on flesh and pitching his tent among us as a dwelling place forever. It is the day God disappears into our flesh, sinking deep inside our human nature and beginning the transformation of each and all of us and all creation by his intimate presence among us.

The Orthodox Church celebrates the incarnation of God with many overtures of the crucifixion and Easter as well as salvation and baptism. Nathan Mitchell, liturgist and poet, once interspersed the verses from the "Royal Hours" for Christmas Eve and Good Friday in one of his articles in *Worship* magazine. Every year since, I have read the two together for a deeper sense of how the church has looked at this day's Scriptures and experience, not primarily as the nativity of Jesus, but as the incarnation of God, as the transformation of humanity and history. These verses can serve as meditation points for reflection in the twelve days of Christmas that begin today and end on the feast of Epiphany:

The One who holds all creation in the hollow of a hand
is born today of the Virgin.

The One who hung the earth upon the waters
*   is hung today upon the Cross.*
The One whose essence none can touch
*   is wrapped in swaddling clothes as a mortal.*
The One who rules the angels
*   is crowned today with thorns.*
God, who in the beginning created the heavens,
*   lies now in a manger.*
God, who wraps the heavens in clouds,
*   is wrapped in mocking purple.*
The One who rained manna down on the people in the
*   wilderness is fed on milk from a Mother's breast.*
The One who set Eve and Adam free in the Jordan
*   is slapped in the face.*
Today the Church's Spouse
*   calls forth the Magi.*
Today the Church's Spouse
*   is nailed to the cross.*
The Virgin's child
*   accepts their gifts.*
The Virgin's child
*   is pierced with a spear.*
We worship you nativity, O Christ!
We worship you passion, O Christ!
Show us your glorious Theophany!
Show us, too, your glorious Resurrection!

These interspersed verses remind us starkly of the three-day feast of Good Friday, Holy Saturday, and Easter and let us see more clearly the three-part feast of Advent, Christmas, and Epiphany as one whole piece. And they put in sharp focus the three segments of John's prologue: the first section on the Word of God; the second on John as witness to the light and on the real light that came into the world and was rejected, yet is still offered to all who are willing to accept him; and the final portion that speaks of the one who is "love following upon love," who is the fullness of God, ever at the Father's side.

The prologue of John's Gospel contains so much meaning that it is hard to single out individual phrases or sentences as this season's essence. We will, however, look at a few of the more familiar lines and suggest a few ways of looking at what is being expressed. Perhaps the most famous of these lines is this one: "And the Word became flesh and made his dwelling among us, and we saw his glory, the glory of the Father's only Son, full of grace and truth" (John 1:14). God's dwelling place is among us. This has been the case ever since the journey through the desert after the escape from Egypt. Originally the Tabernacle of the Lord was the space where God's glory dwelled, the Ark of the Covenant that held the Torah given on Mount Sinai, and where the shewbread was given to Yahweh as an offering of thanksgiving. The children of Israel carried this Ark, this house of God, with them as they traveled to their new homeland.

Instead of "made his dwelling," a more descriptive and closer translation of the Greek is "he pitched his tent" among us, a tent much like those the wandering Israelites "dwelled in" temporarily for forty years while they learned how to become people in the wilderness and to trust in Yahweh. Once they settled in the promised land, they built more substantial dwelling places for Yahweh, culminating in the Temple that David began in dream form and his son Solomon finished, a monument of cedar and stone, built to exact specifications. Yet it was destroyed by the Babylonians, rebuilt, and destroyed by the Romans with only a fragment of the western wall, called the Wailing Wall, remaining today.

Now there is a new dwelling place, a new tent for God's presence among us. It is the flesh of a human being, beloved child and sons of God, one of us, born of Mary the Virgin, conceived in her womb and born in a cave near Bethlehem. God has entered the world and stays in a body like ours! Now the Word, the essence of God's soul, has been spoken truly. As at creation's beginning, when the Word and intent of God brought forth all the earth and its creatures, now God's Word becomes human, subject to limitations and weakness, and finally subject to death itself. Now we see this "glory of God" that the angels sang about the night of his birth. It looks like us.

The "glory of the Father's only Son is full of grace and truth." In Luke's Gospel, Mary is addressed as full of grace, favored by God, but this only Son is full of grace and truth, an image that is bound to the history of Israel and God's covenant (see Exod. 34:6). This grace and truth are about love, about "the way things were meant to be." They concern all of us, individually and together in communion, as God's own people. In this only Son we will all be born, adopted, made heirs, and become beloved sons and daughters, the children of the Father God. Our humanity is blessed beyond words in the body of this human being, Jesus, "the glory as of the Father's only Son." God has come home, entered into us as closely and as surely as a child dwells in its mother's womb, and then enters the world at large to live, breathe, love, and die.

There is a fascinating Chinese children's story called "Youchao and the First Dwellings" that can perhaps add to the meaning of "pitched his tent and made his dwelling among us." The story also illustrates why this day is so extraordinary and so transformative for the human race and its future.

> ✳ *It was long, long ago when the earth was very old already, but human beings were still young. Since the beginning people had loved the sunlight and being on the earth. They loved the hunting and gathering, singing as the birds did early in the morning and gathering together as the birds did at night. But when the sky became shadowy and dusk came, there was fear. They could not look for food. They could not see what was out there, if there was danger. They were afraid to sleep, afraid to be alone, afraid of anyone who traveled and moved at night, afraid of animals and creatures of the night. They longed for light to come, and they posted watchers who would cry at the first sound of danger, but also at the first*

trace of light returning. They sometimes hid in caves and under ledges, but it was bitterly cold, and though they were out of the rain and wind and snow, it was a hard, hard way to live.

But God used to visit the earth whenever he had the chance, to see how things were going down below. God would watch and see the people's fear and suffering. This God couldn't bear; it was not meant to be so hard to dwell on the earth. So God sat under a tree and wondered what could be done to help the people in their distress. God dozed and was awakened by the chitter and songs of birds nested in the tree above. Fascinated with the birds, God watched as they flew back and forth with bits of down, grasses and twigs, leaves and seeds, building a nest for the protection and safety of their young. That was it! The pattern would follow that of the birds. Instead of twigs, there would be bent branches of long willow trees. Instead of dry grass, there would be hay and straw. The first dwelling was constructed, and God rested inside to see if it was adequate. Since it was quite satisfactory, God thought to build another and another and another, with variations and new ideas, enjoying making nests for the people.

The people found them and entered them and slept secure, and the word spread like wildfire. Almost overnight, shelters, houses, and other dwelling places were built on earth. They were comfortable, warm, dry, and good for storing food and other necessities as well as for gathering together in peace. They were the people's nests. And so in honor of the God who visited them and gave them rest and dwelling places, they called their God "Youchao," which means "having nest."

Our God has visited us too and has always been concerned for our safety, well-being, and the quality of life on this earth. And God has visited again and again through judges, kings, laws, and sometimes threats, but more often with gifts of freedom and promises of a land, a secure dwelling place, a way of belonging.

December 28, Holy Innocents, Martyrs

I John 1:5–2:2
Psalm 124:2–5, 7–8
Matthew 2:13–18

This is the fourth day of Christmas. And today is a celebration of children, all the children others find threatening. There is no way to avoid the gruesome events that Matthew records in his Christmas story. It jars us, wrenches our hearts, and leaves a grisly shadow behind. It is a massacre of the innocents, those who have nothing to do with existing power struggles, no agendas—they just happen to be in the wrong place at the wrong time. The tragedy begins with the magi, outsiders searching for meaning in a star. They innocently give information to Herod, a ruthless, evil murderer. The magi blindly bring death and destruction, unaware that evil is using them.

It is a horrific story, repeated in one form or another in every age, every generation. In the past few decades, there have been massacres of innocents. In eastern European countries, in what was Russia, in Africa, in Northern Ireland, even in the United States, the innocent, the children, are caught in the cross fire of adults who hate, who seek only to solidify their base of influence and power, and who consider whole groups of people expendable. The Jews believe there is a Pharaoh in every generation. There is also a Herod. They are cut from the same cloth, fed by the same fears, and fueled by hate, nationalism, and personal vengeance for being slighted. We do not know what Herod would have done if the Magi had returned with the further information he had asked them to bring him, but in the end it is their not returning that sets him into a furious rage and sets in motion the carnage that was intended to safeguard him from a child. His reaction to the Magi's disobedience is fast, ruthless, and imperious, a military and political tactic to secure his place in his small kingdom.

The story steadfastly refuses to let us personalize, theologize, or even spiritualize the infancy narratives. It places them squarely in the reality of politics, nationalism, economics, militarism, and evil. People often resist the connection between politics and religion, insisting that one can be religious, spiritual, and good without being sullied with such mundane matters as politics. Or they go even further and declare that religion is just between oneself and God and affects behavior only toward one's own group or those selected to receive one's respect.

Four decades after Vatican II and its declarations on human freedom and statements on church and society, and after many statements by the universal church and by local bishops, many Catholics staunchly adhere to a separation of church and state, religion and politics, a life with God and life lived with other human beings. Never the twain shall meet.

And yet they do meet throughout the Old Testament, especially in the Prophets and Psalms, and also in the story of Yahweh calling Moses to go back into the jaws of Egypt, where there was a price on his head, and confront the Pharaoh and lead his people out to freedom. This Moses, the liberator of Israel, was born under a death sentence—the Egyptian leader had decreed that all Israelite boy children were to be killed by the midwives who delivered them. Moses' sister and mother were traitors who risked their lives and their families to save one child from the death decreed by a reigning power that saw all male children of the oppressed as a threat, fearing the overpopulation of the poor and the declining birthrate of the ruling class. This story crops up again in the massacre of the children at the time of the birth of Jesus. But sadly it is not relegated to the past.

Gustavo Gutiérrez has written an essay called "Jesus Born among the Massacred Innocent of History." He puts the massacre in the context of today.

The Christmas liturgical cycle includes a commemoration that is in danger of being overlooked or misinterpreted: the day of the Holy Innocents, December 28 . . . The birth of a child on the outskirts of a small city worried the traitor Herod. The smell of the stable reached Herod's palace, and the fear the newborn child evoked led him to slaughter many innocent children. Unjust and untimely death cruelly accompanied the life that had just begun. Tragedy surrounded the joy of birth—a foretaste of the blood that would be spilled on the cross by those who would resist the announcement of the God of life by the child-become-adult.

The searing cry of Rachel who wept for her children continues to be heard in our country—it is the cry of the mothers of the 100 out of every 1,000 infants who die in their first year of life . . .

The blood of the innocents continues to drench the history of Peru and Latin America, it constitutes the price, unacceptable to the human and Christian conscience, that the people of this subcontinent are paying in order to sustain what García Marquez calls "the illusion of having our own life within the division of the world's goods." That is the world to which God irrevocably committed himself on the day we commemorate as Christmas.

Life and death. Solidarity sealed with blood. Christmas is, nonetheless, the promise that life will overcome death and that hope is not a vain dream when it becomes flesh in a people. The "peace on earth" proclaimed to the shepherds of Bethlehem is what is demanded if we are to build a just world—a world, as the Bible stresses, that will never cease to link justice with peace.

(*EL DIARIO MARKA*, LIMA, PERU, DECEMBER 26, 1982)

This is the sin of the world, and we all share it, by collusion and by ignoring such political and social realities in our search for a meaningful "spirituality."

From Lent: The Daily and the Sunday Readings

Introduction

✤   *Once upon a time there was a storyteller who loved words: the sound and feel of them, the way they flowed, eddied about, returned, and spiraled down in little currents. Better, he loved stories: any kind really, but especially the ones that caught folks and carried them, casting them forth in a place distant from where they were when the story began. Best of all, he loved telling the stories. He was compelled to it by some power deeper than any force that moved rivers and stirred the seas in their depths. He was most himself in the telling: graceful, free, light, and truthful, obedient to Another, whom he liked to think of as the Word, the Story that all others could only serve and imitate.*

He lived simply and faithfully and told stories whenever he could. Then, one day, he began to notice things changing, or, to be more precise—disappearing. First it was little things: his keys, glasses, notes to himself, pages off a calendar, socks, spoons. Nothing disappeared that was of any importance really, but it was annoying. He thought of himself as forgetful, and he chalked it up to short-term-memory loss and laughed about midlife.

But the problem grew worse, and it became harder to laugh at. More began to disappear: hours of the day, sleep and dreams at night, acquaintances, even friends. Then the pages of his manuscripts disappeared, also notes for classes or talks, his suitcase. Nothing was ever returned or found. He wondered if he might be ill, or losing his mind, or becoming senile. And then he began to notice connections, disconcerting connections. He carefully kept records until he was absolutely sure of his findings, which disturbed him greatly. Everything that had disappeared was closely connected to a story he had told.

So he tried not telling stories, but that didn't work. He tried to monitor the stories and figure out ahead of time what he'd lose. Sometimes that worked, but the logic was not always immediately apparent. There seemed to be another structure of logic and symbolism at work. He tried being detached, unattached, even practicing the virtue of poverty, and soon he realized that this was hard. He grew fearful and apprehensive. When and where would it all stop?

This predicament became the backdrop of his life. Stories continued to enchant him, and there seemed more of them. He found them in books, people's conversations, his mind, observing situations and relationships on the street, traveling. There was suddenly a surfeit of stories. They couldn't have come (or were they presented to him as choices?) at a worse time in his life. He took them in, gingerly, greedily, like a man hungry for food, insight, wisdom, and hope.

Then he began to lose pieces of himself! First he lost his hair, fingernails, toenails: replaceable pieces. One day he told a story— enthralled by it himself as the words flowed from him—and he lost a finger. The next day he lost another on the same hand. It was time to make some major decisions. He couldn't go on like this, at least without consciously knowing what would happen every time he was caught in a story. Still, he was bound to the stories and to the telling.

Soon he noticed another side effect. As he disappeared he be-

came more and more adept as a teller. The stories acquired more power, breadth, and influence. In fact, they began to come true in reality. He began to hope that in losing himself perhaps there was a larger design, a whole that he was contributing to and literally creating out of his own flesh.

That thought sustained him at times, but he kept losing himself and disappearing—legs, arms, hands, feet, shoulders, hips. Not much of his torso was left. He clung to his face, eyes, and mouth, his memory and mind, his ears and lungs, and, of course, his heart. It was all that he had left. Was any story worth losing his sight for? Or his memory? Or his heart? Or his very soul? Was the Story insatiable? Did it really want everything, all of him, down to the last shreds of his body and soul? More to the point: could he and would he give it all up, in trust? Could he?

That is the question. Can we and will we give ourselves up, in trust to others, to the Other? Where is the end, the limit? How much are we willing to lose? How much of ourselves must be emptied out so that the Word, the Story, can come through us?

This book is about Lent, a book of reflections, stories, and questions for forty days based on the daily lectionary readings for the season. Its context is this story. What if this story came true in each of our lives, all of our lives, in the community of the Word? What if every day of Lent we lost something of ourselves so that the Teller, the Word, might flow through us more surely and freely? At the end of the forty days, what would be left? Can we, will we, consent to the story? To the diminishment? To the loss? To the mystery of the ending? To the total trust in the Word? What if there is no end until all time disappears into eternity in the incarnation and the wording of the Story in our flesh now?

Supposedly, after giving a talk in the Far East, Thomas Merton left the room with the words "I think I'll just disappear." They were his last words. Soon he was dead, electrocuted by an electric fan, and shipped home to the Kentucky hills on an army transport plane. Did this monk, who spent twenty-seven years seeking the face and the mystery of God, know something? Did he just disappear with a twinkle in his eye? This Lent, let us just disappear back into the arms of the One who created earth to be a garden, a dwelling place secure for all peoples, a haven for the least among us.

Long before Jesus, a disturber of structures and souls, disappeared into the tomb, he was intent on vanishing into the reverence of God, the shadow of the Spirit, the will of his Father, the service and obedience of his human companions, and the depths of history and time. Let us disappear with him and into him. As we go to die with him, losing ourselves in obedience and trust, so too we will rise with him on the first day of the week, before dawn. . . .

Saturday of the First Week of Lent

Deuteronomy 26:16–19
Psalm 119:1–2, 4–5, 7–8
Matthew 5:43–48

The first reading has Moses speaking to the people. It is full of promise and hope, for it tells us who we are, giving us an identity that can sustain us in all situations and experiences. The people are reminded that there is an agreement being made between God and us, that we are to walk in God's ways and hearken to the voice of God first and foremost. We are now God's possession, a people particularly belonging to God. If we follow God's ways, we will be raised up high in praise and renown and glory before all other peoples, and we will be a people sacred to the Lord.

This reading is not talking about nationalism, but about sacredness and intimacy. God, we are reminded, made all peoples, all nations, but chose one to make this agreement with. God's choice must be remembered and honored with great attention to obey the statutes and commandments. God's promises far outstrip anything we are asked to do in God's name. To live justly and to be in relationship with God bring joy and abundance of life. The people of God were chosen to model for the other nations the possibilities of life that God offers all peoples. The people consecrated to God are set apart for hope, imagination, and creativity, for proclaiming the possibilities of being human in history, and for the fullness of life, thankfulness, and depth of identity. The beginning of this consecration, the place where learning and initiation into a relationship of privilege with God are found, is seeking to know God with all our hearts by walking in the right way of the Lord. Diligence, firmness of purpose, uprightness, thankfulness, a life that is blameless, are sure indicators that God is close to us and that others will see the presence of God among us.

Jesus, like Moses the liberator and leader of his newly chosen people, is intent on making sure that his disciples know what he will ask of them. Jesus begins with the existing law: "You shall love your countryman but hate your enemy." Initially that may sound like a terrible commandment, but it specifically narrowed down and pointed out to the people whom they were responsible for—their own people, their own nation, bound in covenant with the Almighty. But now Jesus breaks the boundaries: "My command to you is: love your enemies, pray for your persecutors." There are to be no limits to love; there is no one we are not required to pray for or intercede for before God. In fact, the new criterion is not our own country or nation or people, but our very enemy, both collectively and individually.

If we do obey Jesus' commandment, we prove without a doubt that we are children of our Father, for God's sun rises on both the bad and the good. God's rain falls on the just and the unjust. If we love only those who love us, what merit is there in that? The world does as much. In fact, sinners and people we think very little of—tax collectors, politicians, corrupt business corporations, or our enemies—do as much. If we are going to imitate God, we are to be as perfect as God is perfect! It sounds impossible, outrageous, even naive. In some translations of this famous verse, *compassionate* or *holy* is used instead of the word *perfect*. Perhaps in our society, which sees the word *perfect* as a negative way of being in the world, the other words are closer to what Jesus is telling us we must try to express in our lives.

When I was much younger, this reading from Matthew evoked in me an image that was strong and powerful. I would walk around in the bright sunshine in a parking lot or shopping mall and look at the people: some were basking in rays of sunlight, dancing in sunbeams; others carried dark shadows or had black clouds trailing along behind them. I thought what a terrible place the world would be if we knew at every minute where we stood before God, whether we were bad or good! In the rain, which I dearly loved to walk in for hours, I thought again of this passage. What if it only rained on us when we were just? We would have no moisture, no respite from the dust and sand and grit, unless we were just in the eyes of God. I couldn't think of a worse way to go through life—exposed, judged, and experiencing the condemnation publicly. There would be no leeway, no breathing space, no kindness or place of sanctuary to reevaluate our position and move toward another. Thankfully we have instead God's kindness, pity, mercy, hospitality, simple courtesy, and gentle invitation to come home—to the sun and the rain and to God. We are to make sure that everyone else knows that the invitation is always there, the door is always open. God is like this; we have to do as much once we have known such kindness and care. We must extend such courtesy and openhandedness to all others.

Exclusion, the making of enemies, the decision to treat human beings with disrespect or refuse them forgiveness, is a curse. It is contempt for God. It is a terrible sin. Loving one's enemies is as natural as God loving us, but it is only with awareness of God's tenderness that this phenomenon becomes utterly apparent. This experience of God, as Simone Weil says, "is not consolation, it is light." Perhaps it is both realities: light that makes us see others with God's gentle eyes, and consolation that the only way we can respond to that love in our own experience of God is to look with such eyes upon all human beings, especially our enemies.

There is a whimsical poem that my grandmother once gave me that recalls this fact.

A Dream

I dreamed I died and Heaven's gates swung wide,
A smiling angel gently ushered me inside.
There, to my great amazement, were hundreds
Of people I had known down on earth.
Some, I judged as unfit and of very little worth.
Immediately angry words came to my lips,
But they were never set free.
For as I looked around, not one expected me.

—ANONYMOUS

Perhaps St. Augustine prayed to this compassionate, perfect Father when he finally came to his senses and turned toward a life he could not have imagined or borne before. It is the life of one who has accepted discipleship and so becomes a son or daughter of God. Niall O'Brien in *Island of Tears, Island of Hope* describes the experience in just one line: "Prayer is contact with God, and when it is authentic the mercy of God touches the searchers and flows out on their fellows, radiating God's mercy and love to them."

This experience in prayer is not a onetime thing, though the first time it can seem to have a magnitude that dwarfs anything previous. But once there has been this contact with Jesus' Father—Compassion, Perfection, Wholeness—there begins a hunger for it in the soul and a fresh awareness of its lack in our lives. Prayer is about that experience, but it is ultimately about sharing that experience with others who are as desperate for its taste as we are. We are not allowed to take from such Compassion without passing it on to another, especially anyone we think of as our enemy. In fact, spiritual writers are quick to remind us that if we truly pray and know God, there is no way we can think of another as our enemy. Teresa of Avila writes:

Prayer is not just spending time with the Lord. It is partly that— but if it ends there, it is fruitless. No, prayer is dynamic. Authentic prayer changes us—unmasks us, strips us, indicates where growth is needed. Authentic prayer never leads us to complacency, but needles us, makes us uneasy at times. It leads us to true self-knowledge, to true humanity.

Prayer makes us see clearly that there are no enemies. There are only others just like us, and the rain falls on us all, just and unjust alike; the sun warms us all, the good and the bad. Even the horrible, according to our standards, are invited into God's love. Luckily our standards are not the ones used by Jesus' Father. Prayer is the place for learning new standards, ones that are based on God's unutterable kindness for all of us, beginning with our enemies and extending even to us.

Sunday of the Second Week of Lent, Cycle B

Genesis 22:1–2, 9–13, 15–18
Psalm 116:10, 15–19
Romans 8:31–34
Mark 9:2–10

God stood behind Jesus, his words, his actions, his life, and his death. God stood behind him and caught him, throwing him back into life, resisting any hold that death could have on him. Jesus' God, the Father, now stands behind us, behind our words, actions, lives, and deaths, and God also stands in between us and what we do that hinders resurrection and good news to the earth. What are you standing behind? Whom are you standing behind in the world today?

Today is sometimes called the day of dreams, for God's dream for creation and for all of us is revealed in the risen Lord Jesus, beloved Son raised up forever. This dream begins in baptism, and it is fraught with risks. I once had an immediate experience of what this might mean. I was swimming in the Pacific Ocean, along a wild and lonely expanse of beach off the coast of northern California. The sea was calm and full of seals playing and swimming around me; I didn't notice the current subtly shifting because I was entranced with the play of the seals. Suddenly I was caught in a riptide. I struggled furiously for a time before remembering that it is fruitless to fight the current. It will just wear you out and then drag you under. You have to submit and let it carry you past the ripping tide. It will take you deeper, farther out, but when the tide passes, you can swim into shore. The seals reminded me. They didn't fight the water but eased into the pull and floated on top. I imitated them and did the same. It was a long swim into shore later, but I never would have made it otherwise. It was a terrifying feeling, yet an exuberant one as well. I had been saved!

God didn't spare Jesus from the ravages and risks of being human, and God doesn't spare us either. In baptism we have been given the privileged relationship that Jesus shared with his beloved father, and that relationship calls us to sacrifice, obedience, trust, and risk as we walk toward God. In that closeness there is pain and suffering, even death sometimes, but the glory shines through. Jesus was full of grace and truth, yet he suffered and was condemned unjustly. We must learn in this season to see the glory of God and the presence of Jesus transfigured in those who suffer unjustly, in the friends of God who give away what is most precious to them, including their lives, and who live risking everything to save others from death, sin, and despair.

The transfiguration story is a way of life that we are called to imitate. We are meant to transfigure earth, our relationships, and the church, and to be transfigured by others. We are to bring life out of suffering and death; liberation and freedom out of injustice, persecution, and resistance to the gospel; light out of darkness; and hope out of despair and encouragement. This is resurrection now, shared with us in baptism and in Jesus present in the world. When we listen to Jesus and the Scriptures, we learn how to obey and how to live with this seed of glory and shining grace.

When I was studying for my master's degree in systematic theology back in the early seventies, I took a course on the resurrection accounts.

It lasted from September through May. It was a grueling course, a heady introduction to exegesis, a comparison of accounts, wordplays, and so on. As Holy Week approached, we were instructed to go individually to a graveyard, tomb, or mausoleum after the Good Friday services and for at least three hours meditate and reflect on what happened to Jesus in the tomb and what resurrection means. It was a bleak, cold, windy, wet day, certainly not conducive to reflecting outdoors on anything, let alone death. I picked a huge national cemetery to get lost in and found myself in an alcove, somewhat protected from the rain and drizzle. In the midst of a half circle of stone benches was a statue, weather-beaten and greened with age and moisture. After looking at it for ages, I still couldn't tell whether it was a man or a woman who was shrouded in mourning and abject sadness. It was haunting, a good prelude to wondering what had happened to Jesus. I sat there for hours, damp and sodden, with the cold creeping into my bones. Then I stiffly got up and headed home, knowing nothing at all.

When asked in class on Monday morning what I had learned, I said that I didn't know what happened to Jesus, that I didn't know how resurrection occurred, that I wasn't all that sure of much. I only knew that somewhere in that cold, gray afternoon with lines and lines of white crosses filling my vision, I recommitted myself to believing in resurrection—as a taste, a sign, a necessary part of my life. I hoped I would grow in understanding or be given some glimpse of its meaning in the coming years. The professor accepted that, but I was left with a hunger to understand, to know, so that I could stake my life on something a bit more substantial.

It was almost a decade later that I got an intuition of what it could be, this mystery of resurrection. Once again I was in class, now studying for a Ph.D. in Scripture. We were explaining resurrection texts and had been assigned to write a three-page paper explaining resurrection. I tried. When the wastebasket was full, I gave up and went for a walk in the nearby park. I went prepared to stay the afternoon; I brought a blanket, water, a book of poetry and my journal, dried apples, and music to take me completely away from the realms of academia. I was more attuned to a flight of fancy. I got settled in my favorite spot, one that gave me a grand view of the ocean and the fog coming in.

No sooner had Mozart started to fill the air than a busload of young boys on a field trip interrupted my fantasy afternoon. They poured out of the bus, equipped with packs, Frisbees, and loud voices. I rolled over on my stomach and surveyed them as I tried to decide whether to move to another spot. But there was something about them that intrigued me. They were all between the ages of six and twelve. They were sharing food out of their sacks. Most intriguing of all, each had a huge helium-filled balloon on a long string tied to his wrist.

They played and I drifted, watching one boy in particular, about seven maybe. He was intent on everything he did. He unwrapped his brownie carefully, and he retied his shoelaces. In the midst of one such maneuver the string slipped from his wrist and the balloon headed for the skies. The boy stood there, a picture of absolute loss and dismay, as he watched his treasure slip away. His fists bunched up and his face contorted. He was just about to let out a good cry when suddenly another boy noticed the soaring balloon. He shouted, "Hey, guys! Look what Joshua just found out! They're better if you let them go!" In a matter of seconds forty or fifty brightly colored balloons were all floating away, with many heads upturned, intent on watching them go. Joshua's face had gone from dismay to near ecstasy. I was stunned.

It was only a moment, but that vision has stayed with me ever since. It is the essence of resurrection. What appeared to be disastrous, without hope, utter loss and desolation for one person was redeemed by another. It was made into something unbelievably holy and delightful by those who saw the pain and let go of something precious themselves, urging all the others to share that gift. And the boy's name was Joshua! Uncanny. I knew in a flash of a balloon soaring away and a sea of bright faces what was possible anywhere, anytime, for anyone who has eyes to see, quick reflexes, and the freedom to risk everything so another might have life. Rising helium balloons, rising hopes, and raised faces were all hints of Jesus' being raised from the dead.

I am forever grateful to that unnamed child who, in a moment of tender regard, set his friend free and taught me what rising from the dead might mean. This is our vocation. This is our command in listening to the word of the Lord. This is transfiguration. This is what binds us to earth and to the kingdom of God. We have been called to live in this sacred mystery of binding and re-creating all the earth to God. It is our glory and our salvation.

Saturday of the Third Week of Lent

Hosea 6:1–6
Psalm 51:3–4, 18–21
Luke 18:9–14

The word of God is plaintive and strong. God is reaching out to the chosen people, beloved Ephraim and Judah, who are far from God, caught in their affliction. God is sure that they will realize that although it was God who struck them, it is God too who will heal their wounds.

If we strive to know the Lord, we can be certain that he will come to us like the rain that waters the earth. But God knows Ephraim and Judah—and us. Our piety is like the dew, which early passes away. We are fickle; our faithfulness is short-lived and shallow. So, again and again, God sends the prophets to us to bring us to our senses and make us see that what God wants, the *only* thing that God wants, is love, not sacrifice. Ritual, liturgy, devotions, and prayers are all a mockery of God. We must learn to be steadfast, humble, contrite of spirit, and to imitate God in our dealing with others. Nothing else is required. Nothing else will be accepted.

All of this is prelude to Jesus' parable of the Pharisee and the tax collector, addressed to those who believe in their own self-righteousness while holding everyone else in contempt. We are familiar with the story. Two men go up to the Temple to pray. One stands before God with his head unbowed and prays aloud, certain of an audience with the Holy One: "I give you thanks, O God, that I am not like the rest of men— grasping, crooked, adulterous—or even like this tax collector. I fast twice a week. I pay tithes on all I possess." The tax collector, however, kept his distance, not even daring to raise his eyes. He just beat his breast and prayed, "O God, be merciful to me, a sinner."

How do we pray? Do we tell God who we are and how much good we do, expecting God to be impressed, certainly more open to listening to us and granting us what we ask for? Or do we see our true relation to the Holy One? Whatever we do can never be enough. The awareness of God overshadows us and fills us with awareness of our sinfulness and lack of love. We do not presume to stare God in the face. We are not sure of a privileged position at all. Even though we are the children of God, we are still sinners and in need of mercy and the Spirit, even to pray, even to approach God.

These are the two extremes presented to us. If they were on a scale of one to ten, with the tax collector a ten and the Pharisee a one, where would we position ourselves? Where would others who witness our lives place us on the scale? Where would God in divine truthfulness place us? Not easy questions. And Jesus' summary of the parable is clear: "Believe me, this man went home from the temple justified but the other did not. For everyone who exalts himself shall be humbled while he who humbles himself shall be exalted."

In God's reckoning everything is topsy-turvy. We can never be sure of our goodness, which is no more than a mote of dust in someone's eye or a raindrop in a drought. We have a long way to go in order to belong wholly to God. This God, Hosea and Jesus tell us, will heal us and bind up our wounds. We need only turn humbly to God. If we do not, then God will strike us with the force of the words in the mouth of the prophet or rend us so that we might turn to God in our affliction. Before we even begin to pray, we need to heed the prophet's word and Jesus' parable. They confront us in our pride and puffed-up sense of ourselves as the center of the universe. Perhaps we will be humbled when we least expect it.

This is a good time to look at what we claim to be. In our baptism we made promises, and we will renew them once again at the Easter Vigil, joined by the new catechumens. The ancient phrases are short and somewhat vague. They are couched in the language of rejection rather than the positive tone that calls forth more and more from us. In the Latin American Sacramentary the promises are more direct and can teach us some humility. The first: Do you promise to live forever in the freedom of the children of God? Free as children bound to the Father, Spirit, and Jesus the Christ and one another? Free for the gospel, for justice, for the poor, for the work of peace and hope? Free in the life and death, the cross and resurrection, of Jesus? Free, full of possibility, free from slavery, from sin, from all death that is unnecessary and destructive, free for holiness and grace?

The second promise is more detailed than the original version (do you promise to reject Satan and all his pomps?). It lists a number of things that we must reject. Do you refuse to be mastered by sin? Do you refuse to be held captive by evil? This question is put to us a number of times: Do you refuse to be mastered by the sins of materialism, nationalism, violence, racism, sexism, selfishness and greed, hatred, militarism and war, capitalism and communism, anything that hinders the coming of God into the world? The focus is on evils that we contribute to or allow to pervade society.

And the last promise: Do you refuse to live under no sign of power but the sign of the cross? Do you promise to live with humility, gratitude, nonviolence, generosity, forgiveness, mercy, joy? Do you foster a sense of community, a sense of companionship, with Jesus and the Spirit and your brothers and sisters?

This is our belief and our covenant. If we look at the promises we have made, where do we stand? Have we been obedient to these promises and our church community? Is it perhaps time to swallow our pride and move to the back of the church, to the back of the group, and cast our eyes on the floor as we realize that we are just like the prophet describes: our piety is like a morning cloud, as dew in the early hours of the day. It lasts about that long and is about that insubstantial. At least when we beg to receive mercy as a sinner, we bind ourselves to all those who share our faith and our gratitude for the mercy of God in the gift of Jesus to the world. We return as part of God's people, hoping for healing for our wounds and the wounds we inflict on others. We hope for resurrection on the third day, grace, and the power of the Spirit to sustain us and make us holy.

It is the eve of the fourth Sunday of Lent, a time for us to take a hard look at where we are and how far we've come and what still lies before us. This day can be a threshold, a boundary that we cross, a turning into the path. We can acknowledge how much we stumble and how much we cause others to get lost by our self-righteousness and feigned goodness.

As we are reminded by Diadochus of Photice, "Baptism revives God's icon and makes it radiant. But to produce his likeness God awaits our cooperation. Then it is that grace starts to fill in this icon with God's likeness." When we go to pray today, will we be radiant? Only others will know, but that is the way it is meant to be. Diadochus also reminded his followers: "All human beings are created in God's likeness. But to be in God's likeness can be properly said only of those who have lovingly pledged him their will." Today is a time for pledges, for promises renewed, and for the surety of God's strength to fulfill our promises.

Wednesday of Holy Week

Isaiah 50:4–9
Psalm 69:8–10, 21–22, 31, 33–34
Matthew 26:14–25

This Isaian reading is, in part, the reading from Palm Sunday. It is the description of the Suffering Servant of Yahweh, of Jesus the crucified One. It speaks of extreme humility, humbled even unto death, death that is preceded by spitting, beating, public shame, degradation. But it is about strength and vindication too. The words are bold and forthright, especially if they are spoken in the midst of torture: "He is near who upholds my right; if anyone wishes to oppose me, let us appear together. Who disputes my right? Let him confront me. See, the Lord God is my help." This is the stance of a prophet reminding those who stand in opposition to his word and presence that God is witness to all that is occurring and that God remembers! God will speak on behalf of those who suffer and will uphold the rights of those enslaved, tortured, and killed. It is a courageous stand against the forces of evil even as evil seeks to stop the heart of the one who belongs to God.

Psalm 69 speaks of a closeness, a kinship with God. It expresses an understanding of why God does not intervene to save people in the face of persecution, and it reveals a steadfast sense of faithfulness. Can we pray like this? Have we even stood up for God's will and the poor often enough so that there would be any reason for us to be caught in this predicament of suffering for the honor of God or the cause of justice?

> For your sake I bear insult,
> and shame covers my face.
> I have become an outcast to my brothers,
> a stranger to my mother's sons.
> Because zeal for your house consumes me, and the insults of
>   those who blaspheme you fall upon me.

Jesus' zeal for his Father's house the Temple has caused him to drive the money changers out, but zeal for his Father's house the community of the covenant has caused him to side with the ones who have fallen through the cracks of society and religious institutions; to heal and aid those who are ill, despised, and insulted; and to keep company with sinners. His revelation of God contradicts the practice and images of the "religious" ones, and they go after him.

The Psalm lists what evil people can do to those who threaten their shallow images of God: They put gall in his food, and in his thirst he is given vinegar to drink. There is no one to comfort him. He is isolated and condemned to suffer and die alone, cursed by human beings, laughed at or ignored by religious people. But the prayer is definitely the prayer of Jesus: "I will praise the name of God in song, and I will glorify him with thanksgiving: . . . 'See, you lowly ones, and be glad; you who seek God, may your hearts be merry! For the Lord hears the poor, and his own who are in bonds he spurns not.' "

This is a prayer of encouragement to others who suffer. And the response used in the liturgy praises and acknowledges what must not be forgotten: "Lord, in your great love, answer me." God is love, and it is love that sustains. This prayer takes us beyond our pain into God's heart.

The story is told of the betrayal of Jesus by Judas. This time the account is from Matthew. We must listen and let it pierce our hearts. Before the Passover Judas goes to the authorities and asks what they are willing to give him if he hands Jesus over to them. This is a business transaction, a deal. Jesus is a commodity, and money changes hands.

Meanwhile, Jesus is making his own plans for the Passover meal, sending his disciples on ahead into the city to arrange for a house in which they will have dinner. An anonymous donor lends Jesus his house. And dinner begins. As it grows dark, literally and figuratively, Jesus speaks: "I give you my word, one of you is about to betray me." The rest of the group is distressed and each asks Jesus the same question: "Surely it is not I, Lord?" This is the question each of us must ask of God in the presence of the community this week.

The ritual gesture of dipping in the same dish with Jesus takes place. In this account Jesus adds harsh words: "The Son of Man is departing, as Scripture says of him, but woe to that man by whom the Son of Man is betrayed. Better for him if he had never been born."

Terrible words. And they are not just about Judas. They are about all of us who have betrayed our faith, sometimes in small ways, unaware of the consequences on others and on our own faltering souls, and sometimes in larger ways that have caused others to sin, to lose heart, or to participate with others in violence and evil. When Judas asks, along with the others, "Surely it is not I, Rabbi?" he receives the answer that none of us ever wants to hear or admit to: "It is you who have said it." Even in Jesus' answer there is an open door, a chance to change. Nothing is set. And the Gospel stops here. "It is you who have said it." We are sinners. Now what are we going to do?

We must look at ourselves clearly, with the eye of God. We claim to love God. We claim to follow Jesus as Lord on the way of the cross. We claim to belong to the kingdom of God's justice and peace. We claim to resist evil and refuse to be mastered by sin. We claim to live in the freedom of the children of God.

The assertion "love is blind" is often spoken glibly. Perhaps we are attempting to avoid responsibility for what we do to those we claim to love. But as G. K. Chesterton wrote: "Love is *not* blind; that is the last thing it is. Love is bound, and the more it is bound the less it is blind." Love is bound to God and to one another in God; all that we do affects others. When we sin against God, we sin against one another. We are accountable to the community for what we do personally.

In the same way, what we do or do not do as a community makes us accountable for much of what the world does. The seeds of the world's hatred and violence and lack of belief in God are found in our faithlessness. Instead of being a light to the nations, often we are just another sound in a cacophony.

When I was in Ireland a few years ago, I was driving on a backcountry road and listening to the radio. There had been a short-story writing contest. To make the contest more of a challenge, the story was limited to around thirty words. Some of the entries were read over the radio, and I was half listening, concentrating more on driving on the correct side of the road and not running into the stone walls that seemed all too close. Then this story was read:

Welcome home, son!
Hello, Father.

It is so good to see you. It's been a long time.
Yes, Father, a very long time. It was hard.
Hard as nails. Hard as wood.
I know. What was the hardest?
The kiss, Father, the kiss. (Long pause)
Yes. Come in and let me hold you.

I nearly drove off the road. Within seconds I was crying and had to pull over. It hit me hard. I was overwhelmed by the realization that sin is evil and terrible, but some sin is more evil and more terrible: the sin of those who claim to be friends, disciples, companions. My sin, the sin of the communities I was part of, and the sin of the church were the most devastating of all, like that kiss.

That night, as I sat under a great tree in an old abandoned monastery reading poetry, I came across this line: "Let your heart melt towards me, just as the ice that melts in spring leaves no trace of its chill" (*Kokinshu*). It was the remedy for the morning's aching pain. And a few days later I was listening to a Buddhist monk in exile from Vietnam speak. A piece I managed to jot down seemed connected as well: "No argument. No reason. No blame. Just understanding which leads to love" (Thich Nhat Hanh).

This is the way God is with all of us. Today, as individual Christians and as the church we pray: "Lord, in your great love, answer us." Today we are all called to be reconciled to one another so that the body of Christ, whole and in communion, can celebrate the Triduum together. All of us, together with the catechumens, are to meet together at the door of the church, forgiven and reconciled, to enter into the mystery of our salvation, belief, and freedom as the children of God.

Officially today is the last day of Lent. Our journey is complete. Now we go to celebrate Easter. Alexander Schmemann, a great liturgical scholar, writes:

Even though we are baptized, what we constantly lose and betray is precisely that which we receive at baptism. Therefore,

Easter is our return to our own baptism, whereas Lent is our preparation for that return—the slow and sustained effort to perform, at the end, our own passage into new life in Christ . . . Each Lent and Easter are, once again, the rediscovery and the recovery by us of what we were made through our own baptismal death and resurrection.

Mystery now comes over us and we disappear into it, much as Peter, James, and John disappeared into the cloud that overshadowed Jesus at the transfiguration. For our part, we must make sure that all that is evil or halfhearted within us disappears in our desire to walk the way of the cross with Jesus and come home to the Father, to the kingdom, and to the community of those who seek the company of Jesus.

Holy Thursday: *Mass of the Lord's Supper*

Exodus 12:1–8, 11–14
Psalm 116:12–13, 15–18
1 Corinthians 11:23–26
John 13:1–15

Today is often called the feast of friends, the friends of God. But it is also a night of "re-membering," of putting back together the body of Christ, the church, the community of those who gather around the story (the word) and the bread (the flesh and blood) and become what they eat. The Jews begin Passover with the story. The youngest asks the question: why is this night different from all others?

The ritual of Passover tells the story of terror and death, when the angel of God passed over the doorways marked with the blood of the sacrificed lamb, and also tells about the wonder and marvelous works that God did for the chosen people in leading them out of Egypt, away from slavery and repression, through the desert of Sinai, and into the promised land. The ritual ends with the passionate cry "Next year in Jerusalem!," a blessing and fervent prayer for the fullness of the promises set in motion so long ago.

Remembering is the essence of the ritual. It makes present in history the story and the promises. What God did in ages past for the chosen ones, God will do now for those gathered at table. The story continues in every generation. God waits for us to come. This is the ritual that the Holy Thursday Mass is based upon, and yet there is more, for Jesus made significant changes in the ritual on the night before he died. We celebrate this night in the shadow of betrayal. It is a bittersweet night of intimacy, gifts given, and love expressed.

The first reading begins with the account of the rite that is to be celebrated as a memorial in the first month of the Jewish calendar. It details the ritual slaying of the lamb, which is to be shared by the family alone or with other households so that the entire lamb is consumed. The lamb is slaughtered during the evening twilight, with the whole assembly of Israel as witness. Those who are to eat together take some of the blood of the lamb and mark their doorposts and the lintel of every house. How they are to eat the meal is specified and the foods are named: roasted lamb, unleavened bread, and bitter herbs to remind them of preparation in haste and the bitter, long years of slavery and oppression when they could not worship their God. They eat the meal standing, with their belts and bags around their waists, sandals on their feet, and staff in hand, "like those who are in flight." Because they are. They are in flight from death, from slavery.

This is the Passover of the Lord, because on this night God will go through Egypt and strike down the firstborn, human and beast alike, executing judgment on all the gods of Egypt. This is a night of listening, believing, and clinging to others in fear and hope. It is a night of death that is the prelude to the beginning of life for a whole people. "Seeing the blood, I will pass over you; and no destructive blow will come upon you." The blood, seeping deep into the wood of the lintels of the doorways, is the mark and sign of salvation. And salvation is about bread, justice, and hope. This day is a memorial feast, a perpetual institution that all generations are commanded to remember, to celebrate the coming of the power of God into the world with freedom and lasting justice for those who cry out for help.

The images of unleavened bread, the lamb of God, and the blood marking those saved are woven through the Christian ritual as well, and yet they are more personal because the bread, the lamb, and the blood are the person and the body of Jesus and what we become: the body of Christ in the world, a source of freedom and hope in the midst of terror and death for all who cry out to God.

We remember the dying and the rising of Jesus and, on this night, his last meal with his friends, and his gift to them: his own flesh and blood. This memory is steeped in forgiveness, reconciliation, and atonement for the sins of the past, and rebirth. This night is a meal among friends, the sacrifice of the Lamb on the cross, and the resurrection—all braided into one reality. Johannes Metz calls this story the dangerous memory of the passion of Christ. It is dangerous and subversive, because what is seen as judgment and death by some is believed to be salvation and life by others. We must remember this night that the words "body of Christ" describe the Eucharist and us, the people of God; we are to become bread for the world with the bread that we share this night.

It is not just the bread that is this rich source of strength and sustenance, it is also the blood. The Psalm sings: "I will raise the cup of salvation and call on the name of the Lord."—Ps. 116:13 This reminds us what we are to do with our lives so that the ritual gestures of our worship are truly expressive of our self-giving. We are to make a return to the Lord for all the good that God has done for us. We are to take up the cup of salvation and call upon the name of the Lord—and we are to drink the cup of wine, blood, suffering, and salvation.

There is an immediate connection between eucharist and death: "Precious in the eyes of the Lord is the death of his faithful ones" (Ps. 116:15). All of our deaths are one in the dying of Jesus. All of us are servants, sons and daughters whose bonds have been loosened by our God, and so we offer a sacrifice of thanksgiving, vowing our lives to the Lord in the presence of one another. Our blessing-cup taken and shared proclaims that we trust in the blood that heals and reconciles the aches and wounds of the world caused by sin, evil, injustice, and violent hatred. The blood of Christ is poured into our wounds and we heal, scarred over and mindful of the suffering but able to understand the pain of those who suffer unjustly and to share in their struggle to be free and whole. St. Paul reminds us: "I have been crucified with Christ . . . I carry the marks of Jesus branded on my body" (Gal. 2:19, 6:17). In this ritual of eating and drinking with Jesus, we are in Christ, not just repeating his sacrifice and modeling our lives on his, but living in the wounds and heart and very body of Christ, together.

The Gospel continues the story. The ritual is based upon the lived experience of Jesus in the world, with his disciples and those who came to believe in him. In John's Gospel there is no specific ritual of the breaking of the bread and the sharing of the cup of the Last Supper. Instead, there is another eucharistic ritual, another telling of the story: the ritual of the washing of the feet of the disciples by Jesus. Both rituals are rooted in the same reality. For John's community—and for all the church—getting down on our knees in humble obedience, following Jesus' example of a lifetime of serving and performing those tasks that are needed in the world, is remembering Jesus, putting him back in our communities and uniting us as a holy people belonging to God.

The story is simple. Jesus intends to show his disciples how much he has loved them before he leaves them, reversing the relationships. He, the master, washes their feet. This is the way to honor God, by honoring one another, and especially those among us in need of healing, care, and tenderness, let alone justice, freedom, and hope of living at long last as human beings.

Jesus comes to Simon Peter. Sometimes we read just the name Simon—his name before he met and encountered Jesus. At other times it is simply Peter—who he is after being converted to Jesus and the kingdom. At other times, like tonight, it is Simon Peter, where he is of both minds and hearts, acting more as he was before he followed Jesus, yet in the presence of Jesus, who renamed him. He resists: "Lord, are you going to wash my feet?" And Peter is told that he does not understand what Jesus does to him and for him in this gesture of obedience and submission. He resists more forcefully: "You will never wash my feet!" Jesus is patient and yet persistent: "If I don't wash you, you'll have no share in my heritage." It is time for Peter to reconsider, and when he does, he lunges forward in his typical way: "Not only my feet, but my hands and head as well."

Our society is out of touch with such rituals of hospitality, welcome, service, and honor, and so the depth of what is happening and the reasoning behind Peter's outburst often go unrealized. Washing a person's feet was onerous work. People wore, at most, sandals in a world of heat, loose garbage, and animal droppings. People's feet were crusted, smelly, and repulsive, and even worse if they were diseased or had sores. Even husbands could not demand that their wives wash their feet. It was something that was necessary, but it was done as a courtesy, an honor for a guest arriving in a host's house, or in love, affection, dedication, or submission freely given. Sometimes a disciple washed his master's feet, an honor that expressed a level of trust and intimacy between the two, but never did the master wash the disciples' feet. Never! This is more than the reversal of fortunes spoken of and proclaimed in the good news. This is a reversal of what constitutes worship of God. Submission, obedience, service, bending before others is bending before God, because now, in the mystery of the incarnation, we do indeed bend before God when we serve one another's needs and tend to one another's wounds.

After washing their feet, Jesus reclines once again at the table and asks them, "Do you understand what I just did for you? You address me as 'Teacher' and 'Lord,' and fittingly enough, for that is what I am. But if I washed your feet—I who am Teacher and Lord—then you must wash each other's feet. What I just did was to give you an example: as I have done, so you must do." This ritual is not just a momentary or onetime experience to impress upon the disciples the depth of Jesus' love for them. It is a moment that ritualizes and intensifies his entire life and the life that is at the root of all his actions.

This night is about bread and wine, about bodies and blood, about feet and washing, about intimacy and unbounded, unexpected love, about a God who bends before us hoping that one day we will treat each other with the same regard and dignity that he has always lavished upon us. This is what the new covenant is about. This is what reality and religion are about. This is what community and love are about.

Some theologians and preachers say that basically Jesus was killed because of the way he ate, whom he ate with, and what he encouraged people to do for and with one another as a sign of their allegiance to him and to the kingdom of his Father.

There is an old story told among Zen teachers:

✻   *Once upon a time there was a family, the relatives of a poor sick samurai, who were dying of hunger. They approached Eisai's temple, and the good monk there took the golden halo off the image of Buddha and gave it to them, telling them to go and sell it and buy food for themselves and find shelter. When others heard about it, there was the cry of "Sacrilege!" What reckless and dangerous behavior! What kind of precedent was set for the temples!*

But the monk calmly reminded them of the story of the Chinese master Tanka, who burned a wooden image to warm himself. And he preached to them: Buddha's mind is full of love and mercy. If the Buddha had heard the plight of these people, why, he would have cut off a limb if that would have helped them in their pain! What's a halo or anything else that's available in the face of a human being's suffering and need?

We are invited to eat and drink at the table of the Lord, to have our feet washed, to enter the wounds and heart of Christ, to be as his beloved friends. And we are told to do as Jesus did. We must wash each other's feet. Jesus expressed his love in service to the world. Now that is our task.

Poetry

From *Dancing with Angels: Selected Poems*

God is an elephant
Lumbering,
taking up so much space
useless, massive, so ungainly,
awkward, here on earth.
A stampede in the wild
An act in the circus
A ride in the zoo
God is an elephant
What is he trying to make
us remember?

Day after Christmas, for Michael
Day after Christmas, for Michael
cold street corner on the edge of Berkeley
off University. Under streetlights
and flashlights, they come in ones
and twos and sometimes threes. In cabs,

on bicycles, on foot. Stopping by, being
cool, acting at ease. Thursday night.
Needle exchange. Illegal but somehow just.

They come, some furtive, eyes searching
in quick darting glances, seeking acceptance.
Especially the women, dark eyes shadowed
with liner and deeper lines drawn. Our
fingers touch as I hand the bags with clean
needles over to them. Exchanges in the street.

Some come with the smell of cheap wine
heavy between us, weaving only slightly
eyes too bright, tongues glib, they turn
their heads aside and spit, muttering behind
their scarves. Mostly though they are all
incredibly polite, careful, even grateful.
I keep thinking, seeing past eyes to rooms
and veins pierced in harsh light or in shared
shadows. Aches too raw, too crowded to be
contained. Needle ghettos that defy geographical
or social boundaries.

I stand with a dear friend and a couple of
strangers, men, all gay and the angel Ariel
in the night. We chat, stomp feet to keep
warm, pass the time, the cold creeping in
under sweats and gloves. The strong light
sits in a baby stroller with the litany of
who exchanges—male, female, black, white
asian, indian, hispanic and the brown bags,
not lunch—but new syringes, information on

counseling, aids, alcohol, and condoms.
They hardly ever have a woman with them
on these nights.

The women's faces all look weary, fearful
hard and vulnerable. We speak only a few
words: hi, evening sure is cold, thanks, we
appreciate you doing this—how many you got?
count them out, put them in here. Careful
you don't get stuck, be safe. bye. Simple human
exchanges. It's the day after Christmas, on
the street with the poor folk, the outsiders
still no room for them. Lives squandered
needle by needle, drumming despair, singing
blood, plain needs, shooting up. Who cares?
Dim sorrows at such terrible losses. And I
am inordinately grateful for this night, this
exchange. Somehow this is incarnation.
Divine/human exchange.

The most ragged roses smell the sweetest
the fragrance pulls my face down close
—memories of an old woman dying
my nana telling secrets to her granddaughter
who believed in druids and angel graces
and watched her face death unflinchingly
though fear-filled and alone.
My only friend was leaving.
I learned the lesson of loss
the roses remained in the room
long after she left. I remember the roses
and broke the glass in grief.

Going through old mementos, boxes of saved treasures
I had forgotten
the Green Beret, the purple heart
missing in action.
It was early in that long war.
he volunteered. I screamed. He left.
We both went off.
He to war and I, to do battle with God.
We were both novices in the art of dying.
They brought it to the convent in New England
on a day in late march, old snow still piled high.
I was nineteen. He was twenty-three.
Now so many years later, at forty-five
warm tears move silently gently
We were both so young for such final agreements,
taken so far beyond our words.
I have trouble remembering his face
but the pain for a few moments was still so fresh
so singular, so raw.
Every death and each first kiss are so alike.
I hadn't known that before—then
I do now
I close the box. Refold the beret
and put it back on the bottom underneath
all the letters, photographs, and roses.
It was so long ago. I wonder—
am I any more adept in the art of dying?
or are we always novices in that regard. . . .

A Trappist funeral reminds me. . . . I want
bare feet, a white shroud or coarse cloth
a wedding dress of gray or white against the dirt

to match my hair long ago turned.
To be laid deep in the ground
for I have so loved earth.
A moment of clear blue turquoise sky above
to gaze on me and then the slap
of red New Mexico earth in my face.
I will be lowered awkwardly unevenly by friends.
Only one small change. Mix in flower seeds
at the very end so folk will have unexpected beauty
when I am gone away.

GETHSEMANE, 1990

I write all these lines with angels looking over my shoulder.
They scratch out words and throw in images of their own.
The handwriting changes noticeably, as they pull on my hand,
leading me by wild subterranean paths. They bring me memories
like ripe cherries, just picked and then, if I'm not attentive,
they add a thorn or thistle to the bowl and smile ruefully,
as though tending to an errant child.

They know I need nests, belonging spaces and they bring
twigs and threads and down for the makings. Their wings
comfort, the sound opening and closing like doors on carpet
to closed rooms. They let me in to stay awhile, especially
when the pain is strong and broad.

The meanings are sifted through angel hair. They do not
understand heartache and grief but they see its shadow
and they are drawn as moths to flame sensing a place
to touch with unfurled light.

Crooked fingers carefully unbent so I can sign this space
with rain, with a gust of wind, with tears and only a slight

tremor. Hope is hidden in each phrase. Their work
is done so freely and without ruse. I smile when I read
it later and know I was in their company all along.

I read in a book once
it was a long time ago.
about an angel who fell in love with earth
but she needed someone to believe in her
in order to stay visible.
I wonder often these days
if I were caught in the same predicament
if I'd be forever disappearing.

I write to remake the world.
I write to make the world right.
I write to get beyond survival to life.
I write for the right to life for all,
    beginning with earth and creatures and all things that begin
    in seed and seek to sprout and change form, mature, grow old
    gracefully, and die well, finishing their stories themselves.
I write to keep breathing, walking, relating, praying.
I write to worship.
I write to keep the Word enfleshed, to keep incarnation in
    history, to make the Word come true.
I write to make love easily understandable, tangible, simply
    acknowledged.
I write to make love gratefully to the One who spoke once in
    human flesh and whispered "you are a letter that gives heart
    to my soul—write me."
So I do. Until forever. My words become flesh.
The story is true, it is the only story I serve, the only story I ever
    tell,

it is the place, the only place I ever dwell.

*I notice I've started to kiss the Book, press my lips against the
      leather*

*when I retrieve it from its place. Pages opened, I bend and honor
      silently*

solemnly the words printed black.

*When did I start caressing the Word, touching the unspoken
      sighs of God*

with my tongue. I care not if others notice,

*This is ritual, a secret limit breached, a face without flesh
      fingered,*

*a breathing together and the words coming singing out of my
      mouth.*

*It is fervor, piety, reverence or more, something other—I do it
      even in public,*

*more than ease and familiarity, even more than long marriage
      and faithfulness.*

It is the fruit of endurance, the child of passionate devotion.

*It is presence extending beyond the silence. It is seeking me out
      and drawing me*

*in, this body, this text of the only God I know with limb of script
      and story form.*

It has become necessity before speaking even one word.

I am concealed in the spaces between the letters.

I kiss the door coming into home, the only home I know.

I want my words to crack diamonds

shatter hearts the way a soprano's voice

breaks glass sending hard splinters to cut

and draw blood and salvage the truth.

I want my words to remain as subversive relics

wild witnesses to cruelty's callousness

warning of hope's death, trammelled on by careless
phrases and deadly intents. People must
be able to trust again what they hear.
It is the only authority I will obey
The Word made Flesh that dwells among us still.

Some Things I Wonder About. . . .

Do angels scream at all the violence, the innocents' deaths?
Does some old Indian spirit, uncle, or grandfather bring back
    the spring?
Do the trees' roots move like fingers through the soil's flesh,
    blind yet seeing, knowing it in intimacy?
Does the first bird each morning know it announces hope
    restored with its wild trill of song?
Does mystery want us to stumble into its embrace as much as we
    want to be held securely?
Do our eyelids really imitate wings and is learning to fly like
    seeing and opening our eyes?
Is the Spirit always stroking the very soft spots on the top of our
    heads but we think it's just the wind in our hair?
Do angels ache when we make God weep again in all the
    enclosed gardens of the world?
Are crows and ravens and cormorants really broken-off pieces of
    night wildly free?
Is being created more limitless than we ever imagined? What do
    we want to be?
God, I hope these are all more true than false.

Evading the cloak of death
the old women slide across the canyon floor
like ghosts with bare feet and voluminous skirts.

I see them only inches ahead of me
but they are so silent that I do not trust my senses.
I give up trying to imitate their ease and swiftness,
their fluidity and stare at their long hair
disappearing in the vellum of the night.
They've become reins and I obediently walk behind them
until morning explodes across mountain stone
and swirls their skirts in reds and golds,
old patterns of their homes.
Was the night a trance
a dance, a long march, the road back
the way I lost once?
As the day draws on, I feel oddly at ease on earth.

(REMEMBERING GUATEMALA)

From Marrow of Mystery: Selected Poems

Introduction

When I was young, my brothers and sisters and I would all converge on our Nana's apartment in New York. It was a Sunday noon ritual after church. We crowded around her table. The treat was always the same: hot boiled marrow bones specially requested from the butcher down the block. The smell hit you as the front door was opened. Sweet and strong, but basically indescribable. Great slices of dark bread nice and warm lay waiting on the table.

Standing in her apron, her white hair pulled back in a bun, Nana would eye us each in turn and fish the marrow bones out of the steaming pot onto a plate. Then she would scoop out the insides. They looked gross, awful, and ugly. She would smear them, slather them, on the bread. Each of us would be served and immediately we would bite into our bread, running our tongues over the marrow. But always, the youngest or anyone sickly or weak, would get served first and got the biggest bones and the most marrow. We never spoke, only smelled and sniffed and sighed and made slurping noises as we ate.

I could never put together something that smelled and tasted that good with what looked so icky and awful and came out of bones. We ate the insides of bones! But I learned early about many mysteries around that table. Silence is the appropriate response to such goodness—no talk after eating. What is ugly can belie appearances, give meaning, and take you places you never dreamed was hidden there. Marrow was meant to be shared—but first it was to be given to the weakest, the youngest, and those most in need of such infusions of life. And there are rituals that make religion meaningful. Being the one who ladled out the goodness and spread it around meant that you didn't eat yourself, but my Nana never seemed to mind much. Her delight was in watching us eat.

But what has stayed with me most is: mystery has to be dug out of bones, looks ugly, tastes luscious, but really is indescribable—beyond words—but oh, the sheer delight in digging and smearing and letting others feast on it.

These poems could be called autobiographical, and some are, but many are more to the heart of just being human and having either stumbled into the marrow of life or been handed outright, for no reason at all, a piece of thick homemade bread smeared with the marrow of mystery by so many generous folk.

I travel ten, eleven months of the year—to Asia, islands galore, Canada, the South China seas, Celtic green dollops in an ocean of blue, the United States, and Latin America. I crisscross earth going backwards and forwards in time and place. It is exhausting and exhilarating and, although I usually go as the teacher or the preacher or the storyteller, I am always the one taught, caught up in wisdom, and called to radical altering of my life and thoughts.

But I always come back—back home—a place of wild light, a small place in northern New Mexico—a place of high sky, enchanted mesas, and blood-of-Christ mountains, to a land close by wilderness. And that wildness strays often into my path and backyard, and I lie in wait for it. It feeds me more than anything else, even more than words and music: it is silence, solitude, loneliness loved, wildness visited—in hawk's eye, wolf's howl, raptor and reptile and skunk, and the way land, sky, and weather all come together. It seeps into me and I need it as though I need a transfusion. That is why there are so many poems that are triggered by storms, lack of rain, seasons shifting, and places apart from usual human habitation. I cannot stay away too long from places off the beaten path. If I can't get home, then I must go off into the unknown wherever I am traveling.

After months on the road, coping with 40 degrees Celsius and monsoon rains, sitting on runways delayed, days of gray cold, hordes of people, words, and translations—and being a stranger, a visitor, a foreigner, a guest—I have to come back to being a monk, a hermit outwardly for a while since I am really always that internally. And in those travels there is violence, haste, ignorance, injustice, horror, betrayals, as well as enduring graces, faithfulness in the face of brutality, snippets of unrepeatable glory, ordinary courtesies, and gross inequities. Billions of human beings brushing shoulders, caressing one another, and shoving one another aside must be absorbed somehow. It's osmosis—and after such dense periods of absorption, there has to be utter silence, a time to brush all spirits, words, and presences away from one's heart as an old native elder showed me with his dance of hands. It has to be done periodically outside, literally, with the earth and the sky and the waters as witnesses and, in lieu of that, in pockets of solitude, gleaned moments of sanctuary, and more often than not, in words—poems, pieces of stories, images given, memories put on a page, soul and mind emptied out.

These pieces are culled from stacks of journals, reams of attempts and poems just given fully formed. Some of the poems merited titles, some did not. They are bits and pieces, scooped out of bones—the marrow of life's richness found in every human being and all over earth in remnants, ruins, and all that shares this place with us—the beasts and the birds, spirits and schools of fish, light and weather patterns, and the ground itself. All talks. I seek to listen. And sometimes poetry is the residue of the conversations, more often of prayer, of conscious remembering, of the struggle to make meaning or to brush away accumulation of spirit, to empty the pockets of soul. This sort of writing, reflection, and communion is the undercurrent, the daily stuff of life, running under and through the books, the talks, the preaching, and the storytelling. It's just pieces of marrow bones spread on bread. It has nourished me but it must be shared out for mystery speaks most surely in silences shared and when the marrow is dug out, spread on bread—or scrawled on a page. Some of the digging has been done, but the feast is always laid out before us. This book is really just a pot of marrow bones reeking of mystery, given as a gift.

Incarnations

The original Incarnation was God giving form and face to creation, making a place outside, a place other than just God. The Jewish mystics believe God made a space, breathed out, whispered, sighed a sound—and the Mysterious Holy One set in motion all that is and has ever been and will be still.

And Christians believe fervently that after eons of waiting and waiting, God spoke, sighed, and dared a Word that had been there from the beginning, and the Word was God and that Word took on flesh and blood and bone and mind and made earth his dwelling place. This Word has stayed on with us and will until forever, lingering in the absent presence of the Spirit.

Once the Word became flesh. Now all flesh seeks to become word, to transpose the mystery. We are made in the image and likeness of God. Our flesh speaks, sings, weeps, stutters, and gasps as we make meaning with our lives.

There are persons who are clear phrases, a word carefully pronounced, articulating small pieces of mystery. There are people, moments that incarnate a truth, pose a question, blurt out unselfconsciously a wild proposition that is hinged to the Holy and the doors swing wide. These poems seek to remember, to put on paper these incarnations of God walking earth on clay feet, with shining eyes and gestures of radiant clarity. They live and breathe and exhale some detail of Mystery's transcendence through the marrow of our bones.

Elegy for Louis

(*Thomas Merton*)

Twenty-nine years have gone by.
It was a cold gray morning.
In the early dark the radio punctured restless sleep.
5 A.M. New York City, 23rd Street and 7th Avenue,
an apartment across the street from the Chelsea Hotel,
next door to the YMCA. A dump of an efficiency.
Home that year, 1968, teaching uptown in Harlem.

The news came on. Eyes still closed.
Last item—Bangkok, Thailand.
The infamous monk Thomas Merton
was bizarrely electrocuted in a hotel room.
He was coming home from Asia in a military transport,
sealed in a coffin—to Gethsemane. The irony
was not lost on the commentator:
This man had protested that war from the hills of Kentucky
    battling with words,
hunkered down and holding out alone on a grassy knoll.

I kept my eyes closed.
This was too much reality to grasp in
the shadows of another day. The names
rose like warm blood in my throat:
JFK, RFK, MLK, now another: TM
or Father Louis, as he was known.
He was dead. I awoke, weeping.

We've learned to live 29 years without him.
But wonder what we would have become if
he were here today? Joy to you, Louie:
Remember us in your delight face to face!

It was the beginning of wisdom rooted in wood:
the cross contemplating pain, a long loving hard
look at what's grindingly hard to see.
His death: a new seed of contemplation.

—DECEMBER 10, 1998

Bold Virgin Knowing

Quickening, innocence grasped.
She quickens and turns, trembles, harp strings played, delicately
  fingered
and her womb is no longer empty. What wisdom spreads through
  her mind,
limbs, bright joys and old fears, intimations of prayers and a
  nation's hopes?
Unborn child conceived without passion or sex yet intimacy, a
  being known,
knowing intercourse and communication.
Virgin, wild untouched still as forest primeval, undiscovered
  island, sea's
hidden volcano. What seed was dropped softly into your
  acquiescent heart?
As it lay trembling beneath words—covered with the wide hand
  of God.
Covered. Imprint impressed, swelling to ripeness of summer out
  of season.
Nature bypassed. This is mystery, so much humanness and yet so
  much lack—
only female form to make male flesh.
God's refuge in a girlchild's body that will learn grief as the only
  ground under his feet.
She rocks cradling herself and what's to come, singular witness
  for awhile.

Quickening, all eager desire, intent on her lot, her portion, her
    cup.
Over the roofs the swallows and larks drop, swooping and the
    vines climb
trailing fragrances in the night air. The wind barely stirs.
Peace has slipped into the world.
Heat bouncing off the street, sweat running down my back
subway sweat wending way through crowds to shuttle to
    42nd St. E.
A woman in what was once white clothes washed over years
Salvadoran—Guatemalan?
Alone with space around as she walked slowly in her world
Eyes cast down, lips moving. She was praying
As sure as any monk in a cloister, or sitting on a cushion.
Same chi, same sense of reverence in unself-conscious absorption
    of the Holy.
I was stunned—thrown into Your presence as she passed me by—
Oblivious of all yet somehow more solid in her communion with
    you
than any who hurried to their destinations.

I smiled and realized—she's already there, just being here.
When I am old may I pray and walk and be like that, O God
So simple, pure and true to myself and You.
Unabashedly Yours and about Your business, as my life
fades from cleansing like her clothes. Amen.

I want to be remembered for having wove the Word
subtly through every fabric and design, hiding it and then
uncovering detail, color, thread and line.
Wrapping all of earth and all its creatures in a cloth
fair, delicate and fine, that held a people's hopes and bread

and fragments and pieces of heart to raise the dead.
I want to be remembered for having shorn the sheep
and gathered wool, and spun and carded and made garments
against the cold. And then to have weathered all the storms
and dwelled in the high mountain passes and found the deep
     and
greenest grasses for their hungers. And stayed, keeping watch
over them, singing and humming them home, with the Word.
     Amen.

—AFTER TEACHING IN IRELAND

In the shadow of Charing Cross I sit
Across from Galileo bent solidly over calculations—
     Intent on measuring the universe. Intense passion.
Inside—treasures of words, scribbles and scrawls of centuries.
The one I cherished seeing most—Gandhi's letter before gong on
     A 21-day fast protesting the violence that followed the salt
          demonstrations.
Eminently legible, untouchable under glass—the measure of a
     human being—
     Meekness—gasping the vital essence of the truth.
My back up against a wall warmed in the noonday sun
I reflect on my words—are they lasting? Or everlasting?
Ahimsa. I too vow and bless the Word made flesh
And cross that altered any measure of what is human in the
     universe.

—LONDON

September Blues

porcelain vase against the cream wall
old bruises fading on fair skin
herons dusky in late afternoon heat

small flowers part white, part purple
fluttering against dry green leaves.
Eyes of a robin's egg though more lasting;
blurs of memories, faces long and newly dead
silk brushing and sliding liquid against skin
and a feather found in wet grass—a jay's discarded shirt.
Lilies letting go. The line between night and day
veils around the moon on an evening of thunderstorms.
Water in deep caverns leaning heavily towards the luster of
     ebony.
Obsidian wings flashing in bright light while raven and crow
bicker and clamor for attention.
Iris petals light on the fringes of violet.
Lavender and thistle, corn and bells wild in fields
and old veins rich in the arms of a widow
tears on a face allowed to fall
bones of a deer picked coyote-clean
fur on the paws of wolf in a trap
held in steel dull and deadly.
Just blues.
I want to write a hopeful poem
beak open the egg shells with gleaming whites and thick suns of
     courage
and make a cake of brownies rich and chewy.
I want my plants to flower now.
I want to take my finger and touch ever so gently the lined faces
     of friends
and honor the many wrinkles in the old, turning the creases into
     crinkles of laughter.
I want the hate, the rape, the fighting on huge and small scales
     to stop. And
I want peace to be taken up as international pastimes, obsessions
     and addiction.

I want earth and my hearth and community to feel like it's
    home, a dwelling place
secure where the poor can't wait to open the door after the long
    day.
I want hope to roll up her sleeves, stand and resist and cuss and
    sing
and catch everyone off guard. Make it be so.
I want this fall to be one of harvest and hope. Amen.

The Morning of the Magpie

I left
the window wide open, curtains drawn back.
The moon is full and I wanted to be awakened by its intruding
    intimacy as it rose,
but I slept through the night and I was awakened—rudely by a
    magpie sitting (if it was ever for a moment still)
on the window sill inside the window frame.
The room is small
his presence
strong.
I lay in bed, bundled, one foot exposed
It hopped to the bed covers!
I was wide awake.
Two feet from my face
It hopped from foot to foot
It couldn't get ahold of solid ground
but sank into the duvet.

Lord, I thought—how will I get it to the window ledge again?
He didn't seem in any hurry to depart.
I caught the clock's face out of the corner of my eye—4:30 a.m.

The black and white and fierce blue wings rose up V
I expected the loud raucous cry but silence filled the room.
I daren't move—but I wiggled my toes
(the ones underneath—safe from that beak!)
and feared for my other foot!

Then I wanted to laugh—it was all so ludicrous
I was grinning deliciously, giggling like a girl—
Awakening in the morning to find myself in bed with a large
    clumsy magpie.
He must have suspected and became insulted—
(magpies do have that aristocratic air about them)
he turned his back on me,
looking for flight and hopped to the edge of the bed.
Then deliberately he landed directly on my foot
And used it for his jumping-off point—
It looked as though he grazed the window frame but he was
    free—
And I was alone in the bed again.

Trickster—I remembered—
I felt—investigated, probed, visited accidentally, curiously,
    honestly.
Disappointed that I might have rebuffed him by my
    unseeming
        lack of seriousness—
Perhaps his dignity had been piqued?
I slipped from bed and was enchanted—
to find he'd left a feather!
The avian version of Cinderella's slipper!
It is black—blue black.
Delicate soft fierce bit of night wing.

I love its silken feel.
I call this day June 30, the morning of the magpie.

—DUBLIN

Infusions

Blood transfusions, vitamin B shots, vitamin C chewables, heart and organ transplants—unbelievable surges of energy, vitality, medicine for healing and strengthening. The spirit and soul realm has its ways, too—the touch of another coming unexpectedly, a stranger's intimacy, the poor's hospitality, a gentle stroking laid on violence's destruction, tears welling up over a slight detail—these are infusions of hope, peace, passion, freedom, plain graces and love.

The Spirit is the sacrament of the world and is always seeking flesh to use, to touch, to express itself. The Spirit is always seeking us—like a heat-seeking missile seeking its target; an arrow its prey; the eye of an owl for movement and carelessness on the edge of dark.

Infusions that bring soul medicine or bruising realities to bear on long ignored muscles of the mind and heart are in these poems—a story spun out by a spider web of circumstances, laughter erupting, hot lava of anger spilling loose—righteous prophet anger focused on souls too content. Electrical shocks, chi activated, disciplines of graceful motion that loose what is blocked and held bound—these instances are felt as though Spirit touched flesh, flesh touched back, or home was found in a foreign land as familiar as any well-loved place. Mystery goes out in search of friends, accosting and curling up around the unsuspecting. Poems inevitably are spit out, given birth to, wrenched out of such daring games of catch-as-catch can between Mystery and ordinary mortality.

Porch-Sitting

There is a ritual to this porch sitting.
First, if possible face the western sun, sit in a chair that's not too
    cozy

so you stay alert—put your feet up so you're off the ground
but close enough that you can reach down and touch it with
    fingers
stretched.

Bring water, not icy but cold enough.
Listen. Pay attention!, ears up, pulled back.
Don't miss anything, get distracted!
(I'm sure I could teach graduate level courses in this—)
Sweat
feel it run in a trickle down your neck. Soak your shirt.
Don't forget to breathe. Really breathe!
Take it all in. Let it all out. Marvel at it.
The simplicity, constant repetition.
Be grateful. You are alive!

Drift. Pray.
Keep in mind that once you do this—
—commit yourself—
you're going to have trouble coming back in.
Settle. Root yourself.
Feel it go down your spine and into your buttocks.
Stretch!
Make yourself longer.
Resist too much thinking.
A little is OK especially if it leads to dreaming
or a few lines of poetry or humming (you'll attract
bees, butterflies, hummingbirds and Lord knows what else!)

Sometimes you have to do this alone, especially in the beginning
until you get the knack of it—
later you can bring another along but you have to be quiet
—not just not talk. Be still.

Be stilled!
Try being a tree. Practice the seasons.
Smell—send out your senses, like tentacles, widening your
    range . . .
go octopus in a circle tentatively absorbing more and more
Lean into osmosis and then reverse the process
Disappear into this space.
Slide between the veils.
now, you're beginning to know the basics of the ritual.
That's enough for the first lesson.

Now you're on your own
Good luck with resuming your normal life—
Laugh!
at yourself and dissolve all violence.
In returning hold the world very very carefully . . .
Go about making peace.
If you find the edge creeping back in—
Quick! Head for the porch—
Anybody's!
And start again. As tho it were the first time.
like when God first sat on the porch and sighed
and said: oh, this is good, so very very good.

Prayer

I sit and squirm and try to stay still and count the minutes.
My feet go to sleep. My back aches. The ends of my fingers
    tingle.
Nonetheless the volcano bursts and hot lava moves down
the mountain and takes over everything in its path—
But it too departs from the norm—it does not set out to destroy
or swallow up, it lays down a loam, a layer of sediment lush and

life-giving and transforms the sewer sludge into fertile ground.
How it pulls off this fantastic feat—I am at a loss to explain.
   But
I know if I don't try to pray but just sit there, even grousing . . .
all hell does break loose and the sewers back up and what spews
    forth
is deadly. So I sit and count breaths before the Emptiness
and hang on for a dearer life.

                           —AT THE MONASTERY

So many unmanageable impulses, memories, shocks to my
   system.
Violent pieces let loose in my mind. Ping pong balls, with
   magnets
in a confined space, a riot of noise, confusion, movement.
Am exhausted always. Even my body abruptly shuts down.
All from traveling, visiting other countries, being the stranger,
the outsider, rarely the guest. And so much of that other world
I stumbled into hurts. I hurt now, knowing.
My old world has been attacked at its roots.
Now they are bitter roots and I am estranged from myself
and where I've lived so long.

It wasn't just India—but India with its one billion people
overwhelmed concepts with immediacy, with the scale of
   violence,
with misery, with horror and grim reality. The extremes, even of
   weather,
was the norm. Evil's touch squatted in every street and shadowed
   me
in thousands of eyes, outstretched grubbing hands, severed limbs,
scarred bodies—it broke something inside me and left me bereft

of any prayer but "Mercy, God! Why?" Sigh. Cry.
I carried it home with me. They clamor inside.
They live here now.
They seek acceptance. I seek absolution—unaware of them so
    long.
May we all be one in Mercy's arms. Amen.

V o w

I vow
to atone in my own life for all the deaths unnecessary and
    violent
for those deemed expendable.
When life is cheap, their lives go first.
Millions of children in Iraq, India, Iran, Israel, Ireland,
    Indonesia
(the litany of places that begin with I) but the world utters
this kind of killing in every place. Latest: East Timor.

I vow
to speak up, to speak out, on their behalf
for all the ones who suffer in silence, die anonymous, not
    missed,
who took their own lives in despair and lost from any human's
    care.

I vow
never to instill fear, to illicit or use language, silence or
    circumstance
let alone power against another or to aggravate any situation.
To approach what is volatile with Isaiah's description of the
    servant of Yahweh

who suffers—not crying out in the streets, not bruising the
   smoldering wick,
not leaning against the bruised reed, lest it break—

I vow
to beg entrance and acceptance of the stranger, the other who I
   now know
not as just my neighbor to be loved as I love myself but as
   sacrament of
the Incarnation to be tendered as God tends to me.

I vow
to salvage the poor, the ignored, the despised and diminished
and kiss them over and over again like mothers kiss away
their children's hurts, scratches, bruises and bumps, while
   wiping their
smudged and tear-stained frightened faces—
and steadfastly refuse to stop until they collapse in laughter
or giddiness or delight. Why not?
Everyone was created for small glories and daily dignity.

I vow
to search out and adamantly stake every day on the unforeseen,
the stranger come, the absolutely impossible, the miraculous,
the gestures of grace, the silent screaming of the Spirit trying
to distract us from the banal and to proudly and quietly repeat:
"This is the day the Lord has made, let us be glad and rejoice
   in it!"
To practice resurrection, if need be, with a vengeance and a
   passion
heretofore reserved for making love.

I vow

to be gloriously attached to life, to being human, even the
   hardscrabble
Gut-wrenching and groaning parts, the catastrophes—as well as
   the
Stunning and deliciously sweet pieces.

I vow

to praise in words and write ceaselessly, but I will only let
what has been birthed in silences, water and blood be spoken
in my worship and truthtelling.

I vow

to stand witness and not let the extremities people are made
to endure pass by unheeded. I will protest and give vent to
lamentation. I will be a question mark and an exclamation
   point.
Mantra-like whispering and shouting, chanting No! It is not
   allowed!
No more! Enough! Desist! Stop! Don't buckle under or close
   your eyes
or turn away! See! Look! Contemplate and declare!

I vow

to believe in non-violent resistance to all that dehumanizes,
to all that undermines hope and all that sucks the life-blood of
   justice
from another. Along with the stars of night I will stand witness
and remember all those nameless who once watched the night
   sky
and dreamed of kindness and of peace on earth.

I vow

austerity, not the grim and artless kind that decries beauty

and the goodness of all that is made and given over to us to
  share
but the kind that is founded on appreciation, the deeply
  embedded debt
of sheer gratitude.

I vow

to savor, finger, run my heart over and impart spirit to all
that languishes, strip excess to quicken another's failing strength,
learn the bare necessities I need so others can know less need.
I will limit desire and channel even my anger into life-lines
for those slipping away unnoticed and stave off sorrow.
No grasping. Instead laughing.

I vow

to court insecurity that can be remedied by sharing
and community, even reveling in the poor's generosity.
But I will be profligate with hope and all it takes
to set the prisoners free.

I vow

to be pure and live with integrity. I will!

Written, remembering a line: "In such a world, justice is a
  continent
always being discovered by taking soundings." (Wm. Stafford)
These are my soundings late December 1999
I will not relent from living. Not ever! Amen.

Unpublished Poems

The Solace of Old Speech

I hear voices in the rain
hidden peoples' hopes and cries
falling falling on roof and ground
misting, dropping, ceaselessly pleading
—to be remembered
—to be heeded
—warning, soothing?
Spirits, airs, elves, souls?
Loosed or returning with concern
Speaking truths hard to hear
in ordinary daily tongues.
There is a sweetness, a freshness
as it falls on hands and faces
washing out eyes and cleansing hearts.
And there is pain, moans that went unheard
and so were buried in the air,
falling free with cloud bursts.
And listened to intently truth echoes
and repeats with lightening flashes
thundering in a language so precise
it defys mere words for adequate translations.
Brave voices, radiant absences
lingering in lilting and keening sounds.
After days, how can I not hear?
and take to heart such a lyrical literature
of humankind's everlasting ordinary
longings insisting on communion?

Forgive me for not knowing how to utter a word back
and stumbling so along the shore that separates us still.

I pray aloud: keep whispering, singing,
weeping, divining a way to touch home
in every shower and storm.
softly accompanying us
walking with such dignity
filling up the solitudes
so completely.

DUBLIN 06/03/02

Desperate Counter-Measures

Talk of war, dropping bombs
Nationalistic swords raised and rattling.
A million or more on each side
Eye-balling one another through gun sights.
And all caught inbetween, living on a line
are now running, pursued by terror
leaving all behind.
I rant and rage. Fidget, and am frustrated.
I would fling flowers wet with dew
into the world's tense faces.
I would haunt their dreams with images
and wild yearnings for peace
so that they'd wake weeping in their need.
I would send birds from exotic shores
mad with colored feathers.
And drop notes of paper that when touched
exuded a perfume that stunned into stillness.
I'd find a million or more sets of childrens' eyes
to stare wide open into each face
that wielded a gun.
They'd have to yield
or I'd pray they would forget

everything but their first loves,
and off they'd go searching,
dropping their defenses
their arms open wide.
And then they'd only tell of wonder
and of making love
and all the borders and lines
would blur leaving only vague traces
as birds flying across the ordinary blue sky
pursued only by the clouds.

Failing all this
I'd rouse the old magic
and turn them all to trees.
Two forests facing each other
Soon soon becoming one great green wood.
With a bent branch I trace the old script on the ground.
willing the words back into the world.
THERE SHALL BE PEACE
ONLY PEACE
PEACE.

INDIA/PAKISTAN 06/04/02

PART ii

Mercy

✻

Introduction

You have been appointed . . .
to ask for mercy for the world,
to keep vigil for the salvation of all,
and to partake in every means of suffering,
both of the just and the sinners.

ISAAC THE SYRIAN

In all the religions of the Book—Judaism, Christianity, and Islam—the name of God that is most powerful, that summons God to our aid, and that reveals the depth of a glimpse of what God might truly be is the name of Mercy. In Islam the ninety-ninth name of God (the one hundredth is not known to human beings, and if by rare gift it is, it cannot be spoken aloud) is Allah, the most merciful, the most compassionate. The psalms of the Jewish people and the prayer of the Church are laced with the repetitive cry: "Have mercy on me, O Lord, for I cry to you all day" (Ps. 86:3).

The advent of each year in Christian tradition calls upon God our Justice to speedily enter into the world, but when the child comes, along with justice comes "Mercy singing in the night" (Rob Young, ofm). And this child, grown to be a man, teaches of a God called Father who he describes endlessly, not just in terms of justice, but of mercy unbounded, limitless, and inexpressible. In Jesus' litany of those blessed here on earth and in the fullness of the kingdom to come are found those who hunger and thirst for justice who will be satisfied, and the merciful who will be shown mercy. (Matt. 5:6,7) At the end of each of the teaching sections of Matthew's Gospel, Jesus exhorts his disciples to be like the Father, and it is always in terms of mercy. At the conclusion of the Sermon on the Mount, Jesus tells us that we must be "children of your Father in Heaven. For he makes his sun rise on both the wicked and the good, and he gives rain to both the just and the unjust. . . . For your part you must be righteous [just] and perfect [merciful and compassionate] in the way your heavenly Father is just and merciful." (Matt. 5:45–48)

When Jesus calls the tax collector Matthew to be one of his own followers and Matthew throws a party for Jesus to meet his friends, Jesus is slandered and criticized for associating with such scum, those who are irreligious. But Jesus responds with "Healthy people do not need a doctor, but sick people do. Go and find out what this means: What I want is mercy, not sacrifice. I did not come to call the righteous but sinners." (Matt. 9:12–13) This line is embedded in the message of Yahweh to Hosea (6:6): "I desired mercy and not sacrifice." Somehow, whatever the laws and tenets of Jesus' religion and the tradition of Exodus and the prophets are, they have underground sources and wellsprings of mercy. Mercy is often translated as steadfast love or tenderness, and is always wedded to forgiveness: the forgiveness of God towards all of us and the forgiveness we are to extend to others, all others because of God's mercy. From the beginning of God's calling forth a people, this characteristic of mercy is stronger than any other in God's gestures and work among the people. Even when the people rebel against God, there is punishment for three generations but steadfast love and mercy is given down to the one thousandth generation for those who love and keep the commandments. (Exod. 20:6)

One of the most often-repeated descriptions of God in the Psalms and the Prophets is this: "God is merciful, gracious, and just." (Exod. 34:6) More than four-fifths of the Psalms speak of God's mercies and how God does mercy, gives mercy, showers mercy, and pleads for mercy among his people. Perhaps one of the most often-quoted lines of a prophet are these: "This is what I ask of you: to do justice, love tenderly, and walk humbly with your God." The translation could just as surely read: do justice, do mercy, and walk humbly with your God.

But what is mercy? Mercy is forgiveness and more. It is forgiveness given becuause of the goodness and love of the one who offers it. Mercy is love that is given to all, beyond all reason, over and over again. Mercy is love unto death. Mercy is nonviolent resistance to evil and the embrace of all: just and unjust, sinner and those who have turned from evil. Mercy is sweet, unexpected, hardly to be believed, shocking, freeing, given when there is no hope. It is always undeserved, overflowing, and embarassing. There is no way to repay mercy and the only response can be that of gratitude. Mercy is God become flesh and blood, a human being to be one with us, live with us, save us by presence and touch, die with us and at our hands, and free us by sharing resurrection with us. Mercy is the crucified one stretched out to encompass the whole world and whispering forgiveness for all in a dying prayer. Mercy is the presence of God among us still in the poor, those who suffer at the hands of others and those who stand up for and stand with those who are forgotten and destroyed in the world. Mercy sings and weeps, cries and dances. Mercy is the wildness of God's love for our enemies, for us, for the victims, for all that has been made with such tender regard.

Of course, all of that seems vague until we are exhorted to love our enemies, do good to those who persecute us, give to all who beg from us, and pray for those who harm us. Most especially Mercy shadows us when we are told that we must forgive and forgive and forgive seventy times seven, everyone for everything, no exceptions, no strings attached, no deals because that is how Mercy, our God deals with us. Mercy is a power to be reckoned with when we are shown that we must lay down our lives for one another and be willing to die for our beliefs, but that we are not allowed to kill anyone for any reason, and certainly never in the name of Mercy, our God. It seems then, that Mercy becomes hard as nails to live out, impossible to practice, and even dangerous in a world that sees Mercy as weakness and as crazy. Mercy reveals that human be-ings are made in the image and likeness of a God beyond easy definition, whose understanding of what it means to be human is also what it means to be divine and stamped with the icon of the Holy One. Mercy like God's and like those who imitate God is usually hidden, secret, outra-geous, nonviolent, and intent on transforming the world by grace, free-dom, and truth beyond mere words or expression. The practice of Mercy alters the universe, opening rifts in the world where God can slip in un-awares and visit, leaving behind the scent of paradise and wondering awe at what we might be, let alone what God might be. Mercy says: Be care-ful! Your idea of God, your experience of God may have absolutely noth-ing to do with God at all! What if you haven't even begun to know God, or holiness or refuge or love at all?

Mercy is the rain of God, the reign of God, the rein of God. Mercy gives birth out of death. Mercy comforts and fills up with what is lack-ing. Mercy heals. Mercy not only forgets but remembers, re-members and puts back together better than originally. Mercy is best described by poetry, by music, by psalm, prayer, story and silence. Mercy is the echo of the holy lingering, absent still among us. Mercy is God's hope and prayer for us. Paul often begins or ends his letters with the blessing: "May grace, mercy and peace be with you from God the Father and Christ Jesus our Lord." (1 and 2 Tim. 1:2) If only we knew that it is only by giving mercy that it becomes more visible in our own lives. The native peoples of this land have a saying: A gift is not a gift until it has been given twice. Mercy is the gift given again and again to us. Oh, to learn how to return the favor of such mercy! What a world this would be!

From Leave Her Alone

Introduction

Every letter of Torah has the power to revive the dead. Believe it.
For one soul, . . . one heart, . . . I give up everything.
—RABBI SHLOMO CARLEBACH

How much does it take to cover up the sun? Put your finger over
your eye—you can't see a thing.
—BA'AL SHEM TOV

These two statements confront us with the two ends of a spectrum of the way we can approach the Scriptures: with a wide-open reverence for mysterious power that conceals as much as it reveals; or with suspicion born of individual and stunted vision. The reflections in this book begin with the first attitude, assuming that the text is inspired by God and that it holds a key that can unlock underground passages and loose unparalleled power into our lives. Thus this book rejects the second attitude—the individualistic interpretation—as limiting and distorting. Only when the text is seen and reverenced in a context, a community of believers that struggles with its meaning and their lives, can there be true sight. Between the text and the community there must be reciprocity.

Scripture stories are not just about characters or history; they are more about what we are being inspired to do with our own lives as individuals and, even more important, as a community of believers. The text is good news; therefore, the interpretation must be founded on hope and the possibility of a more graceful and liberating reality for those most in need.

We should read the texts through a veil, as it were, a veil that filters out selfish intent, personal agendas, or anything that validates dominant and oppressive arrangements. The veil is that of suffering and mercy, born of the memory of the Suffering Servant, the crucified One raised from the tomb by a God who is faithful to life. Just as the prophets heard and proclaimed the Word of God through the experience and eyes of those most in pain and without justice, so the texts must remind and challenge us to read them through the eyes of the masses of people who do not know life as good news or the presence of the God of justice, truth, and life in our midst. Such a reading will bring comfort and solace, encouragement and righteousness, but also crisis and conflict, confrontation and harsh reminders that we have sold our birthrights as the children of God and chosen instead our culture's power and promises.

All the texts must be read with the bright shadow of the resurrection bent over us. This reality must cast its terrifying and holy power on our lives, as once the glance of Yahweh struck terror into the forces of the oncoming army of the Egyptians, as we are told by Miriam, who raised her voice in the people's victory song. And so we will look at a number of accounts of this cornerstone of our faith and lives, as found in the earliest Gospel, that of Mark. We begin with the theme of this book: a charge that confronts us in our blindness, fear, hesitation, ignorance, lack of understanding, or weakness of faith. They are words of Jesus to his disciples: "Later Jesus showed himself to the Eleven, while they were at table. He reproached them for their unbelief and stubbornness in refusing to believe those who had seen him after he had risen" (Mark 16:14).

This appearance is Jesus' last in Mark's Gospel. It is preceded by three other recorded appearances. The first, the longest, is the announcement by an angel (a young man in a white robe?) to the three women who went to the tomb when the Sabbath was over: Mary of Magdala, Mary the mother of James, and Salome. The angel announces that Jesus is not in the tomb, but goes before them into Galilee. They are commanded to "go and tell his disciples and Peter: Jesus is going ahead of you into Galilee; you will see him there just as he told you" (Mark 16:7). The account of the second appearance is much shorter, and it is specifically to Mary of Magdala. It is characterized as being the first appearance of Jesus himself, and the text records that Mary obeyed the summons to report what she had heard and seen, but "they" would not believe it (or her) (Mark 16:9–11). It is thought that this is a short version of the account given in John 20:11, when Mary is weeping outside the tomb and does not recognize Jesus as he approaches her, until he calls her by name. And then, in the shortest of the appearance texts, Jesus shows himself "in another form to two of them [no names], as they were walking in the country" (Mark 16:12). There is speculation that this allusion is to the appearance to the two men on the road to Emmaus, which is recorded in great detail in Luke's resurrection accounts. In Luke's first account, those who return from the tomb and state that Jesus is alive are greeted just as they were in the Markan text. It reads: "Among the women who brought the news were Mary Magdalene, Joanna, and Mary the mother of James. But however much they insisted, those who heard did not believe the seemingly nonsensical story" (Luke 24:9–10).

The accounts are confusing regarding names, events, and sequence. But it is clear that at least four women are named, the two that appear in both being Mary of Magdala and Mary the mother of James. This Mary of Magdala is *not* Mary of Bethany, the sister of Martha, and is not the woman who anoints Jesus in any of the Gospels. Is Mary the mother of James the mother of one of the disciples, James the lesser (not the mother of James and John)?

And other persons are mentioned. Earlier, at the death of Jesus, we are told that the only witnesses to the crucifixion were women, though it is the captain of the guard detail that supervised the execution who proclaims at Jesus' death, "Truly, this man was the Son of God" (Mark 15:39). In the next verses we are told:

> There were also some women watching from a distance; among them were Mary Magdalene, Mary the mother of James the younger and Joses, and Salome, who had followed Jesus when he was in Galilee and saw to his needs. There were also others who had come up with him to Jerusalem.
>
> (MARK 15:40–41)

These are members of Jesus' community, disciples and friends. These are the faithful ones in terrifying circumstances. They stood at a distance because the soldiers cordoned off an area around the crosses, keeping everyone at bay. The scene would have been one of horror, eerie silence, screams of the victims, and taunts of bystanders. This was a public denunciation of those executed and was meant to be an unforgettable lesson for family, friends, and followers. The general rule was that the soldiers guarded those writhing in agony until they were dead, keeping anyone from them, and then continued to guard them so that relatives could not take the bodies down and bury them. The corpses were to hang there until birds and animals ate them. Any display of mourning was strictly forbidden: no weeping or lamentation, no words of comfort or displays of concern. The eleven disciples of Jesus were in hiding because known association with the one executed could result in one's being executed as well.

And that is what is remarkable about the presence of all these women, in the crowd, at a distance, silent witnesses to all that happens. And then they are still bold enough to risk going to the grave to anoint the body. Even today around the world it is sometimes forbidden that relatives, friends, or those connected to any religious group bury the bodies of those cut down in the struggle for justice and freedom. It is so in El Salvador and Guatemala and was the case in South Africa and many other countries.

These are the witnesses, cowed, dazed, full of fear, but intent on anointing the body of Jesus, affording his body their final service, a corporal work of mercy. They have no idea how they will accomplish it. Their talk is of the huge stone that will block the entrance to the tomb, because they had waited around until after the body had been placed inside. Then came the Sabbath and its demands for laying aside all other concerns.

The account of their bending down to enter the tomb and of encountering the young man who tries to calm their fears gives only the announcement of what has happened. The messenger proclaims: "Don't be alarmed; you are looking for Jesus of Nazareth who was crucified; he has been raised and is not here" (Mark 16:6). And the text says they don't obey. They are alarmed. They don't say anything to anyone else at first. They probably fled and later regrouped and began talking excitedly, exclaiming all at once. Grief had turned to wild hope and terrible confusion: Where was he? Was he alive? And eventually they did go to the others but were not believed.

Jesus reproaches the Eleven, who are in hiding, for their "unbelief and their stubbornness in refusing to believe those who had seen him after he had risen." The story is told, and told again, and still faith is blocked like the tomb with the huge millstone that fills its entrance. Three, four, five women tell the story, yet those who said they were Jesus' friends refuse to believe them. They stubbornly cling to their unbelief and refuse to admit that another has been given something they ran away from. The two walking in the country—one of whom is later named Cleophas and the other of whom many believe was his wife—tell them the story, and they are steadfastly resistant to a word of hope. In some ways it does not matter who tells the story, just that it is told, over and over again, until it begins to seep in through cold stone hearts and warm them again. Though these stories appear to be about women, they are about human beings, about all those who need the story of resurrection, of life and truth, and who need people who believe in it and put it into practice.

The text is like dough that needs to be squeezed, floured, kneaded, unraveled, wrapped up, combined with other ingredients of prayer and life, ritual and justice, and baked before it can be eaten or shared. The text, in the technique of midrash, talks to those who listen. It is not a one-sided dialogue on our end. Rather, it's a bit like a spirit retrieval, a journey where we find our way back into the stories and texts, following a spiral on ancient shells and fossils, finding in the remnants left behind a trail that draws us back and down and in.

A friend of mine has an old woven rug that is a cherished possession, a gift from his grandmother. It hangs on a wall in his study, and he intends to be buried in it, as is his people's custom. It is more than a hundred years old, frayed and worn in places, but the pattern is still strongly defined in its texture. You have to look closely, even know where to look, to find the Spirit line, a place where the pattern is unfinished and left open. It is both the way the Spirit is let out and the way one enters the rug. The text is like that—one has to know it intimately to find the entrance to it and the place where the Spirit seeps out, looking for us. Perhaps our attitude has to be the same: we have to intend to be buried in its mystery and believe that its full meaning lies beyond our own lives.

For instance, at the end of Mark's Gospel we read that Jesus "speaks to them and was taken up into heaven and took his place at the right hand of God." Then comes what is now the last line of the Gospel: "The Eleven went forth and preached everywhere, while the Lord worked with them and confirmed the message by the signs which accompanied them" (Mark 16:20).

That's the last line in the book as we have it now, but it's apparent that there were originally other "last lines." It is widely accepted that the original ending came at Mark 16:8, which reads, "The women went out of the tomb and fled, beside themselves with fear. And they said nothing to anyone because they were afraid." Do both endings speak the truth? Does one say more truth than the other? Let's dig a little. We know the women did eventually get past their fear and tell the Eleven, who didn't believe them. They were told to go back to Galilee, which is about ninety miles from the site of the empty tomb in Jerusalem. And the three women, all the others who had come up with Jesus to Jerusalem, and the Eleven did return to their homes. What did they tell? What memories were shared? Did they go back to the beginning, when they first met Jesus in Galilee, and confess their conversions, healings, forgiveness, doubts, and struggles to continue following him? Among the community, overshadowed by the resurrection's reality and the presence of Jesus' Spirit among them, did they wonder if they had heard or understood anything he said at all?

Does the text itself turn in a spiral, back to the beginning for us, so that we can reread, reponder, reevaluate, and reinterpret what we once were so sure of in light of what happened to Jesus: crucifixion, death, and resurrection? Does the text itself tell us that the meaning of all things for us is different now that we have experienced crucifixion, death, and resurrection in our baptisms and confessions among his followers? What are we to do now? What's back in Galilee?

Let's go back to the beginning:

This is the beginning of the good news of Jesus Christ, the Son of God. It is written in the book of Isaiah, the prophet, "I am sending my messenger ahead of you to prepare your way. Let the people hear the voice calling in the desert: Prepare the way of the Lord, level his paths."

(MARK 1:1–3)

Are we now the messengers, sent ahead to prepare the way for the good news of Jesus Christ, the son of God?

John's Message, 12:1–11

"Leave her alone." Jesus says these three words in response to Judas' evaluation of Mary's anointing of Jesus' feet with costly perfume and then wiping them with her hair. They are a command from the Master to a disciple who is out of line, who is speaking out of malice, ignorance, or blindness. Even without the context of the story, the words are about freedom and noninterference. And they infer praise, infer allowance for Mary and for her behavior and intentions. These words announce that Mary has been recognized and accepted—and so, defended and protected.

I often say that "in the hearing is the meaning," and particularly in the context of John's Gospel, it reveals layers of meaning and insight. "Leave her alone" is a corrective. It can even be a chastisement for a self-righteousness that defends one's own agenda and so severs connections with and condemns another. The command to leave her alone stops that process sharply and has inherent in it a positive judgment in opposition. It is a demand to desist, pointed personally and yet also collectively at "you."

Leave her alone. Leave her be. Leave her to her work. Don't hinder or interfere. Don't ridicule or belittle. Leave her with me! She's bound to me, not you. Leave her alone. Like the doctor's adage "to do no harm," this is a moral imperative. It is a testament regarding who really sees, who has insight, who senses truth, who acts righteously, and even who can learn from whom.

Even more so, it is a confession, a statement of whose side the Holy is on, whom Jesus sides with, who is privileged in closeness, who has caught a glimpse of holiness, of wholeness, and wants to draw closer to it—who is therefore in relation to, and closer to, God. But the words are also a confrontation with what is not true, what is evil, false, sinful.

Leave her *alone*. The tenor of the words is the pivot of the story, and the story is about reactions: To people. To relationships. To what Jesus has done by raising Lazarus from the dead. The sound of the words is utterly human, and they reveal communion with another, with one who, like Jesus, is an outcast. The words bind Jesus and Mary together. One of the definitions of religion is relink, rebind, bind together at the root, and so this story is about religion at its root and questions us in whom and what we bind ourselves to and why. This "identification with" reveals our own identity, our self-knowledge.

We will look at this story of Mary anointing Jesus' feet while Martha, Mary's older sister, waits on them at table. We will examine what provokes Judas' judgment as well as Jesus' judgment in retaliation and his defense and affirmation of the one so meanly singled out. Jesus' words sound like a corrective, yet they also express his understanding that his presence and power have evoked distress, gratitude, and confusion in Mary, the sister of Lazarus, whom he had raised from the dead. This deed of his has shattered her identity, her vision of life and death. Jesus' presence and actions are an intrusion into her life, her soul—a welcome intrusion, but one that is awesome and even disconcerting, that unleashes emotions and reactions that seem abnormal, out of place, senseless, even tasteless.

This is not a woman relating to a man. This is a woman who is on the edge of discovery, the edge of belief and faith, the edge of transformation. She is on the edge of consciousness of what *is* and *is not,* of sinfulness, lack, and inability to express what is welling up inside her. It is the story of a woman who is one sensing, beginning to believe, that this man is more than man—that he is holy, other, powerfully bound to life and death, and intimate with the defining moments of life in ways none of us have ever known. And that makes him singular, alone in the midst of his friends—Mary, Martha, Lazarus, and the disciples. Her action is a gesture of reaching to touch, to root herself again in reality. She is asking: Is this man human? Is this man my friend? Is this man of God? Is this man bound to me? Is this man going to die? Is this power, this person, dangerous, attractive, world-altering, shattering, freeing? If he raised my brother from death and decay, then what will he do with my life and the life of others?

Let us read the story in John now and listen to the meaning, remembering that the meaning is in the hearing and that reading aloud reveals what cannot be heard or known in the mind alone:

Six days before the Passover, Jesus came to Bethany where he had raised Lazarus, the dead man, to life. Now they gave a dinner for him, and while Martha waited on them, Lazarus sat at the table with Jesus.

Then Mary took a pound of expensive perfume made from genuine nard and anointed the feet of Jesus, wiping them with her hair. And the whole house was filled with the fragrance of the perfume.

Judas, son of Simon Iscariot—the disciple who was to betray Jesus—remarked, "This perfume could have been sold for three hundred silver coins and turned over to the poor." Judas, indeed, had no concern for the poor; he was a thief and as he held the common purse, he used to help himself to the funds.

But Jesus spoke up, "Leave her alone. Was she not keeping it for the day of my burial? (The poor you always have with you, but you will not always have me.)"

Many Jews heard that Jesus was there and they came not only because of Jesus, but also to see Lazarus whom he had raised from the dead. So the chief priests thought about killing Lazarus as well, for many of the Jews were drifting away because of him and believing in Jesus.

(JOHN 12:1–11)

The first and last paragraphs bracket the story, giving it a foreground and putting it in a perspective of resurrection (life being given back to Lazarus) and killing (the intention to kill not only Jesus but Lazarus because, now raised from the dead, he is the cause of others coming to believe in and follow Jesus more closely). We are told that it is six days before Passover, which would mean that the city is swelling with pilgrims and Jews from the Diaspora, those scattered among the nations returning to the Temple in Jerusalem in expectation of freedom and liberation once again. In John's Gospel the Passover falls on a Friday, so this is the Sabbath, Jesus' last Sabbath meal with his friends and disciples before his death. In the previous chapter we are told that the city and the religious officials are seething with hatred and intrigue, plotting how to arrest Jesus, just waiting for the right moment in the confusion of crowds and activities that marked the feast day. We are told, "Meanwhile the chief priests and the elders had given orders that anyone who knew where he was should let them know so that they could arrest him" (John 11:57). This incident—so personal and intimate, in a household of friends—takes place while others are conspiring to kill Jesus. Time is running out. Jesus has six days before the conspiracy closes in on him and he is betrayed and murdered. The raising of Lazarus from the dead has complicated matters: now it seems best to kill both of them. Association with this man Jesus is becoming life-threatening, for the officials see Jesus as disturbing organized religion and acceptable practices of temple worship, sacrifice, and prayer.

And in the midst of this we are told simply: "Now they gave a dinner for him, and while Martha waited on them, Lazarus sat at the table with Jesus." This is the Sabbath meal, a ritual within every Jewish household, a time of blessing, of prayer, and of shared dreams and hopes for freedom and liberation. Because this is the last Sabbath before the feast of Passover, the meal and prayers have an added significance and power. The community gathers around Jesus while the powerful plan death. This community is thus a protest against killing, hatred, and any religious practice that would condone destruction of human beings.

Jesus' small community of twelve disciples and his three close friends would have sung the Psalms, read the Torah portion, and feasted on the promises of God, while they wined and dined at the table. Lazarus, we are told, sat at the table with Jesus in a privileged place, by his side, guest of honor, intimate with the one who raised him from the dead. He was close to the presence that had summoned him forth from the tomb, close to the voice that had broken the barrier of death and decay and commanded him to "Come forth!" into life, into the light again. He knew that voice as the voice of his friend, and he would have hung on every word that Jesus spoke. In short, he would have been adoring this

man who had power over life and death, his own life and death and those
of all others. The dinner party would have crackled with energy, with a
trace of fear and wild expectations. What would Jesus do next?

We are told clearly that Martha waited on them. Martha, the head
of the household, the eldest of the three friends of Jesus, has obviously
sent her servants away and honors Jesus by waiting on him and his disciples. It is her way of expressing her gratitude, her joy at her brother's
return to life. She graciously shifts her relationship to Jesus—she shifts
from being the hostess to the one who serves at table. She humbles herself before Jesus and those he brings with him to her house, not servilely,
but with genuine love and devotion. It is her way. She would have been
the one to light the candles, summon the presence of Shekhinah, and begin the ritual celebration of the Sabbath meal. It is now time out of time,
time made holy and sacred unto God, time for the visions and dreams of
Israel to take their rightful place in the minds and hearts of the community. It is Sabbath, and it is Jesus' last Sabbath with his friends.

And now Mary enters. She takes a pound of perfume, incredibly expensive, made from genuine nard, and goes to Jesus at the table and
anoints his feet, then wipes his feet with her hair. "And the whole house
was filled with the fragrance of the perfume." Whenever guests entered
a house, they removed their sandals before reclining at the table on long
couches or benches. They would lie on their sides, their heads facing in-
ward toward the table, their feet out and away. Mary obviously had access to wealth. In other translations we are told that the perfume cost the
equivalent of 365 days' wages. She is making herself poor for Jesus, as
her sister is making herself a servant for his sake, in gratitude for what
Jesus has done for their beloved brother, Lazarus. The roles are shifting
in response to the altering of life and death among them.

The word that is used is important: she *anoints* Jesus' feet with the
perfume and then wipes off the excess with her hair. Her hair is unbound. In her own house she would not be expected to cover her hair
with a veil or a cloth. And, as was the custom, her hair would have been
long, uncut for years, her "crowning glory," as it is often referred to in

Mideastern cultures. She would have been bent over his feet, with her hair hanging down over her head. She is making an act of obedience, of devotion, of respect, a passionate one, one that is founded on gratitude. Her response is born of what is inexpressible.

In Hebrew society those who were anointed were priests, prophets, and kings. Mary is recognizing and ritually confessing that Jesus is prophet, king, and priest in Israel. The prophets Elijah and Elisha had brought back people from the dead. Kings had power over life and death. The priests mediated between God and the people. Jesus, for Mary, has become all these and more. He graces her home with his presence and calls her, her sister, Martha, and her brother, Lazarus, friends. She knows that he loves her, loves them all, having put his life in jeopardy when he raised Lazarus. In giving Lazarus life, he has endangered his own. They lived less than two miles from the inner city of Jerusalem, and their household was visited by many, the curious and those truly concerned. She has heard the rumors and knows about the growing hostility in the city—all of it centered around Jesus and aggravated by the raising of Lazarus.

To unknowing and unseeing eyes, she is acting rashly, imprudently, even, as Judas will say, wasting perfume that could have been sold for a market value of three hundred silver pieces. Later, as we know, he himself will sell Jesus out for a mere thirty silver pieces. He is indignant at such extravagant waste of resources. His rationale at first seems innocent, even righteous enough: it could have been sold, the money then turned over to the poor. The gloss on the Gospel text informs us, however, that Judas could care less about the poor and that he is a common thief, taking from the common purse that was used to give alms to the poor—in essence, he steals from the community, from the poor, and from God, because almsgiving was a part of Jewish rituals and atonement. This description of Judas illuminates his accusation about Mary's deed. It reveals greed and a mean-spiritedness that must publicly try to shame another's good deed.

At this point, we are told, "Jesus spoke up." There is a sense that Jesus will not allow such a statement to go unchallenged. He speaks up, loudly enough so that all in the room, no matter what they might be thinking, will know precisely what he thinks of the situation and Mary's actions. He is not just a guest of honor at a meal in Martha, Mary, and Lazarus' house—he is a teacher, the Master of the disciples, and Lord. His words vindicate Mary's intention, behavior, and her relationship to him, but also sets a precedent and takes what seems to be a very personal and singular response to his person and adds a theological and sociological reality—Jesus is making a statement about future judgments about money, excess, and actions that are borderline worship and unusual in the community. His words are pivotal to his own person and how we are to love him, how we are to respond to his presence and absence among us.

"Leave her alone. Was she not keeping it for the day of my burial? (The poor you always have with you, but you will not always have me.)" These are loaded lines, and they have been used in the most bizarre ways to self-righteously defend behaviors that Jesus would never have endorsed. They have been quoted to mean that the poor will always be with us so there is nothing we can do about it, revealing a lack of faith, revealing selfishness and noninvolvement with the needs of the poor. They have been used to validate spending enormous amounts of money on houses of worship and extravagant accessories while the poor go hungry. However, exegetes and other scholars of the Scriptures often view the line as John's rendering of Matthew's chapter 25, the parable of the sheep and the goats, with its famous lines: "Whatsoever you do to the least of your brothers and sisters, you do to me" (v. 40) and "Whatsoever you fail to do to the least of your brothers and sisters, you have failed to do it to me" (v. 45).

Jesus is acknowledging Mary's gift, her generous, openhanded, and open-hearted giving in anointing him for burial. The wealthy kept nard, aromatic spices, myrrh, and aloes for their own deaths and burial chambers. Mary takes what she has kept for death and honors him in life. She anoints him not only for death but also for priesthood, prophecy, and kingship in God's sight. The highest act of mercy, the most meritorious corporal act of mercy, in the Jewish community was anointing for burial, because it made the ones who performed it unclean themselves, for they had touched death and become ritually impure. In turn they had to remain apart from the community while they performed the ritual of cleansing and purification. Mary has unknowingly or with partial knowledge aligned herself with one who is already condemned to death, a religious and politically dangerous criminal, one who is poorest of the poor in the eyes of the Jewish community.

Jesus is declaring for his followers, for his community, that anything we do for the poor, who are always with us, we do for Jesus, who is always with us now, by his incarnation, suffering, and death, in the poor in our midst. We will always have Jesus now, in the poor. Whatever we passionately desire to do for Jesus, for God, in worship, obedience, and devotion, we can passionately, devotedly do by obeying the need of the poor and honoring them in their flesh.

It must have been an uncomfortable moment at the dinner party, a glitch in the ritual celebration of a Sabbath meal. A rift opened, between those who would stand with Jesus as he was arrested, condemned to death, and crucified and those who would refuse to believe that such a thing was happening, let alone those who would betray him in deed, in word, and in running away to save themselves in fear and confusion. The setting of murderous intent, conspiracy, and betrayal has moved into the household, among friends and disciples.

Mary has a glimpse that this is Jesus' gift not only to her brother, Lazarus, but to her and her sister, Martha, and to everyone. She has witnessed resurrection and comes to believe that nothing will ever be the same again, that life can now blossom forth even out of death, out of inhospitality and dishonesty, out of murder and hate. This man Jesus and his Father now stand behind her life and the lives of all people.

Leave her alone! She is truly at home for the first time in her life. And for a moment while she anoints his feet and wipes them with her unbound hair, bent over his body at table, Jesus also is truly at home.

God has been given welcome in the hearts and household of his three friends, Mary, Martha, and Lazarus. All other holds are broken.

Slave Girl

We begin with a maidservant, a young girl captured and enslaved by Aramean soldiers. The story is found in 2 Kings 5. The text is primarily about Naaman the leper, but we will look at events from the vantage point of the conquered one, the young woman. The story begins:

> Naaman was the army commander of the king of Aram. This man was highly regarded and enjoyed the king's favor, for Yahweh had helped him lead the army of the Arameans to victory. But this valiant man was sick with leprosy.
>
> One day some Aramean soldiers raided the land of Israel and took a young girl captive who became a servant to the wife of Naaman. She said to her mistress, "If my master would only present himself to the prophet in Samaria, he would surely cure him of his leprosy."
>
> Naaman went to tell the king what the young Israelite maidservant had said. The king of Aram said to him, "Go to the prophet, and I shall also send a letter to the king of Israel."
>
> (VV. 1–5)

It is remarkable what this one woman sets in motion! She is a captured slave, an indentured servant, dragged off in a raid, exiled now in enemy territory, far from her own people and religious sanctuaries. Yet she is bold enough to declare her belief in the prophet of her own people, whom she honors as holding the Word of the Lord, a power and a presence of the Holy unique among the other nations. Her suggestion passes from her mistress, the wife of Naaman, to the general of enemy forces, to the king, and then to the king in Israel, who sees it as a ruse to start a war between the two groups.

But Elisha, a prophet in Israel, knows what Yahweh is planning. Elisha sends word to the king in Israel to send Naaman to him, so "that he will know that there is a prophet in the land of Israel." Naaman goes and Elisha tells him to go to the river Jordan, plunge into its waters seven times, and he will be cleansed, his flesh becoming as it was before. Naaman is furious. The order is stupid, without meaning for him. Why the river Jordan? Why not one of the rivers in his own land? He had expected to be touched, seared with power, dramatically healed, or at least Elisha should have cried out to his God and called on the power of God's name: Yahweh. And again, it is the servants (other Israelite captives?) who reason with him, saying, "Father, if the prophet ordered you to do something difficult, would you not have done it? But how much easier when he said: Take a bath and you will be cleansed" (v. 13). Is his wife's maidservant in that company, traveling with Naaman, as a guide, encouraging him to obey?

Naaman is healed utterly, and he takes back to his own land sacks of earth from the land of Israel to build an altar so that he can worship the true God, Yahweh. Even in his own country. He begs Elisha to pardon him because he must still accompany his king when the king goes to worship his god, and Elisha sends him home in peace. Naaman is gracious with his gifts and sure now in praise of and belief in Israel's God, the only God.

What of the young maidservant? She has known horror, fear, and loneliness in her young life, and most probably she has experienced physical and sexual abuse, being subjected to the soldiers' humiliation and contempt. Yet eventually she is bought or brought to the household of a prominent man. Her life would have improved immensely as a captive, although she is still a servant, an exile, and far from her own people. But more than anything else she is a believer in the power and presence of her God and knows that her God works in all lands, for all people who obey his commands as they are expressed through the prophet. She is an outcast and recognizes Naaman, for all his power and prestige, as an outcast because of his leprosy. She has compassion on those who own her.

God works through her, and she is the source of Naaman's being led to the prophet in Israel and to the experience of healing and wholeness.

Was Naaman generous enough to release her from her servitude and send her home? We know from Naaman's plea for forgiveness that he had to go back to his world and that he and his household would be alone now in their worship of Yahweh. But we do not know if he freed the maidservant. The slave girl is never mentioned again. We lose track of her, yet we know that she is a leader, a model for behavior under persecution and hardship. She is worthy of praise. True authority does not only or primarily reside in the mighty of the land, the leaders of armies or those respected among their own. True authority is more powerful, deeper, and truer than Deborah's, more hidden yet more pervasive, crossing borders, healing and offering hope that makes friends and equals out of conquerors and enemies. This servant girl knows the power of the poor and the presence of God with those who suffer and lives with dignity in spite of what she has experienced, preaching the Word of God no matter her circumstances. She is in the tradition neither of Deborah nor of Yael. She is, rather, in the tradition of Jesus, who commands the man born blind to go and wash in the pool of Siloam and among those called blessed because they are peacemakers, merciful, and see God everywhere.

Wives and Warriors

When Mrs. Einstein was asked if she understood her husband's theory of relativity, she answered, "No, but I know my husband, and I know he can be trusted." While many may smile at this anecdote, others may not. Instead, they may be annoyed and retort that the statement limits or devalues women and their abilities. In the recent past some women have criticized what they have interpreted as the tendency in the Bible and the church to remember and refer to women in the contexts of their primary relationships to others, especially the men of their lives. Thus, contemporary women believe that to be known as someone's wife, mother, sister, grandmother, aunt, or even friend somehow disparages one's person. Women are, they say, to be seen as individuals, independent of their relationships to men. And yet if we are not remembered for our commitments, our loves, our bonds to one another, and our place in relation to others, what are we to be remembered for? It could be answered that we could be eulogized for what we accomplished, our work, our art, but if it is done primarily for our own benefit or self-expression, does that not reveal the narrowness and the limited boundaries of our world?

I was once sent a Valentine's Day card with the children's characters Winnie the Pooh and Piglet. I have kept it for its wisdom and deep understanding of love. It is a short conversation between the two:

> Piglet sidled up to Pooh from behind.
> "Pooh," he whispered.
> "Yes, Piglet?"
> "Nothing," said Piglet, taking Pooh's paw. "I just wanted to be sure of you."

Perhaps in our deepest and truest moments we are seen and known by those who are sure of us and those we are sure of in our lives.

Ba'al Shem Tov, a great Jewish storyteller, mystic, and prophet of the eighteenth century, wrote of marriage, although not the marriage of convenience or the marriage contracted for children, inheritance, or legalized sex, or even the marriage based on romantic love. He wrote of marriage as something intrinsic to each person's soul and ultimate meaning: "From every human being there rises a light that reaches straight to heaven, and when two souls that are destined to be together find each other, their streams of light flow together, and a single brighter light goes forth from their united being."

This connection, this sense of being one, beyond customary attachments, is a form of love that is honored in many of the stories of the patriarchs, the prophets, and their wives. It is a bonding born of faith, of enduring together, of knowing and experiencing the presence and power of the Holy in their lives together. In a sense, these relationships cannot be described using the categories and words available to us today. In the Bible these intimate connections are often only hinted at in the public accounting of events, in the naming of a couple's children, or in asides apparently dropped randomly into the text.

The Wife of Isaiah the Prophet

In chapter 8 of Isaiah we are introduced to Isaiah's wife, who has no name:

> I went to my wife; she conceived and gave birth to a son. Then Yahweh said to me, "Call him 'Quick to Plunder–Booty Is Close,' for this is Yahweh's word: Before the child knows how to say 'father' or 'mother,' the wealth of Damascus and the booty of Samaria will be carried off by the King of Assyria."
>
> (VV. 3–4)

She is not described as wife; the word used, *nebiah,* indicates a prophetess. But what about this woman, the prophetess who is wife to Isaiah, the towering prophet and suffering servant of Yahweh, the voice of the poor and those in distress because of others' sin? Who is she and who was she to Isaiah and to God? She is effaced behind the overwhelming presence of her husband and only surfaces in the shadows of her children's names. They reveal an ongoing relationship bound intimately to the fate of Israel as well as to God in the covenant bond. This bond and relationship are experiencing trauma, struggle, and a time pregnant with both the peace of the one promised to come and the wars and torture of a world that refuses the healing rivers and gently flowing waters of Shiloah (Isa. 8:6). Isaiah will go on to say: "So I will wait for Yahweh who hides his face from the people of Jacob. I will hope in him. Here am I and the children he has given me. We are signs and portents in Israel from Yahweh Sabaoth, who dwells on Mount Zion" (Isa. 8:17–18). Yahweh hides his face from his people, and Isaiah's wife hides her face as well, an apt image of the loving, faithful, ever-present, tending God they both serve. One serves by speaking, and the other serves by being silent and hidden, like the pauses and rests in between words and notes of a musical score. Both are essential to the message and the music that are made.

Isaiah will endure terrible sufferings, walking for three years, naked and barefoot, and though once he was of noble birth, he will accompany Israel through some of its darkest hours. His end is unknown, except that it is thought to be a horrible one, torturous and bloody, as the songs of the suffering servant attest. And this woman who loved him suffered and prayed with him on behalf of the stubborn people.

The essence of the prophet or prophetess is sacrifice, pain that comes from conscience and seeks to dent the hardness of others' consciences, and it is never bitter or self-serving. Its anger is always on behalf of others, and those who speak also accept pain as an inevitable reaction to their words—pain inflicted heartlessly by those who resist hearing the truth. Prophecy is about displacement from culture, nation, and the norm, wherever it is found, because it invariably leads to the destruction of those who do not "make it as things are constructed." These people are called out of any normal life and consecrated to defying the majority and the mainstream while siding with those who by their very presence shout at our deaf ears that we are not honest, not holy, and not living with integrity. There are many hidden prophets among us who are the backbone of those who stand up front. Like the young woman Thérèse of Lisieux, who died at age twenty-four in a cloistered convent in France and is now a Doctor of the Church, we must learn that there is another order besides the dominant one or the contemporary one. She wrote, "Each small task of everyday life is part of the total harmony of the universe."

Isaiah's wife was a prophetess. The prophetess or prophet is about giving bread and word to the poor. They are about reminding us of what it means to be human beings, made in the image and likeness of God. Whatever this essence is, it is beyond description in terms of masculine and feminine. It is more basic than being a woman or a man. Archbishop Desmond Tutu tries to speak of it from the perspective of his culture:

> *Ubuntu* is very difficult to render into a Western language. It speaks of the very essence of being human. When we want to give high praise to someone we say, *"Yu, u nobuntu"*; "Hey, so-and-so has *ubuntu."* Then you are generous, you are hospitable, you are friendly and caring and compassionate. You share what you have. It is to say, "My humanity is caught up, is inextricably bound up, in yours." We belong in a bundle of life. We say, "A person is a person through other persons." It is not, "I think therefore I am." It says rather: "I am human because I belong. I participate, I share." A person with *ubuntu* is open and available to others, affirming of others, does not feel threatened that others are able and good, for he or she has a proper self-assurance that comes from knowing that he or she belongs in a greater whole and is diminished when others are humiliated or diminished, when others are tortured or oppressed, or treated as if they were less than who they are. (Desmond Tutu, *No Future Without Forgiveness*
>
> (DOUBLEDAY, 1999 P. 31)

Perhaps the prophets and prophetesses could express this essence and call people to it because they had first known it in their own flesh and known it together in their own marriage relationships, and with God.

Mary and Eve

Mary's story has suffered almost as drastically from lack of imagination as has Eve's story. Most interpretations have simply cast Mary as the antithesis of everything Eve was seen to be or not to be. Yet we know little specifically about Mary. We are given geographical locations, an isolated village in a backwater region of an occupied territory, and we are given her place in a genealogy that purports to go back to the very beginnings (Matthew 1). She is remembered as being in the line of kings through her husband, Joseph, and she is remembered as the mother of the long-awaited one. The text reads: "Jacob was the father of Joseph, the husband of Mary, and from her came Jesus who is called the Christ—the Anointed" (Matt. 1:16).

Mary's and Eve's stories seem all about how they conceive and why and who their children will be for the people. But the how is a bit different: "She [Mary] has conceived by the Holy Spirit, and will bear a son, whom you are to call 'Jesus' for he will free his people from their sins" (Matt. 1:20b–21). This all happens to fulfill prophecies made eight or nine hundred years earlier. The information is relayed in a dream, and there is no "knowing" between husband and wife. The knowing is between God and a woman. In this rendering of the story in Matthew, that's about all we know. When this woman appears in the text, she never speaks a word. She does not do the naming, as was the custom. She is always described as being seen with the child and being Mary, the mother.

Then the child and the mother are in mortal danger from Herod, a man who has made choices that make him more and more inhuman. His choice, like Cain's, is murder. He is afraid of this child's life, of stories that reek of hope and the promise of freedom. So he chooses to kill the child. An angel tells Joseph, the father, of Herod's intention, and the family flees. Herod "gave orders to kill all the boys in Bethlehem and its neighborhood who were two years old or under" (Matt. 2:16). In response, "a cry is heard in Ramah, wailing and loud lamentation: Rachel weeps for her children. She refuses to be comforted, for they are no more" (Matt. 2:18). The threads woven between Eve, Rachel, and Mary are plaited with blood and cries for comfort, justice, and life. When the immediate threat of Herod is over, because of his death, Joseph takes the child and his mother home to Israel. And that's one of Mary's stories.

We know the end of her child's story. He is killed, murdered by others in cold blood. She knows suffering, injustice, helplessness in the face of others' choices, loss that cannot ever be replaced, although in another story she is given, like Eve, another son to take as her own. As her first-born dies, he gives her into the care of a younger disciple, John, and with another mother named Mary they become a new kind of family, a family born of a relationship of word, life, hope, suffering, and death.

Like Eve, Mary chooses, takes risks, and walks into the unknown. She is young, but then Eve certainly was too. Unlike Eve, Mary has an-other woman, a friend, to go to in her need and with her questions. She greets Elizabeth, and the air is full of Spirit, children dancing inside wombs, and freedom aborning. There are recognition and singing of the praise of God. The old, the barren, the unborn, the virgin, the women, the children, and two men who will not know women in the usual ways are writing a new story altogether with the Spirit of God. And it's worth singing about. So the song, the story, tells of souls and spirits that seize hold of the flesh that exalts. It says that servants and the lowly and the ones blamed in the past are now blessed and looked upon with great de-light by the eye of God. And this God has been hiding and trying to get into the story at every juncture since the beginning, and always it was mercy that was trying to gain entrance into those who lived in his pres-ence (unlike Cain, who departed from Yahweh's presence).

And there is more. The proud, the mighty, the knowledgeable, and the sure are going to be put down. Those who were rich, who had more than the others, who hoarded, who acquired and did not give the best or share, will know emptiness, and those who were hungry and in want, aching in emptiness, will know good things. What a reversal in the story as it's been told so far! Of course, there were always other stories, hidden in bits and scattered remnants, but now the story of life is rising and be-ing remembered, coming true. It is mercy's story, a story that was trying to be told from the beginning.

Mary stays with her woman friend, who understands and shares some of her wonder for a while, and then goes home to live apparently as everyone else does, until it is time for the story to be born as a human being. The child is born, away from home, with strangers who provide shelter and with angels singing and dancing like stars in the sky.

Then she and Joseph take the child and offer him to God, in obedience to the laws of old, and they meet ancient ones with stories of what will become of this child and how his choices will have consequences for Mary especially but also for all who come into his presence. He will be the cause of many people's rise or downfall, a sign of opposition and contradiction to what has become acceptable and known. Mary will know something else as well: "A sword will pierce her heart and soul so that the secret thoughts of everyone will be brought to light" (Luke 2:35).

In all the Gospels except John's, this is the last we see of her. The Acts of the Apostles mentions her once, when she is with Jesus' followers after his death and the Spirit came again. The text says: "All of these together gave themselves to constant prayer. With them were some women and also Mary, the mother of Jesus, and his brothers" (Acts 1:14). Wherever she appears in the larger story of the good news about her child Jesus, Mary is found with the Spirit. She knows the Spirit of God in her heart and in her flesh.

In the Gospel of John she stands witness at a public execution. It is a heart-wrenching and all-too-human story:

> Near the cross of Jesus stood his mother, his mother's sister Mary, who was the wife of Cleophas, and Mary of Magdala. When Jesus saw the Mother, and the disciple, he said to the mother, "Woman, this is your son." Then he said to the disciple, "There is your mother." And from that moment the disciple took her to his own home.
>
> (JOHN 19:25–27)

This is the last will and testament of a man in agony, making sure that what he loves has intimacy and care after his death. It is a new form of genealogy, of giving birth so that life is passed on and given to the future. It is not based on blood ties, birth, or marriage, but on a shared re-lationship between people who know each other in love, in this person Jesus' flesh and spirit, and in the Father's will. Mary is first described in the text as Jesus' mother, standing with her sister and another woman friend of his, Mary of Magdala. Then she becomes "the Mother" when Jesus sees her there with the disciple. She stands in Jesus' presence, knowing he will die, but he still has work to do. In the midst of his pain, he separates himself from her as mother/child and makes her mother to all the disciples. She is to be mother to all those who stand with him in death, and they are to take her home as their mother. She has become the mother of all those who live because of this human being, this man's life, his death, and his soon-to-be resurrection. She's become the mother and the grandmother of life that cannot be indelibly harmed by suffering or even by death.

Her silent lament has been heard as clearly as Eve's wail of pain at the reality of death chosen by one human being for another: murder. And the compassion of God has answered again by giving new relationships and new life, stronger than death, stronger than biological generation or old kinship ties. There is another family now, another possibility to the story, another choice with freedom and imagination and life never dreamed of, even throughout the times of the old stories. Suffering and death are as intimate with life as are delight and joy. Perhaps it was meant to be from the very beginning. But both these women have much in common: They are both the mother of the living. They are both the mother of all sorrows. They are both the mother of all those who make choices, both terrible ones and ones that are good and holy. They both sing and lament, know living and dying within their own bodies and spir-its, know God, and know love and intimacies as well as isolation and loneliness, emptiness, and mystery.

The only difference is that Eve had no stories to go by in her life. She made them up as she lived and others lived and died around her. Mary had many stories, songs, poems, lamentations, and memories to go on as she lived. Both knew the dark night and the bright dawn, just reversed in time: Eve knew these in the beginning of her life, Mary at the end of hers. We both know their stories as our own; and because of them, our lives are bright darkness and life that knows both death and resurrection. But neither of them is the whole story; not even together do they begin to tell it all. We do have an intimation of the story's end. It's found in the book of Revelation:

> A loud voice came from the throne, "Here is the dwelling of God among men [human beings]: He will pitch his tent among them and they will be his people. God will be with them and wipe every tear from their eyes. There shall be no more death or mourning, crying out or pain, for the world that was has passed away."
>
> (REV. 21:3–4)

Until then, suffering and death will constitute an essential part of our lives. Eve was confronted by the serpent and chose. Mary was confronted by the angel Gabriel and chose. Each of us is confronted by the serpent and the Holy. Each of us must choose. As with Eve, Mary, and Jesus, suffering and death are the contexts for choices that can lead to new life and understanding.

Like Eve's and Mary's stories, our stories are stories of choices. None of the stories are scripts to follow. Each of the stories of these women simply roughs out options, sets precedents, and warns us about knowledge and its consequences. Each of the stories is a mirror full of mystery and wisdom, knowledge and wonder, a mirror that helps reveal our true selves.

Lately, as I have been writing this book, I have a recurring image. Mary dies, and as she enters heaven, Eve is standing at a distance watching all the jubilation. But Mary has no interest in all the glory whatsoever. She's intent on looking for someone. She spies her, over on the side, in the shadows, and goes to her, ignoring everyone else. She reaches out, and they fall into each other's arms like old and dear and long-lost friends. Eve and Mary hold on to each other and weep. Each had wept at morning's light and with mourning's loss. Each had cried out in agony and anguish over what their children could do to each other. Each had been amazed at how life turned out. Each had sought new words and im-ages for what they experienced and came to know in life, in birth, in suf-fering, in joy, with others, alone, and in death. Now together they have a song to sing, tears that flow freely, and laughter that spills out of their mouths. The HOLY ONES listen and are well pleased. And to everyone's surprise, Mary and Eve walk off together away from the crowd. Oh, and did they have stories to tell and worlds to share! They still do. Amazingly it is up to us now. Our lives, our choices, and what we do with the uni-verse and all our children, as well as our sufferings and deaths, make up their stories. Grandmothers. How they love to talk about their children to one another still. Once upon a time. . . .

From The Bride (Foreword)

Icons: The Eye of God in the
Eye of the Beholder

The icon is God in a human house. It can be seen as an enclosure of divinity in a small window or a door that humbly invites those who bend before it in body or spirit into the realm of faith. Icons are celebrations, proclamations of the mystery of the Incarnation: flesh and bone rendered in gesso and gold paint painstakingly, truthfully expressed both in the finished form and in the process of the making. The making is a deliberate work, an intense labor of emptying out, of absorbing the Holy and letting the remnants remain behind on board and wood. The iconographer strains muscles, bending to draw near the features he seeks to portray, momentarily making visible what is invisible to the human eye. The iconographer sits, sees, stares, and tries not to blink as truth, a speck of truth, is made manifest, made clear to those who stop and gaze upon it.

The icon declares: Halt! And what brings us to a halt makes us cease emotion. All emotions are portrayed, yet all somehow are brought to a full stop: terror, grief, utter isolation, violence, joy, rage, tenderness, even prayer itself. When emotion is held still, then prayer itself stops and is sustained or held before the mind and body. In this stasis it is sometimes called contemplation. An icon is fashioned to portray a person's meaning through God's eye—so an icon demands that we slow down, stop, be still, stand, barely breath. It is the presence of the Spirit coming through the eyes, and it hovers before us silently screaming: Be still—you are in the presence of the Holy. You are now on holy ground. Be attentive!

The work and vocation of an iconographer are therefore described as "wording or writing an icon." The icon is akin to the evangelist's gospel, the preacher's sermon, the teller's story. Each builds a small house for God . . . or better yet, an inn, a wayside rest, a corner of the world that becomes inhabitable, a sanctuary in the midst of rabble and more useful objects. Sometimes icons are done in threes—a triptych—three to a house where friends who were together in the realm of the Holy can now visit others who seek after the Holy hidden right before our eyes in the world at large. We can linger in their company, their presence, for awhile. Triptychs give the same sense of what is known when a locket is opened and a loved one is caught sight of, or when a place is designated a refuge, a state of mind and soul that speaks of God-in-flesh, an image where humankind can be embraced by God and can bend back toward that presence that holds us near and dear always.

At the same time an icon is confinement, like a seed in the ground, a child forming and expanding in the womb, and it is meant to give birth to Another in our midst, in our souls. Icons are mirrors, often small enough to be hand held, that pull us close, not only to our own faces but also toward the faces of those who now see face-to-face with God, as we all mightily hope to do ourselves one day. These countenances can appear intimidating, fascinating, off-putting, freeing, frustrating, purifying, indwelling, even drawing us to gasp for air or incline in worship. But there is no way to ignore them. Their presence is far too strong.

Who are these people depicted in icons—faces, eyes wide-set, long noses, high brows, hands positioned ritually, looking at one another, pointing, looking straight out at us? Who are they who question, challenge, comfort, and demand that we become conscious of ourselves and of God, and in so doing become true, become human, become holy, become those who belong to God? They are our forebears, ancestors in the faith, patriarchs and matriarchs of old, prophets and dreamers, models, old friends, believers who struggled and made it home free, companions on our way, guardian spirits concerned with our safety, our bodies' and souls' well-being, our communities and churches.

They are fellow travelers, strangers, anonymous or even unknown saints who sinned and repented, agonized over evil, and repaired their portion of the world. Mary Oliver, a contemporary poet and winner of the Pulitzer Prize and National Book Award, in her book *Winter Hours: Prose, Prose Poems, and Poems* writes of her own mentors, teachers, and luminaries. She is describing writers and poets, the voice she hears when she writes, but she could be describing the faces and persons depicted in icons for us as well:

> . . . spirits whose influence and teachings I am now inseparable from and forever grateful for. I go nowhere, I arrive nowhere without them. With them I live my life, with them I enter the event, I mold the meditation, I keep if I can some essence of the hour, even as it slips away. And I do not accomplish this alert and loving confrontation by myself and alone, but through terrifying and continual effort, and with this innumerable, fortifying company, bright as stars in the heaven of my mind.
>
> (*WINTER HOURS: PROSE, PROSE POEMS, AND POEMS*
> [NEW YORK; HOUGHTON MIFFLIN] 1999, P. 20)

These faces of the friends of God question us: and question us in such a way that what is posed, proposed to us, is at root unanswerable. Do you know who you are? Do you know who you belong to? Do you know what you were made for? Do you know how to live, to suffer, to die? Do you want communion, holiness, and ultimate freedom from death? You're seen—all these images sound us out silently. They are truth-tellers, revelations and confessors intent on laying bare all our raw and well-concealed places of spirit and soul that hide and refuse to grow gracefully. And of course, these faces comfort us, hold us in our pain and regard us and surround us with tenderness, drawing us gently and firmly into the company of those who suffer and who reach in their desperation, isolation, and agony for God's succor and strength. They, with God, seek to redeem all humankind and creation. They are about the work of transforming even terror and of wresting hope from humanity.

To look upon an icon, to gaze, to search its detail, to sit before it, to contemplate and enter its eyes, is to acknowledge, often in spite of our rational analysis, another domain, another realm altogether than the one that us visible. Like the mystery of the Incarnation—God's grasping of our flesh as presence—an icon is a covenant, a bond, a pact between God, who is limitless, and all who are created and limited, between what is unmade and what is becoming reality and truthfulness by grace's intent within us through our maker. We in turn, are seen into through and through. We are accosted and we are invited to renew our vows, to declare our intents, and once again to kneel and to bend and to obey the demands of our God who thrives in our flesh and loves our form even unto appropriation, crucifixion, transfiguration, and resurrection.

That is why in ritual response to this presence, it is natural to approach the icon, bend, cross oneself three times, and kiss the image—in gratitude, in need, and in affection. Wood once again becomes a bridge that can cross the distance and let us, however fleetingly, touch the Holy. Or as the Native Peoples used to say—the wind on our fingertips is the Great Spirit kissing us; the wind in our hair is the Great Spirit caressing us and laying a blessing upon our heads. One must, of necessity, respond to an icon: obey its summons, if only by avoiding the niche or corner where it resides or by turning away in frustration, disgust, or ignorance. As the Celts once carved in their doorways: Bidden or unbidden, God enters in. It is so with icons as well.

From the beginning our God has been about the work of saving us, of asking us "Where are you?" (These were God's first words to Adam and Eve when they are outside the garden). God has been about the work of trying to draw us closer again to him and to assure us of his presence and intimacy in spite of not knowing our sin and reluctance to be touched and held by the Holy Unutterable One. In his presence no words are needed anymore. The icon has been written to say it all: mercy. Mercy. Mercy singing in the night, seeping through our minds and flesh and lingering like a fragrant smell in the world at large.

The icon is God's silent, boundless mercy. The icon is God's poem and song without words. The icon is God's touch, a kiss, and then the empty place that calls forever after to us—the icon is the echo of God's incarnation once and for all time upon the earth. The icon is a rest stop on the way home, a small sanctuary, a protection, a movable feast that makes us tremble. Blessed be the Name and Form of the Holy One. Blessed be all that God has made. Glory, glory, glory in it. Amen.

From Mary, Mother of All Nations

Introduction: Face to Face with Holy Presences

The word *icon* (*eikon*) simply means "image." But in reality icons are much more. Almost as old as Christianity itself, they are intent on drawing the one who watches and sees into the very presence of the image "written" on the wood.

Always there has been a secret to really seeing. The Book of Exodus recounts the story of Moses seeing Yahweh face-to-face, with glory shining on Moses' face so strongly that the Israelites begged him to cover it. They could not bear to look at him after he had been in the presence of the Holy One of Israel (Exod. 34:30). And so Moses covered his face with a veil to hide the radiance. In 2 Corinthians, Paul writes about seeing with this veil removed from our eyes—seeing with the eyes and light of the Spirit:

> Now this Lord is the Spirit, and where the Spirit of the Lord is, there is freedom. And we, with unveiled faces reflecting like mirrors the brightness of the Lord, all grow brighter and brighter as we are turned into the image [*eikon*] that we reflect; this is the work of the Lord who is Spirit.
>
> (2 COR. 3:17–18)

Icons are soul windows, entrances into the presence of the Holy. Like sacraments in the Western church, they are somehow, mysteriously, the reality that they image. Like the Word of the Lord—inspired by the Spirit of God—which evokes the presence of God as strongly as the Eucharist (bread and wine that are the body and blood of Christ), icons are believed to be sacraments that evoke this presence by sight and by faith. In the words of the Orthodox theologian Paul Evdokimov: "in a nutshell, the icon is a sacrament for the Christian East; more precisely it is the vehicle of a personal presence."

And it is a deep, abiding silence, the silence of night, the silence of resurrection morning, the silence of a mother enraptured by the eyes of her newborn, the silence of a father first seeing his child. It can fill a room as small as a monk's cell or as large as a cathedral—or a corner in the room of a house. It is an unassuming presence that seeps in gradually until it soaks through one's soul and heart and mind.

This presence heeds all the courtesies of friendship and the art of coming to know another with intimacy and depth. It teaches yearning, it can instill quiet, and it calls us to linger. Yet it is an epiphany as indelible as Sinai or the Mount of the Transfiguration, for it is divine light loosed momentarily into the world, and it does not fade. It beseeches us to turn within and view ourselves with truthfulness, and it opens space within us that does not close up ever again. It is a bit of this world that had passed from it, and, paradoxically, it returns again to this world and saturates it to its very roots. In the presence of an icon one senses God's carefulness with human beings, and yet one can tremble with a sense of the unfamiliar and the Holy reaching out to clasp us in an embrace of great tenderness.

An icon speaks a language: one of awe, reverence, canticles of blessing, litanies of detail and gladness, lament and sorrow that lead to adoration without words. Icons can introduce us to "Jubilate Deo" and the profundities of incarnation and resurrection with all the glories of the first freshness of morning in the world. And yet they can similarly touch us with unbearable suffering, the isolation of pain, and unending destruction. They can evoke within us compassion, surging waves of sorrow and grief, recognition of what evil can do to human beings. They can summon up the fury of a prophet's anger or the fury of faithfulness and justice. They incarnate one still point of the divine and let it linger, inhabit, and move in to dwell and stay with us, taking over every room in our minds and souls. In the presence of an icon we are never orphaned. There is always one who whispers in our inner ear and comes like a breath of wind, caressing our cheek, as once Yahweh sought intimacy with the prophet Elijah at the entrance to his cave.

The Irish poet Sean Dunne wrote a grand poem about Thomas Merton's hermitage in Kentucky. It is called "Five Photographs by TM." In one of the "photographs," called "Icons," Dunne amply captures both the sense of familiarity and the ancient wisdom and otherness that icons reveal. In a room they dwell with us, yet remain somehow in the presence of the God of heaven. In the mediums of wood, egg tempera, and gold leaf and in the disciplined expressions of archetypal figures, we are met by the old and new friends of God whom we are called to cherish as the children of God who are still on earth. Whether the icons are of Christ, the Mother of God, the Trinity, the descending and transforming Spirit, the beloved Father, or one of the many angels, saints, and prophets, they all are about revelation. They all invite us to meet face-to-face with the presence portrayed—"written"—on the icon. Theology, belief, spirituality, and prayer all merge in the one who sees and is seen by the presence on the icon. To look, to contemplate, and to begin to pray is to be transformed, to be radically altered, and to draw near to the holy ones of God. We are invited to become part of the icon, part of the story of God, and to know and be known by the Holy. In a sense, one is read by the icon, seen through, exposed. It is humbling, excruciating, freeing, and rapturous. We are taken to the source of what we see.

Icons are a work of *tikkum olam:* they repair the world. They are a remedy, a radical reminder of the good, a proclamation of hope incarnate, standing and judging the world that kills, maims, destroys, and humiliates humankind and selfishly wastes the earth's resources. An icon reweaves a small portion of the universe into communion and makes holy the here and now. Icons whisper, "Remember! Come together again, as it was in the beginning and will be once more."

An icon is a prayer. It is God's prayer and supplication to us to heed once again the command to "Know that I am God . . . There is no other before me" (Exod. 20:2–3). Icons remind us that we are God's possession and God's beloved. Or as Merton wrote: "We are all one, but we have forgotten. The task of religion, of all living is to once again make us One, to reveal that in our flesh in our times and upon the earth." It is *the* task of the human race, as it was the task, the mission, and the good news of the Messiah, the Word of God made flesh of the Virgin and dwelling until forever among us.

An icon is a talisman, a protective wooden scapular, a lifeline in the face of evil and bloodletting. It is a silent witness and an unsingable song of redemption proclaiming that we are blessed creatures, destined to become like God once again. These icons call us home, call us back to ourselves.

The poet Rumi tells a story that we should consider before we contemplate these icons:

> A friend of Joseph's went to visit him after returning from a journey. "What present have you brought me?" Joseph asked.
>
> "What could I bring you," his friend replied, "that you don't already have? But," he added, "because you are so beautiful, and nothing exists in all the world more beautiful than you, I have brought you a mirror, so you can know the joy at every moment of seeing your own face."

Rumi comments:

> Is there anything that God doesn't have already that you could give him? Is there anything that God could need that you could

possibly provide? All that you are here for, and the entire meaning of the Path of Love, is to bring before God a heart bright as
a mirror, so God can see his own face in it.

The mirror is held up before us. Come, look at your face, your true face,
and sit still and know God. Know God without a veil, in Jesus, face-to-
face in a glimpse, a glance, of love. Hear deep in your soul the words of
the Holy One: "Be still and know that I am God." (Ps. 46:10) I am your
God and you are mine. All of you are mine.

My grandmother used to say, "God never takes his eyes off you, dear, because you are so dear to him." Sit now, in the presence of the holy ones,
and be seen through. Let these be the images engraved upon your heart.
And "dare to see [your] soul at the White heat" (Emily Dickinson). For
as the gospel craves a listener, the icon craves a seer. And it is a seer, the
seeker, who completes the icon as it pries us open and shares with us its
silent, unspeakable language. Here the holy comes to inhabit us. This
page is the threshold. Turn the page and see where silence reigns. Keep
company with the holy ones of God. Pray. Here the chasm closes. We are
riveted to this refuge, this solidarity, this compassion that discloses itself
and then encloses us.

A Prayer to Mary

Stillness of God, settle in our souls. Breath of God, move
through us. Light of God, illumine our nights and dawn
in our hearts. Shadow of God, fall over us as once you
bent over the face of Mary and sow the seed of holiness,
of justice, and of mercy within us.

Whisper of love and truth in our waiting hearts. As
we have gazed on these faces and forms of light, make us
icons of your reflection for all the world to see. Mary, you
who learned the wisdom of mercy and lived in its mystery,
share that knowledge with us. May we hear again your
words to all of us: "Do whatever HE tells you!" (John 2:5).

Give us the courage to walk through the world, intent on giving birth to your Word, your hope, and your love, steadfast until we find ourselves gathered into you, O Trinity, at home with this woman who believed, exalting together in the fullness of the freedom of the children of God. Amen.

From Not Counting Women and Children: Neglected Stories from the Bible

Introduction

Words do not disappear. They are indelible—whether they are written on paper, inscribed in hearts, or hidden in memories. A Jewish legend says that if all the earth were quiet for just a moment, then we could all hear the voice of God echoing from Mount Sinai, speaking the words of the Ten Commandments. The sounds, form, and style would roll like waves throughout time and space, catching us today and washing over us.

The words of God never disappear. They hide among us. They have a home among us, waiting for us to recognize and hear them again. They do not disappear because they are truth and they have a life all their own, in relation to all of us and to earth. And so part of our tradition is the telling of stories, the need to say the words again and again for all generations. These words and stories have the power to pry open our minds and our hearts whenever we hear them spoken aloud. Telling the story, saying the words, and listening is a holy enterprise, both worship and expression of life together. This is our religion, what ties and binds our lives together.

This belief that all is story and that the story never ends is the basis for these reflections on *The Book,* the Scriptures. These reflections are a continuance of the words once spoken, of the Word spoken in flesh and blood among us. For the Jewish community this ongoing process and life of the text, written and spoken, is called midrash; technically midrash is an exposition of the underlying import of the text. There are collections of midrash—or commentary—on the text, and then commentary on the commentary. It is a tried and tested method of theologizing and reflecting on the Scriptures. It assumes some knowledge or understanding of the original setting and meaning, but moves on from that point, spiraling out through history and spirit to the here and now.

Midrash looks at words and phrases packed with layers of meanings and associations, with webs or networks of symbols and connections that all reveal the mystery behind the words—the reality of God speaking to us. There are many meanings in translations and interpretation, but they all tell us one truth, the original meaning: God, the Great Mystery that has invited us all to dwell within this presence and share this way of life and community as one. The words are all about us, and they keep expanding to encompass more—more of meaning, more of people and life experiences and situations. They draw us beyond any boundaries of time, space, awareness, identity, or possibility—beyond and into the mystery that surrounds and envelops us. This art and science of sacred storytelling and interpretation is at the core of our religion and practice of belief as God's people.

In the traditional Jewish sources a page of Scripture is a map through history and through different expressions of belief. On one page we can find the original text, then questions and responses down through the centuries. The Mishnah (second century), and Gemara (third through fifth century)—the oral tradition—are cited by Rashi (an eleventh-century exegete) and other scholars from as late as the sixteenth and seventeenth centuries. David Wolpe, a scholar and teacher, calls it a "thicket of text" designed to be endless—to remind the reader and hearer that there is no true beginning or end to the journey of language, of study, of speaking sacred words. The journey continues in our lives, as our experiences and interpretations are added to those of other believers and storytellers and storymakers. These words and interpretations become lifelines for us, our loved ones, and others who come after us. They are transmitted, passed on, become confession, practice, and hope, so that others can build on our beliefs and lives of worship.

My reflections in this book are midrash, commentaries on the stories of the Scriptures. They are carefully selected and chosen stories that are often forgotten, and the comments and reflections are by people who are often ignored and not asked for their thoughts and beliefs about their place in the stories. *Not counting women and children*—two massive groups of people in the world. Yet just being a woman or a child does not necessarily put you or me in that category of people. To belong to this forgotten group, those who reveal meaning through the community's experience, we must become like Jesus, the child of God, the Word that seeks out the lost and sides with those who have not been listened to or taken seriously as theologians.

The stories are all about Jesus, who is woman, child, and man of God—poor, midwife, mother hen, a weeping human being, and always a beloved child, vulnerable and growing in his relationship to God. The stories and images reveal to all of us how to become more human. Of course, there are many other stories, not told here, but I chose these carefully as foundation stories to get us thinking like a child, a woman, a man of God, one of the poor, the not counted, the forgotten, and so they are some of God's best-loved stories. Turn the page and begin once again. "Once upon a time," as the story goes.

Not Counting Women and Children

When Jesus heard this, he withdrew by boat from there to a deserted place by himself. The crowds heard of it and followed him on foot from the towns. When he disembarked and saw the vast throng, his heart was moved with pity, and he cured their sick. As evening drew on, his disciples came to him with the suggestion: "This is a deserted place and it is already late. Dismiss the crowds so that they may go to the villages and buy some food for themselves." Jesus said to them: "There is no need for them to disperse. Give them something to eat yourselves." "We have nothing here," they replied, "but five loaves and a couple of fish." "Bring them here," he said. Then he ordered the crowds to sit down on the grass. He took the five loaves and two fish, looked up to heaven, blessed and broke them and gave the loaves to the disciples, who in turn gave them to the people. All those present ate their fill. The fragments remaining, when gathered up, filled twelve baskets. Those who ate were about five thousand, not counting women and children.

(MATT. 14:13-21)

"Not counting women and children." People react to that phrase in different ways—some with laughter, others with anger, sadness, or disgust. Especially when read aloud, that phrase hangs suspended in the air, like bait on a hook for a fish. One person responds, "I feel excluded." Another complains, "Women and children are put in the same category." Such responses are countered, "But we are all the children of God" (theological reaction to emotion). Or, "But they all were fed and everyone was satisfied, full."

I have always loved this story. It is amazing that in a culture where we characterize men as the dominant group—and men are still dominant in the church in many ways—that the line is even in the text. It reminds us that the Scriptures are inspired by the Spirit. With a line like "five thousand, not counting women and children," perhaps the Spirit is telling us that the group that is the core of the experience is the specific group that is mentioned—women and children—not the one that is left out. Furthermore, sociologists say that when you gather a crowd of men, women, and children, the ratio of women and children to men can be as high as five or six to one. So the story is really the feeding of the thirty-five thousand. Now, if we have missed these points all these years, then what else have we missed?

That's what this chapter is about, but in truth, it's what this whole book, this collection of Scripture stories, is about—what we've missed all these years in reading the stories, for ourselves and in community, because we have been reading them from our own perspectives of dominant cultures, races, beliefs, and assumptions. We have reacted to them without letting the Spirit loose in the text and in the context of the listeners.

Here are some other questions to think about: where did the twelve baskets come from that all the leftovers were collected in? We always remember the extra food, but what about the containers? Maybe they came from the same place that the food came from—the women and children.

Let's go back and look at some of the details of the story. There are unexpected and often unnoticed lines like that one are scattered throughout the Scriptures. If we go hunting and are attentive to them, they can lead us into the wild places of the Spirit where God dwells and where truth resides, waiting for us to discover it anew. Let's go to the very beginning of the story: "When Jesus heard this, he withdrew by boat from there to a deserted place by himself." This is the immediate context for the story. It is the boundary, the setting, and the atmosphere that sets the tone for all that follows. What does Jesus hear?

He hears of the execution of John the Baptist in prison, his beheading during a banquet where Herod was entertained by Herodias' daughter Salome. In response to her dancing Herod offers her a gift, anything she wants, and what she wants is what her mother wants—the head of John the Baptist on a platter. John, the prophet who goes before the face of the Lord, the herald of the long-awaited one, is murdered at a dinner party because of a powerful woman's rage. The demise of the greatest prophet of the Hebrew Scriptures is demeaning, humiliating, and part of a much larger political intrigue in which the coming of the Messiah, conversion, and the possibility of hope for the poor and the masses of people (never taken into account) are ignored. John is dead. His disciples carry away his body, and then they come to inform Jesus.

Jesus reacts with sadness, sorrow, anger, fear: he seeks aloneness. John is his cousin and the one who cleared the way for him—the way is now wide open. What Jesus does now is crucial. It sets in motion all future events. There must have been many things in Jesus' heart and on his mind. First and foremost he felt grief at John's murder and its utter stupidity and callousness. He felt a mixture of anger and righteous rage at the killing of the prophet, the cutting off of the voice crying in the wilderness, giving hope and calling to repentance and conversion. Fear rises inside him; he knows that what happened to John will most likely happen to him if he picks up John's mantle of justice in the prophetic tradition and begins to assert himself as the preacher of hope and the coming of the kingdom of God. To grieve, Jesus goes off to a deserted place; he goes by himself. It is the natural, usual reaction of many people in such a situation. He needs to pray, to weep, and to remember; he must reflect and decide what he himself will do.

But the next lines tell us that he can't get away: "The crowds heard of it and followed him on foot from the towns. When he disembarked and saw the vast throng, his heart was moved with pity, and he cured their sick." Jesus was baptized by John. John had many disciples and many more followers. The people, the masses of the poor and those who hoped for the coming of the Messiah and the possibility of a new life—religious, economic, and social—are left without a leader, bereft and alone, panicking and without direction. But they know of Jesus, for he has already been preaching. As soon as John is dead, the crowds turn to Jesus and will not allow him time apart. John's disciples and even Jesus' own disciples are disoriented, grieving, frightened, angry. Jesus sets out across the lake, and the crowd is so desperate that the people follow him around the lake on foot and are waiting for him when he reaches the other shore.

This story is told in the context of death—needless death, death that is carried out in cold blood for political and personal reasons, death that affects thousands of people. This story situates Jesus in a political reality, a sociological reality, and a religious setting while recounting his personal reaction to the death of John. What Jesus does now sets up the rest of Matthew's Gospel. His reaction will affect his own disciples, the crowds, and so all of us as well. What kind of a person is Jesus? He is human. And at this crisis in his life he is sorrowful, in need of solitude, wanting to get away from everyone. He needs to pray and be with his Father, grieving. But Jesus sees the vast throng and his response is *pity*— "his heart was moved with pity, and he cured their sick."

In that one phrase the kingdom begins in earnest, and Jesus' decision is made. He pities a vast throng, and instead of taking time for himself and dealing with his own very deeply felt desires and needs, he turns to the crowd, knowing that when he does, he sets in motion his own eventual confrontation with the political and religious establishment and his own death. What motivates Jesus' actions, choices, and response is pity. When we grieve, we want to go off alone, to take care of ourselves. When others come after us in this situation, many of us run. But Jesus turns to them, returns to them, and spends the entire day with them. The story is about great lack, great emptiness, and great human needs in the face of suffering and death; in the face of political intrigue, manipulation, destruction; in the face of personal loss. The cry and reach of human hope in the face of life that can seem so terrible is found in this story.

Pity. This word causes realms of reactions—most of them negative. Many people don't want to be pitied. They want to be befriended, cared for, respected, attended to, ministered to, taken compassion on, but not pitied. It is a relentless word, a powerful emotion. In our culture it often connotes looking down on someone, a position of being above another person, an impersonal reaction to a problem rather than a positive response to a human being in need. But Jesus pities a vast throng of people and spends his day with them. What kind of depths does Jesus tap into in his own soul?

What is this pity that moves Jesus, even as he grieves and mourns for John the Baptist and is worried about his own future? The word *pity* in ancient languages and in today's culture has two very strong meanings, both of which can be applied to this text. The first is a gut reaction: the sight before us makes us so sick that we want to throw up. This is not what it means to live, to be human. This is not the way the world should be. This is not the way God created us to live and be with each other. It revolts us. It literally makes us sick; it moves our stomach muscles to throw up anything in our systems. Our bodies and our minds recoil and reject the situation before us. This is what Jesus feels—he looks at a vast throng and wants to be sick. The other meaning is just as strong and evocative. The sight makes us so angry that our stomach muscles (the same ones that make us want to throw up food) begin labor contractions and bring forth something new—give birth to an alternative of hope and profoundly alter the reality before us. Jesus feels this too, and his pity can encompass a massive crowd of people: men, women, and children, all directionless, afraid, lost, without hope, desperate, and in need. And Jesus spends the whole day curing the sick. Jesus spends the day with the crowd. It's a crowd of five thousand—if you don't count the women and children. So we can picture a group of about thirty-five thousand people on foot, heading out of the towns, around the lake, trailing a man they hope can help them. They are women, children, the elderly, the poor, and all manner of others. The crowd undoubtedly includes merchants, beggars, travelers, the curious, the sick, the lame, the blind, lepers, public sinners, prostitutes, tax collectors. There are probably scribes, teachers, Pharisees, lawyers, and others as well. It is humanity—a great sea of people—and they spend all day together because of Jesus' presence. They don't want to leave him. They have touched some sort of hope, some possibility of change, of graceful living, in the midst of their questions, confusion, and pain. But the disciples have other ideas. The disciples have been with the crowds all day too, and they want Jesus to themselves.

But Jesus' reaction is clear, even blunt—probably devastating to his followers: "There is no need for them to disperse. Give them something to eat yourselves." This is the central line of the story. And as often as this story is discussed, everyone tries to avoid this impossible line. Jesus *can't* mean what he says to the disciples! "Give them something to eat yourselves." It is not a suggestion. It is a command. It is a direction, a course of action, one that will change everything, even their thoughts about what they can and cannot do.

We too are disciples. Jesus is also telling us to feed the crowd, telling us to do the seemingly impossible. When Jesus sees the vast throng and has pity on them, he decides to act. What he does next is a model for the rest of the Gospel, the rest of his life, and the life of all of his disciples. We are called to the kingdom of the poor.

"Then he ordered the crowds to sit down on the grass. He took the five loaves and two fish, looked up to heaven, blessed and broke them and gave the loaves to the disciples, who in turn gave them to the people." This process, this pattern, is simple—and simply unbelievable! He orders the crowd to sit down on the grass. He begins by organizing chaos, by putting them into small groups as they sit down together. Then he takes the disciples' food, small and inadequate to feed a multitude, and looks up to heaven and blesses and breaks loaves and gives them back into the hands of the disciples. He takes, blesses, breaks, and distributes them through his disciples to the people seated on the ground. The meal is served by his followers.

Of course, as someone always says, "That's the liturgy! That's the Eucharist! That's what we do every Sunday at Mass!" Yes, exactly. Feeding the crowds with what we ourselves have is exactly that—liturgy. Jesus takes whatever we have, and even if the gift is reluctant, blesses it, breaks it, and passes it around, giving it away graciously. How simple! And "All those present ate their fill." There was enough—not only enough, but all those present ate their fill. They were satisfied, filled, content.

What did happen? Let's go back to that phrase we began with—"not counting women and children." Even today when women and children go anywhere, out for the morning or afternoon, shopping, on errands, to the baby-sitter, the women take provisions in bags—diapers, food, juice, water, change of clothes, toys, pacifier, odds and ends that they and the children consider necessities. Now, women and children haven't changed much from two thousand years ago. If women and children were in the crowd, they would have had water in skins or jugs and food—bread, fish, cheese, fruit, things that could be carried easily in a bag or in the pockets of robes and other clothing. And just as people today always take along more than they need, they would have had extra. And remember, these are people carrying their sick on pallets, with bedding, slings, medicine, water, bandages, and so on. This is a motley crew, a crowd, a vast throng of unwashed poor, desperate, hungry, and sick people.

Who was counted? Who made up the five thousand? Today when crowds are counted, who's considered important, who's included? Even in the census there are thousands of people who are not counted: illegal immigrants, the poor, those who can't read, those who do not belong to a verifiable group, the homeless, those with no insurance, no Social Security number, all those who fall through the cracks of society. The text says "not counting women and children," but we can't assume that means *literally* women and children; it also means the sick, elderly, the prostitutes, lepers, tax collectors, the unacceptables, the strangers, Gentiles, and outcasts within Jewish society. It means, in fact, the bulk of the crowd, the majority of the throng of people who are the followers of Jesus, desperately in need of good news, of curing, and of being fed and given attention, love, dignity, and understanding, and hope for the future.

The numbers of those not counted in our church include all those who don't come but are baptized, those who come intermittently or when they are in desperate need, the separated and divorced, the gay and lesbian, the sick and terminally ill, the old and poor, the illiterate, the unemployed, those unable to drive, those who work when we schedule events, those who are considered not acceptable for whatever reason (wrong religion, weakness, sin, addictions, associations with others, all those we don't want to be caught with—in a crowd, at a dinner party, or in church). Sometimes we don't even like to go to certain liturgies or parishes or be associated with groups of religious people—because we don't want to be categorized as one of them. Them—the uncounted, the unnoticed, the unacceptable, the unwanted, the problems, the masses of people in the world—that is what the good news is about, that is what this story is about, that is what Jesus is about, that is what liturgy and ministry are all about.

Everybody present ate. The disciples must have been shocked, over-joyed, elated, surprised, confused, bewildered, at a loss. What happened? Perhaps with the help of the Spirit, Jesus took the food of his friends, gave it away generously (in fact, had to give it away), and the crowd saw what they were doing and brought forth their own food and supplies and shared them with those who didn't have anything or enough. And everyone was satisfied. There was enough for everyone's need. Not only that: "The fragments remaining, when gathered up, filled twelve baskets." Ah, yes, the baskets—where did they come from? The women and children, the poor who carried them (with the food) into the deserted place at the beginning of the day.

The disciples have two jobs in this story—they distribute the food, and they collect the leftovers, twelve baskets full. Twelve, symbolic of the twelve tribes of Israel or the twelve disciples—or the whole world—more than enough to feed everyone. Miracle? What is the greater miracle—that Jesus multiples food unnaturally or that the people see, trust, risk, hope, and share with one another? After all, this is the pattern, the ritual of liturgy. God takes our often reluctant gift—all that God's friends and disciples have—blesses it, and gives it away to those who are in need. God uses the disciples as a model for behavior, of risking and trusting in a new order, a new way of being with one another and together with Jesus, who orders us to sit down together and eat with him. This story is about liturgy, about ministry, about life among the friends and disciples of Jesus in the midst of the vast throngs of people in the world, those upon whom Jesus has pity.

Remember, all sorts of interpretations are true. And there are all kinds of levels in understanding any interpretation. But it is an old adage that the one that is most true is the one that calls a person to a more radical following of Jesus, a more radical conversion of life—singularly and with others. It takes time, it takes practice, it takes change.

Unless You Become Like a Little Child

In Near Eastern cultures—among Bedouin tribes and in Palestine even today—the place of the child is marked and fixed within the community. These cultures and many others see the child not as an individual with rights, but as a part of the community, fitting at the bottom of society. In fact, the word in Aramaic for "child" and "servant/slave" is the same. Society at the time of Jesus too was structured and developed hierarchically and in strict adherence to the community and its needs. It was a tight-knit group that knew and operated on levels, and on obedience and belonging—and children were at the bottom.

There is an example in Thomas Aquinas' *Summa Theologica* that illustrates this point, and many exegetes refer to it when teaching about Hebrew culture in the time of Jesus. Thomas asks a theoretical question: if you were in a burning house with your mother and father, your wife, and your children, and you could save yourself and only one other, which one would you save? Of course, the question was directed to men only—but it makes the point. When I ask this question today, the answer is either the spouse or one of the children. No one answers mother or father—not ever. And yet Thomas' answer is father, then mother, then wife, then child—in that order, the order of priority of love and obedience as understood in the past and in many cultures today.

It is a very modern concept in the Western world that the child—the future—is important and in a position of privilege. In the past the child was seen as belonging to the father, the group, the community—not the future. The father—the head of the household, the spokesman for the family and the group—ruled. Many times in the Acts of the Apostles and in other places in the Christian Scriptures we read of a man and his whole family being baptized. In Africa and other countries today, when a man is baptized, his wives and children, his whole household, cousins, aunts, uncles, and in-laws are baptized as well. Culture dictates the group response held by the one in charge, the one responsible for the others. Obedience is usually immediate and unquestioning. Western culture is drastically different, oriented toward the individual and the future, and so such choices and behavior are seen as unacceptable, intolerant, aberrant, confining, and so on. But it was the norm in ancient societies and is still the norm in many cultures.

Historically children were the property of the parents and had no rights, no life besides survival and connection to the adults. Child labor, which still exists among the poor, migrants, factory workers, and others in many countries, attests to the lack of awareness of the individual's rights, especially among adults who have no rights. The children of the poor are doubly endangered.

All of this background is crucial to understanding the power of Jesus' words about being a child and his use of children to describe and illustrate belonging in his kingdom and his Father's house. Children were the hope and solace and comfort of their parents in their old age, but life was hard and sometimes no more than mere endurance. The struggle to live was communal and familial, unlike the individuality of today and the small nuclear families or single-parent families of much of present Western society.

In Matthew we find this concept of childhood and its importance in Jesus' kingdom even more clearly outlined:

> Just then the disciples came up to Jesus with the question, "Who is of the greatest importance in the kingdom of God?" He called a little child over and stood him in their midst and said: "I assure you, unless you change and become like little children, you will not enter the kingdom of God. Whoever makes himself lowly, becoming like this child, is of greatest importance in that heavenly reign."

(MATT. 18:1–4)

The greatest kingdom is the lowest and the lowly. This turns upside down the existing social structure and ideas of power and authority, of influence and wisdom. Jesus singles out the most unlikely, the most forgotten and ignored of people, the most useless in a society that looks on abilities and contributions to society as critical, and he says that unless we become like this, we will not enter his kingdom. It is a call that does not sanction upward mobility and independence; it calls us to downward mobility and servanthood, to be obedient to everyone. The story in Matthew then continues with a warning:

> "Whoever welcomes one such child for my sake welcomes me. On the other hand, it would be better for anyone who leads astray one of these little ones who believe in me, to be drowned by a millstone around his neck, in the depth of the sea."
>
> (MATT. 18:5–6)

Welcoming a child—this is where it becomes more obvious that Jesus is not just talking about children newly born and up to the age of fifteen, though they are included. Welcoming a child is welcoming Jesus, when that welcome is done for his sake—in obedience to need, in service and in kindness, in outgoing love, in presence, in response to requests, in bending to honor. This passage is more clearly defined in Matthew 25, when Jesus tells the parable of the sheep and the goats at the judgment of the nations, when the Son of Man separates all the peoples of the earth into those in the kingdom and those outside of it. The criterion for belonging in the kingdom forever is this: "Whatsoever you do to the least of your brothers and sisters you do to me." This means corporal works of mercy: feeding the hungry, giving drink to the thirsty, healing and visiting the sick, burying the dead, setting the prisoners free, sheltering the homeless, clothing the naked—in short, serving the needs of others as a child would wish to be served and taken care of, freely and with dignity.

The second half of Jesus' warning is clear: to lead astray a little one, to lead astray those in need, the poor, and the helpless, those fallen through the cracks of society and our parishes, is to merit death—a judgment that is harsh and complete, expulsion from the dream of living in the kingdom. What is done here is just repeated and echoed there forever. To lead children—the least in the world according to the world's standards—astray, to contribute to their demise and their destruction and loss of dignity and hope, is to do the same to Jesus. Exile from the kingdom is the response of the Son of Man. A child, this son of man, this child of man, this child of humanity, our judge, is God's reflection in humankind. This child who judges is all the poor, the lost, the forgotten, and the forsaken of this world. This child stands before us with God, and together they cast the ballot either in our favor or for our expulsion from their presence forever.

Perhaps the segment of the Gospels that is alluded to most often in this context of children is related in Mark 10 and Luke 18:

> People were bringing their little children to him to have him touch them, but the disciples were scolding them for this. Jesus became indignant when he noticed it and said to them: "Let the children come unto me and do not hinder them. It is to just such as these that the kingdom of God belongs. I assure you that whoever does not accept the reign of God like a little child shall not take part in it." Then he embraced them and blessed them, placing his hands on them.
>
> (MARK 10:13–16)

In Luke there are a few details that are different and significant:

> They even brought babies to be touched by him. When the disciples saw this, they scolded them roundly: but Jesus called for the children saying: "Let the little children come to me. Do not shut them off. The reign of God belongs to such as these. Trust

me when I tell you that whoever does not accept the kingdom
of God as a child will not enter into it."

(LUKE 18:15–17)

These passages are found in the segments on what is necessary for
discipleship—the practice of the virtue of poverty and taking up of one's
cross and denying one's very self. It is the idea of making oneself very
small, a servant, not noticeable or having great authority, but humble and
unobtrusive. In both Gospels this encounter among the disciples, the
children and their parents and families, and Jesus is immediately followed by the story of the rich young man or the story of one of the ruling class who asks, "What must I do to share in everlasting life?" Jesus
points to the virtue of poverty: making oneself poorer so that the poor
might be less poor. The way of the cross is crowded with children—the
poor and those poor for the kingdom.

Often someone mentions a story about St. Catherine of Siena in
these discussions about spiritual childhood, poverty, and authority. It
seems that on one of the streets of Rome there is a statue of the saint,
barefoot and on her way to the Vatican. She is shown coming out of the
poor district of the city, where she cared for plague victims and the incur-
able and the poor. She would go back and forth between the poor, the
least of the city of Rome, and the pope in the Vatican. Her work and the
love and the service of the poor, which was a result of her mystical relationship with Jesus, the crucified One, gave her the power and authority
to approach the Vatican, the highest source of power and authority in the
church. She called it back to the gospel, to the virtue and practice of
poverty, and to its true position as a child of God, a servant of the church,
and one of the poorest. It is interesting to note that the poor did not know
that she was on her way to the Vatican. They only knew her as the ministering angel, the visitor who nursed them, washed them, and treated them
as beloved friends and children. She too was one of those children that Jesus embraced, put his arms around, and held as models for his disciples.

Our God became human, became a child, and dwelled among us. The birth story in Luke is an announcement by angels to shepherds in the field (definitely in the children category). They are told that they will find the child "lying in a manger, wrapped in swaddling clothes" (Luke 2:12, 16). This passage has echoes in the Hebrew Scriptures, especially the book of Wisdom:

> *In swaddling clothes and with constant care I was nurtured.*
> *For no king has any different origin or birth,*
> *but one is the entry into life for all; and in one same way they*
>   *leave it.*

(WISD. 7:4–6)

This passage is about our common humanity, our mortality, our vulnerability—now shared by God, the Son of Man, the Son of the Most High, the son of Mary. But there is another reference that is often forgotten or overlooked. It is about Jerusalem and Jerusalem's unfaithfulness. At your birth "your navel cord was not cut; you were neither washed with water nor anointed, nor were you rubbed with salt, nor swathed in swaddling clothes" (Ezek. 16:4). Swaddling clothes symbolize constant care, tender regard, nurturing, and attention. Jesus begins as loved, as attended to and cared for, first by Mary and Joseph, then by shepherds and astrologers and angels, and then by his Father God and the Spirit. At Jesus' baptism and transfiguration it is the voice of God that announces and tells those who can hear: "This is my beloved son, child, listen to him, upon him my favor rests!" Being such a child is living in a relationship of trust, of affirmation, of nurture and belovedness, and it can be dangerous.

Our God is childlike, vulnerable in a manger, running from ruthlessness, growing up in an out-of-the-way place, off the beaten path, in a neighborhood not known for what it produced. He became the Suffering Servant of God, obedient even unto death on a cross. The face of our God is like this kind of child.

Sarah and Hagar: Who Is Our Mother in Faith?

God is the God of slaves and Egyptians and foreigners and those not wanted and those feared by the Israelites, but it will take a long time and many stories to teach God's people that reality. God is just as concerned about the hopes and dreams and future of those who are not Israelites as about those chosen to stand out among the other nations. All nations and all peoples are God's children.

Those in oppression and poverty today hear the cries in the story of Abraham and recognize their own voices, their own rejection of slavery, servitude, and inequality. When asked by the messenger of the Lord, "Where are you from and where are you going?" all Hagar can answer is, "I am running away from my mistress." I'm running away from slavery, from life without a future, without hope, and without dignity; a life without tenderness and friendship. When she is instructed to return to an abusive situation, she obeys in order to guarantee a life, a name, and a place for her son, her child who is half slave and half free.

So Hagar stands up, stands up for her child, her life, and her future, her hope and her freedom and the vision of what is to come. Even in her vision she could never have imagined the extent and power of the vision of Yahweh, which would be revealed in another woman's child looked down upon and rejected, Jesus, son of Mary, wife of Joseph. Like Hagar, Mary will spend long years alone with her child, after the death of Joseph, her protection in society and Jewish culture. Hagar is like many women who are refugees and immigrants and illegal aliens, barely tolerated and sometimes even persecuted and hunted down. She reminds us as well of their sisters, mothers, cousins, and friends who are left behind and struggling alone to care for their families because of the death or disappearance of their husbands, brothers, and children. Injustice, slavery, oppression, racism, and hatred are still common in the world.

But the story ends well. Hagar, her child, Ishmael, and their descendants are free—free of Israelite slavery and free from fear and domination. Theirs is a miniversion of the larger story to come when Yahweh will hear the cry of a whole people in bondage and lean down to their cries as God leans down to this woman and child, unwanted and thrown out in the desert to die. Ishmael (the name means "God hears") is the hope, hidden but potent and waiting on the time when God will burst forth as the hope of all slaves and oppressed peoples. This God who hears the cry of the poor will not fit into any neat categories of theology and meaning.

What makes a woman of faith? Is it giving birth in a chain of miraculous events, events that are taken out of the context of a life and other relationships? Or is a woman of faith constituted by a discipline of hope, of trust in God, in refusal to give up, in courage, in leaning on the word of God because there is no one else to lean on or aid her children? Or is a woman of faith not defined by boundaries of culture, religion, race, and economic status, but rather by steadfast clinging to life, protecting the unborn and young of her family, even to the point of enduring abuse and mistreatment humbly so that the child of her promise has a chance at life? What makes a woman of faith? Is it association and bloodlines in the community of those called the people of God, those who will become the Israelites? Or is a woman of faith anyone, even an outsider, a slave, a rebellious woman, who resists servitude and is given the sight of God, the word of God, her own covenant and vision of the future, and the ability to survive in spite of some of the other chosen people? Perhaps we do have a mother in faith, but not Sarah, the bitter, unbelieving, and cynical woman driven by jealousy and fear, a woman who does not see her slave Hagar even as a woman like herself but as something useful for a time for her own security. Perhaps our mother in faith is Hagar, the Egyptian slave woman, mother of Ishmael, the firstborn of Abraham, our father in faith—not because she is anyone's mother or concubine or slave or maid, but because she is poor and oppressed, reliant on God, the one God chose to give hope to all the struggling peoples of the world unnoticed, unappreciated, and thrown away carelessly, even by people who are learning faith in God, but are slow and stubborn about sharing that faith in justice with the rest of humankind.

Often in discussions of this story, someone says, "Well, it seems Sarah is still treating Hagar the same way today. Things haven't changed much." Maybe the issue isn't just feminism in opposition to patriarchy. Maybe the deeper sin is racism and classism. After all, Hagar and Sarah are both women, sisters, and still Sarah treats Hagar as dirt, as not human, certainly not as equal in any regard. Sarah treats Hagar as many women say men treat them. The real issue is about power, security, and privilege—control over one's own life.

Many of the liberation theologians of Latin America, including women theologians, are convinced that women's oppression is determined above all by their social situation and that their position in society determines the kind of oppression they live under. This differs from one group of women to another. The struggle to break out of oppression does not begin with institutions, but with poor women who are forming groups of twos and threes, trying to break out of the cycle of misery, poverty, no choices, and no future. They struggle to change their own immediate lives, to acquire basic necessities, but also to change society's consciousness of why they have to live this way. They often seek to change the consciousness of other women who share their same oppression and women in other sectors of society who have more power in the institutional structures of economics, politics, academics, and the church.

The immediate environment of culture and economics defines more brutally what oppression is. Anyone can aggravate the situation and be insensitive to it and their plight—other men and other women of higher social classes and education and culture. Women employers, women professors and writers, women with the freedom to do research and travel, women who hire other women to clean their houses and take care of their children, are often blind to the treatment of poor women, including the ones they are bound to, and especially to the plight of women of color. Poor women do theology differently from well-educated, comfortable, and wealthy women of a culture that dominates the cultures of minorities (who happen to be the majority of people and women worldwide). The voice of the poor, especially poor women, is often unheard by sisters better off, more secure, and benefiting individually from the dominant culture's systems and priorities.

Many poor women do not believe that gender is the basic problem. It is more complicated than that—as the issues between Sarah and Hagar remind us. It is an interlocking set of oppressions. Sarah dominates as thoroughly on an individual level as patriarchy does on a systematic level. Sarah is just as dangerous and disheartening as the system, perhaps even more so because of the common bond that is destroyed in the encounter—that of sisterhood. Liberation, of its nature, is communal. God hears that cry of Hagar and her child in the desert, but as the story grows in power, God hears the cry of God's people in Egypt and bends to them, and finally in Jesus God answers the cry of all the poor, of all people marginalized, ignored, or treated unjustly.

Hagar's story is not what we are used to seeing. It jolts, it disarms, it rages with pain and rejection and loneliness, and it questions what needs to be questioned: What ties us together? What binds us as one? What is our religion? Is it the word of the Lord, the imperious command to life, life ever more abundantly for all human beings following in the vision of Jesus? Is it faith, not just in one people but in all people, any people, especially those who most need faith and a response to their cry to God? Our mother in faith, Hagar teaches us that faith breaks all boundaries of sin, of injustice, of race, religion, social class, nations, and structures.

Our mother in faith is a black slave woman who refused to be humiliated, who saw God, who knew in her flesh a promise and the reality that God is revealed to those most desperate as well as those chosen to be God's people. Our mother in faith is a woman stumbling in the desert while her child clings to her for life, who is befriended by God when everyone else abandons her. Our mother in faith foreshadows the woman Mary, who will sing of freedom and be great not simply because she is the mother of Jesus but because she is the first to believe in the word that was spoken to her.

Perhaps women along with men must learn in their flesh what the tenderness of God is. Perhaps Hagar, our mother in faith, reminds us that being human is the first and critical reality of faith. Perhaps the next time the messenger of the Lord asks Hagar, "Where are you from and where are you going?" she won't answer that she is running away from her mistress, from another woman. Perhaps it's time to change the story and to change any theology so that it's done together by all women—rich or poor, slave or free, whatever nation or race or religion—and with men. Perhaps that will be humankind's best theology ever.

Jerusalem

There are two short pieces in the Gospel of Luke that reveal Jesus lamenting over the city of Jerusalem and lamenting its people, who have missed his coming because of their blindness, stubbornness, and hard-heartedness. The first segment is addressed to the city, and so to the nation, its leaders, and its people:

> "O Jerusalem, Jerusalem, you slay the prophets and slay those who are sent to you! How often have I wanted to gather your children together as a mother bird collects her young under her wings, and you refused me! Your temple will be abandoned. I say to you, you shall not see me until the time comes when you say, 'Blessed is he who comes in the name of the Lord.' "
>
> (LUKE 13:34–35)

Reactions to this passage are mixed, as are the metaphors in the text. Jesus sees himself as the one who has been sent to the city, a prophet rejected and about to be slain. Yet there is the great tenderness and vulnerability in Jesus, who sees himself as a mother bird wanting to draw her defenseless young under her wing. The image of gathering, collecting his own about him recalls a shepherd gathering sheep, or the church gathering for liturgy and worship. The reference to the temple that will be abandoned, as Jesus will be abandoned, adds another layer to the sorrow and utter sense of helplessness. Jesus is mixing both the warning and the starkness of the prophet's words with a plea for repentance and acceptance of the word of God, even now.

Jesus is both the prophet of Israel, the Word of the Lord come again to the people, and the Suffering Servant, the one who will untiringly seek to draw his people back to God at any cost. He is the mother bird that will give its life to the snare trying to save its young, giving them time to fly to safety on their weak wings. The image is old in the Jewish tradition, often in reference to an eagle's wings. This image is full of comfort and the promise of protection.

Eagles mate forever, faithful until death. They build their nests high on cliffs and rocks away from any predators. When the young are born, usually no more than three, they are large, ungainly, and awkward, unable to fly, helpless and in need of constant protection, watchfulness, and feeding. The eagles hunt for food and chew it up and put it into the mouths of the young eagles hourly until they are strong enough to fly. When they are ready to be taught how to fly, the eagles dump the nest over, sending the young ones out into the air. They flap wildly, in a panic, and then almost get the hang of it, but they are weak, unused to flying, and they begin to fall. Then one of the adult eagles swoops down and comes up under the young one that is falling and lifts it on its own wings, higher and higher, giving it a needed rest—and then pulls up abruptly again. And the young one goes at it again, until it tires. Again and again the mother and father birds lift their young on their own wings and carry them until the eaglets have learned the strength that is dormant in their own smaller wings. It takes about fifteen minutes, and then all three of the young can fly, and not one has come anywhere near the ground.

Is this the image of the mother bird that Jesus has in mind: the mighty and proud soaring eagle? Or is he thinking of an ordinary hen, a weak and vulnerable bird that can also be fierce in its protection of its young, fighting and pecking at its enemies, moving quickly to gather its own in clucking gestures and outspread wings? Either image fits Jesus, for he will gather his own for the eucharist in this last week of his life and they will later be scattered and run for fear. Jesus will be destroyed, hung outside the city, crucified on the city's garbage heap, the abode of carrion birds. But he will also know the glory of the eagle in the wings of the Spirit in the rising morning sun of resurrection and new life. Jesus' tears of sorrow and lamentation, human tears of rejection and sheer frustration—he has given his all, his best, the word and presence of the Lord, the image of his Father, merciful, just, tenderhearted, and seeking only the life of the sinner. Now he will give his last word, his blood, his body, his life, in this last attempt to get the people to listen to him.

As Jesus begins the last portion of his way of the cross, there are a few who watch and respond with weeping and mourning:

> A great crowd of people followed him, including women who beat their breasts and lamented over him. Jesus turned to them and said: "Daughters of Jerusalem, do not weep for me. Weep for yourselves and for your children. The days are coming when they will say, 'Happy are the sterile, the wombs that never bore and the breasts that never nursed.' Then they will begin saying to the mountains, 'Fall on us' and to the hills, 'Cover us.' If they do these things in the green wood, what will happen in the dry?"
>
> (LUKE 23:27–31).

The women weep for Jesus, and yet Jesus turns their tears away from him, back toward themselves and their children, toward those who are to come after them. It is here that Jesus points out to us that the way of the cross is not just his, but ours and others. The women express compassion and remorse in groans, beating their breasts in sadness, sorrow, and mourning; it is a time for feeling for and feeling with others, with Jesus. There is a shared horror at what we do to each other in violence, in fear, in rejection, in sin. There is a communion in suffering that is not connected to friendship, or even knowing the person, but recognizing another in their deepest place of vulnerability—as another human being. But Jesus' words deflect their pity away from himself and his sufferings and humiliation. It seems there is something worse in the world than this kind of innocent and unnecessary suffering. Worse are those who do injustice to others, those without pity or compassion, those who are responsible in their actions and deeds for stopping life and inflicting pain and horror on others, those who practice evil while claiming to believe in God, those who sin. What eventually will come upon them, in the fullness of God's time and judgment, will be worse than this suffering of the innocent, this crucifixion of the Word of justice, mercy, and hope. Even in the midst of his pain Jesus reminds the women and us of what is most horrible and pitiable: human beings who are not human, not obedient to the heart of what it means to live—that is, to give life and sustain that life and share it with others.

Tears of compassion must also be tears of penance, of the wrenching that comes with change, of crying out against insensitivity, self-interest, lack of concern. Of collusion with evil institutions and structures and personal abuses against others. The spiral of violence must be arrested by compassion that becomes admonition, penance publicly atoning for and with the victims. The tears must become the lamentations of the prophets, with Jesus weeping over Jerusalem, because a city, a nation, a whole people, missed his meaning, his presence and power, and the possibility for change, for hope for others. It is Jesus' lamentation over the church, over us. We must look to and know who inflicts death, deals with death and destruction, and profits by it. We must acknowledge how to participate in it and weep for our own complicity and what we do that causes others to suffer needlessly.

We have to go to the heart of what causes misery and injustice here and now. Too often we adapt to things as they are, only weeping and being touched when injustice gets close to us personally. We cannot just weep over situations. We have to learn how to intervene. We have to learn not just to stand there, like the majority of the people in the crowd. It is the moment for conversion. Compassion is a dead end if it does not lead us to life, to move, to denounce prophetically why this misery exists, why the human condition has gotten this far out of line, why there is this terrible destruction of human life and dignity. And if we don't, it will affect us eventually and our children.

Jesus, the crucified One, is the image of the One not counted, forgotten, cast aside, rejected. Yet this Jesus is the One God raised from the dead. Now this Jesus remembers all those not counted and puts them at the head of the parade. And all women and children and men, all humankind and earth and its creatures, sing for the "great things this God has done for them." This is the way God's stories go. This is the Word of the Lord.

From Angels Unawares

Preface

The first time I encountered an "angel's kiss" was in Llangollen, Wales, this past year. It was dusk with a wild swirl of sky, storms, and near night. The angel's kiss was warm and tasted of fire; I sighed before every sip. This angel's kiss: two parts brandy to one part Benedictine.

The next day wandering the wet Welsh hills we found an old church, the Chapel of Rug. Its garden was blooming with medieval plants, one called angel's blush. I took seeds to plant half a world away in New Mexico.

Then, the very next night in Liverpool, we had angel-hair pasta and angel food cake! What is this universal enchantment and fascination with angels?

In 1 Enoch (Enoch is thought by many to be an angel himself, as he is taken to walk with God forever), four angels are presented by name: Michael, the merciful and long-suffering; Raphael, set over diseases and wounds of the children of the earth; Gabriel, set over all the powers, especially word and revelation; and Phanuel, set over the repentance and hope of those who inherit eternal life (and so, set over death as well). This last angel, sometimes called Ariel or Azrael, is veiled in a thousand veils before creatures and holds between his hands immensity. He often has four faces, one before, one on his head, one beneath his feet, and one behind, and innumerable eyes. When one eye closes, it is said, someone dies.

Angels are associated with ends, judgments, reckonings. They obey and execute God's decisions and the results of our choices, escorting souls to heaven or thrusting them into hell. They divided the vaults of heaven in the domes of the churches into four, inviting the soul to contemplation and union with the divine, becoming lost in all things, disappearing into adoration, in communion and union with God. They form ladders, ascending and descending, and are given the souls of humans to care for and lead to God. "It is a teaching of Moses that every believer has an angel to guide him as a teacher and shepherd" (St. Basil).

Angels announce birth and attend ascension. The poet John Milton says that they have to fight and resist with great effort to stay down. They rise, fly, appear in trances, visions, and dreams. They lift souls in ecstasy and take up Elijah in his fiery-wheeled chariot. They rise with Jesus (who, tradition says, left his footprint lingering on the hill) and question those left looking up to heaven—gawking—"Why are you looking up to heaven?" Now the Presence resides on earth in the Spirit's children, until the coming of the kingdom.

Angels are creatures of ethereal loveliness but also represent an almost terrifying vision of ultimate Truth. They rarely resemble fat, playful cherubs; more often they are flaming swords unsheathed, intimations of the Holy One who made them, pieces of transcendence drawing near. They are universal, it seems, almost familiar, but uncannily strange, disturbing even to one such as Mary. They tear the heart out of time, alter the pattern, demand the aid of humans. They are, simply, servants of the Lord.

Angels, mysteries of God's imagination, invitations to obedience, and servants visiting earth, are the Creator's call to each of us to reconsider, change, be transformed. They urge us to turn again toward each other and love. They watch and wait for us at home, knowing we are crucial to the heart of God incarnate. They care about us and come to visit and deliver God's word to us. These angels of God are envelopes waiting for our replies.

Introduction

Angels? Just what do we believe about angels? According to the Scriptures, angels appear in a variety of roles and activities. They are guardians of nations, sanctuaries, churches, holy places, and of each individual. They are worshipers of God as well as God's companions, messengers, protectors, watchers, and witnesses. In the Hebrew Scriptures they are called the host of heaven, a court, the Sons of Elohim (in Job and Psalm 29 and Daniel). In the letters of Paul and Peter angels are connected with the cosmic order and with social forces that may be hostile to the gospel. No matter how they are described, the "principalities and powers," the angels, are always subject to Christ and always obey the word of God.

It is Christ who is the center of the angelic world. The angels serve him, belong to him, worship him; their songs and praise resound throughout the church's liturgy and public prayer. Just as Jesus' life was filled with angels—prior to his birth, at his coming into the world, and again at his leaving—angels are present in the life of the church and with believers in the crucial moments of birth, baptism, struggles with temptations and evil, and at death. St. Thomas writes, "The angels work together for the benefit of us all."

The belief in angels has been an ancient and honored tradition of the church from its earliest days and struggles. According to medieval tradition, it was on the first day of creation that angels were made, crafted of light by the Holy One and found to be good.

In the final book of the Christian Scriptures, Revelation, we hear of other beginnings that are also part of the common belief: the war in heaven between the opposing forces of angels. This is the old tradition, told in stories and legends and spiritual treatises. Some of the angels re-

fused to obey the will of God and honor Adam, the first human created
by God. They refused to bend before someone they considered beneath
them. In so doing, they refused to bend before God, who, in the divine
plan hidden from the beginning, would come among us as one like us,
subject to trial, suffering, and death, even death on a cross. These angels
refused to honor the wisdom of God, which would be revealed in the creation of human beings and fulfilled in the mystery of the Incarnation,
God becoming the least of our brothers and sisters, human and vulnerable, and yet revealing God in ways unimagined and unheard-of by the
angels.

In the New Testament when Paul writes of angels, he is adamant
about God's closeness with human beings in the person of the beloved,
Jesus Christ, who is obedient, firstborn, and Son. For Paul there is no
comparison between the angels and Jesus; the angels are servants of God
sent to help those of us who shall be saved. Angels worship God by helping humankind be saved. This part of the infinite plan of God was hidden
from the beginning but revealed gloriously, strangely, compassionately, in
Jesus.

Contrary to our usual images of winged creatures, those obedient
angels who watch over us are bodiless. While some are known to us by
name in a familiar way, angels are distinguished from one another by
function rather than by material characteristics. There are traditionally
nine orders of angels in three hierarchical sets: the highest are the cherubim, seraphim, and thrones; next come dominions, virtues, and powers;
the lowest orders are the principalities, archangels, and angels. It is these
lowest orders that we feel we know so well. The archangels most known
by name in the Western church are Michael, Gabriel, Raphael, and Ariel
(or Phanuel). The Eastern churches name three additional archangels:
Selephiel, the archangel of wisdom; Varachiel, the guardian of truth and
courage in the face of persecution and opposition; and Yegovdiel, the angel of unity, who knows all the languages of the world and all its creatures.

Angels instill in those who see them or hear them a violent need to obey the Truth. Since they stand always in awe before God and worship God, no matter what else they have been charged with doing, that presence of the Holy exudes from them. Sometimes angels have been described as ways by which human beings apprehend the presence, the knowledge, and the will of God.

Angels are evidence that God is taking notice of us. They ask the same always: surrender, obedience, submission, radical abasement, and humility before the Holy One. Some say they make us homesick for heaven. They are always present, ministering, even though we are unaware of them. They hover near wombs, caves, gardens, and tombs, but almost anyplace is made holy by their visitation. They stand in silent rage against inhumanity, knowing that it is up to us, not them, to oppose it. They love earth even more since the incarnation, and they come to visit and linger in the houses of the poor, in the byways, and on the roads. They seem always to be asking us to make alliance with them and so comfort God, who has come to save us all and restore earth to the original dream of holiness. As the angels retie the bonds between heaven and earth, the mysterious plan from the beginning will be fulfilled.

Michael the Archangel: Protector

God posted cherubim and a flaming sword that kept turning at the east of the Garden of Eden to guard the way to the tree of Life.

—GEN. 3:24

In medieval legends this sword is wielded by Michael, an archangel, a member of the lowest order of angels, which consists of principalities, archangels, and angels. This order has been put in charge of human hierarchies and history.

Michael, first named of the angels, and Gabriel, named in the book of Daniel, will be friends and close allies of human kind. Even though Michael is stationed by God at the entrance to the garden with a fiery revolving sword to keep us from entering until the proper time, he also is charged with being the protector of the people of God. The legends about Michael all echo hope and reflect the experience of those who believe not in a God to fear and hide them from, but a God who cares, saves and mysteriously can restore and redeem even choices of evil.

This is one of those legends:

> ✴ *Once upon a time . . . really before our time began, after the war in heaven when Satan and his followers were cast forth from the abiding presence of the light, Michael the archangel was commissioned by God to defend the earth and take charge of the garden where Yahweh God would place Adam and Eve.*
>
> *Just as he had obeyed God and bowed before the image of the maker of all things, Michael obeyed and went immediately to guard the Garden of Eden. For, it is best believed that Yahweh God knew of Satan's intent to destroy creation, to upset the harmony and balance of the earth, to distort the plan of God to lift humankind up from its lowly place below the angels to be God's own friends and children. So God sent Michael to be on the lookout for Satan and to protect our ancestors from their choice and fate as exiles cast forth from the presence of God. But Michael failed.*
>
> *The angel once known as Lucifer, now Satan, was crafty, sly, and devious. He changed form, coming into the garden as a serpent (not a snake, more like a dragon or other fantastic creature). And so it was that Michael, unsuspecting, let him slip by. Thus Satan entrapped Adam and Eve, and they fell from grace and glory. Michael was expecting a creature, an angel of light like the one he battled in the heavens, not one of the wild creatures that Yahweh God had made.*
>
> *When Adam and Eve and all their offspring were exiled from Eden, Yahweh God stationed Michael with the flaming revolving sword at the gate of the garden, charging him to keep them from entering again. And so Michael obeyed. But Michael was crushed, broken-hearted that he had failed God's charge. He had not been*

able to prevent Adam and Eve from sinning; he had not protected the people of God. He stood guard, and yet he had pity on Adam and Eve, who now had to toil and sweat, work and suffer just to survive, and then to die. Yahweh God had made for them garments of skin and clothed them so that they did not go naked into the world, and so Michael thought to give a gift to Adam and Eve as well. In pity for the wretchedness of their lives Michael took his flaming sword and transformed it into a plow, teaching Adam to till the fields and bring forth food from the land. Thus he eased their burden and his own sense of failing God and the people of God.

They say that ever since then Michael has been the defender of the honor of God. Like God, he cares for the poor and lowliest of the earth, the ones who plow the fields and harvest the crops and provide food for others. He defends and guards as patron all those who struggle against evil face to face, confronting it and seeking to stop its power in their flesh and their lives.

They say too that Michael was the first to learn that one cannot fight evil on earth as one does in heaven, and that Michael is the first proponent of nonviolent resistance to evil. It is Michael's experience of Satan on earth that is remembered and echoed and given substance in all the visions, hopes, and promises of the prophets.

Michael and all the angels of God are sent to us to accompany us through suffering and the restoration of the glory of God. All the stories of Michael remind us of the honor of God, obedience to God, trusting in God's wisdom and submitting to the mysteries of the incarnation, the cross and the resurrection. They tell of Michael's presence with the victims of evil and injustice; he stands with those who stand against evil, especially the prophets, martyrs, and the poor. Michael stands against the savagery of the human race and the destruction inherent in disobedience.

Michael, the Angel of Yahweh, is intimate with struggle, suf-

fering and death in the face of sin and evil, and with the souls and spirits of those who seek the honor of God and are known for their love and care for the poor, the victims of injustice and sin.

The Angel of Recidivism

Recidivism, according to the dictionary, is "a tendency to relapse into a previous condition or mode of behavior, especially relapse into criminal behavior." It is characteristically recurring, habitual criminal action. And so the Angel of Recidivism, as Daniel Berrigan calls this angel, is the one who lures, the one who leads us into patterns that upset the social order and refuse to allow history to ignore the reality of truth according to the gospel.

The stories that give rise to the naming of this angel are found primarily in the Acts of the Apostles, chapters 5 and 12. In chapter 5 Peter meets with the believers in Jerusalem. People bring their sick to Solomon's portico hoping that Peter's shadow might fall on them. The high priest and his supporters, the Sadducees, become jealous of the apostles and have them arrested and thrown into the public jail. "But an angel of the Lord opened the door of the prison during the night, brought them out, and said to them, 'Go and stand in the Temple court and give the people the message of life.' Accordingly they entered the Temple at dawn and resumed their teaching" (vv. 19–21). This kind of behavior is what landed them in the clink in the first place!

This angel seems to act as guardian spirit to those who stand in the breach and preach the presence and the power of that Name, that Name that cannot tolerate evil. Prophets are driven by the Angel of Recidivism. They know the hard realities and cannot abide easy avoidance of the issues. Not to describe insidiousness is to whitewash and contribute to the anguish it causes: decay unchecked, despair encouraged, hatred tolerated, unnecessary deaths forgotten, violence romanticized, pollution accommodated, spiritualities developed that desensitize the individual to the pain of others. These are the new rings of hell.

That Angel of Recidivism keeps commanding: go and give the people the message of life. This angel is friend of jailbirds, hard-core "criminals" who obey the Word of God first and only obey the laws of a nation or government when they do not contradict the gospel.

A visit from the angel leaves one disconcerted, drawn deeper into the mystery of God, deeper into the unknown ways of the kingdom of light coming inch by inch into this world, in spite of its resistance. The visit of every angel is terrifying.

This angel is the guardian of jails, patron of religious prisoners, those who practice civil disobedience, tell the truth to power, and seek to protect the innocent with their words and lives laid on the line, always non-violently. Perhaps the way the angels scratch on our souls these days is the scraping sound of sliding bars and prison doors, shackles dragging and the long enduring days and nights of incarceration because of civil disobedience known in more scriptural communities as "preaching the Name." In some historical epochs and countries, that angel is kept busy; in others, this angel barely sees the inside of a jail, for those who call themselves Christians have grown easy with the powers of the world and learned to accommodate evil. When this angel languishes, the faith of Christians is weak-kneed and thin-spirited.

This angel reminds us that the usual boundaries of the natural world are slipping away, being eroded. Even though there is intent to harm those who belong to God and speak with the word of God in their mouths on behalf of others, the presence of the angel is a reminder that there is also blessing, freedom, and hope given in the midst of torture, isolation, and suffering. This angel is attracted by menace, oppression, and the war between the powers of good and evil, always on the side of those favored by God in the conflict and facing terrible odds. The improbable message is constant: Get up! Come! Get dressed: this place cannot hold you long and cannot contain or smother the zeal of your soul!

The Angel of Recidivism does not always visit people in such extremities. Its presence can be experienced breaking boundaries and expanding limits that are much more mundane. Such are the disguises of the Angel of Recidivism. They leave behind a trail of hope and steadfast resolve in the face of injustice and any power that would seek to make life inhuman or any space uninhabitable on this fair earth.

Angels and Hospitality: Our Guardian Angels

Do not neglect to offer hospitality; you know that some people have entertained angels without knowing it.

—HEB. 13:2

For an angel of peace, a faithful guide, a guardian of our souls and bodies, let us entreat the Lord.

—FROM A LITANY OF THE EASTERN ORTHODOX CHURCH

When I was very small, my Nana would say, "Be careful what you say. You never know when you might be speaking to an angel." I would laugh or wonder, and I went through a period of time when I watched people very closely to see if they were indeed angels. But I didn't know exactly what I was looking for, and so I soon tired of the exercise and took people more at face value. Then, when I was about twenty-four, I heard a marvelous story that set me to wondering once again. It was a medieval morality tale told from the point of view of an old, old woman remembering a time long past. It began with the words my Nana had used with me:

※ *Be careful what you say. You never know when you might be speaking to an angel. It seems so long ago now. When I remember that time, I wonder if I imagined it all. But as I think on it, it all comes back so clearly. He was a king. If only I had known that at the time. But that is what the story is all about. I was young and full of dreams and hopes, and I wanted to better my position. I was a shepherd girl and spent most of the year in the high pastures* tending to my father's flocks. But I didn't intend to stay there always. I intended to marry above my station in life. Indeed I had already received an offer from a tradesman in the village.

The king was looking for a wife, and he had seen me in the fields while he was out hunting. I had not seen him. I was busy daydreaming and planning my future life. The king did not want to be married because he was the king, however; he wanted the woman he would marry to choose him freely. So one day he dressed himself in peasant clothes and set out for the fields where I was with my sheep. He laid aside his kingdom for a while and instructed his courtiers to meet him in the field in two weeks' time with two horses and clothes for a maiden. But I didn't know any of that.

He arrived late one afternoon. He said he was coming back from a long journey and would soon be home. He talked of far-off places and things I'd only dreamed about. He could read, and late in the day we would sit by the stream in the cool of shade and he would read to me: poetry, history, geography, philosophy. He was so excited about knowledge—anything that told him of life and the world I considered to be far beyond my domain. The time passed quickly, and he asked me to marry him. We had talked of family and children and the future, and I told him that I already had offers from the tradesmen of the village and that I didn't always want to be just a shepherd's daughter. I wanted more than that, and he told me he could give me more than my heart's desire.

But how could I know? He was dressed as a traveler. He was a stranger to me, almost foreign in his ways of talking and thinking. Then one day he said, "You must decide soon, for I must be on my way."

That day was so long. I cared about him, but I cared more for my position in life and the sure position that I had already been offered. His offer was full of mystery, of hopes and trust. We sat at the *edge of the field, and I finally told him, "I'm sorry, I cannot go with you."*

He looked at me strangely and said, "Can you not trust me?"

"No," I said, "I cannot."

He rose before me. He had seen them coming—his courtiers and the horses. I stood up too and they approached him, calling him king. My heart fell. What had I done in my lack of trust of this good man who made my heart ache and dream, but whom I could not trust? He mounted his horse and told them that the other horse and clothes would not be needed. I watched him ride away. He never looked back.

But it was so long ago, and so much fades in my memory, all but his face when he asked me that question: "Can you not trust me?" I wonder often what my life would have been like if I had trusted that stranger. I never married. I still tend sheep and live alone high in the mountain valleys and wonder if he ever sees me still. If only I had remembered what my grandmother had told me: "Be careful. You never know when you might be speaking to an angel." I wonder if I will ever see him again, for I have lived with him ever since and learned to hope. It was so hard to learn this way. I wonder too if now, after all these years, I have learned to trust.

The story is sad, full of wisdom learned the hard way through experience, mistakes, regret, even remorse. And it has a finality to it, a sense that some things are lost forever in the decision and words of a moment. Angels have that kind of effect, especially if we miss their meaning, their presence, or fail their questioning, Angels and strangers both question us and our deepest assumptions; they call us to risk, to hope, and to trust. Theirs is not a lesson we learn easily.

Angels, Stars, and Dreams of Christmas

Suddenly an angel of the Lord appeared to them, with the Glory of the Lord shining all around them.

As they were terrified, the angel said to them, "Don't be afraid; I am here to give you good news, great joy for all the people. Today a savior has been born to you in David's town; he is the Messiah and the Lord. Let this be a sign to you: you will find the baby wrapped in swaddling clothes and lying in a manger." Just then the angel was surrounded by many more angels, praising God and saying, "Glory to God in the highest; peace on earth for God is blessing humankind."

(LUKE 2:9–14)

These are the angels of the Nativity, the Christmas angels. It seems that angels appear most often at the beginning and end of the life of Jesus: at his incarnation and birth and again at the resurrection and ascension. They are transition times, times of coming and going between heaven and earth. The places of entrance and departure are full of angels. They are the messengers of good news, signals for those open to hope and a possibility of salvation for all peoples.

The angels hover within places of danger and possible death. The boundaries of space, time, and history merge between the forces of this world, which often deal in death, and the powers of heaven, which are intent on giving life.

This world of history, this earth battered by long wars, nationalism, small terrors, and petty sins, is beleaguered and tired, in need of those who walk by starlight, make dreams come true in the daylight hours, and know that the presence of angels is not primarily for one's own protection or gain. Angels are for larger issues of hope, for bringing light into the stifling air of despair, and for escape when necessary from the evil that human beings can do to each other. There is an old saying to heed and take heart from: Only those who walk in darkness ever see the stars.

St. Augustine wrote that "every visible thing in this world is put in charge of an angel." And there is this Jewish saying: Behind every blade of grass is an angel singing "Grow, grow, grow." And just as creation suffered as evil began to spread through the world, now it knows the healing balm and coming sense of peace that this child brings to earth. The land rejoices in his coming.

It is not so strange that the one who made the stars and taught them their songs, who set the boundaries of water, air, sky, and land, would loosen those boundaries by grace and freedom so that once again all creation could play before his face. These are intimations of the coming fullness of resurrection, which this child set in motion, destroying even the hold that death has on humanity and creation. He shatters all the boundaries. But for now the angels of the Nativity teach those who have the eyes to see and hearts large enough to see what is already in our midst. These angels are musicians in concert with the stars of the universe. They are friends to all the great and small creatures of the earth, who know all the same songs. They sing to all human beings who are simple and true enough to hear: all of those who seek after peace and the knowledge of the Lord. The message of these angels, devastating to many on earth, is "Peace on earth to all of goodwill. Peace on earth now."

From Mary, Shadow of Grace

Introduction

When I was little, I listened to nursery rhymes and I was struck by "Mary, Mary, quite contrary, how does your garden grow?" I assumed it was about *the* Mary, the mother of Jesus. I even looked up the word *contrary* and found it meant "opposed to, doing what was not expected, and willful." So Mary, in my small head, was strong and unusual and routinely did the unexpected. Years later I was chagrined to find out that this nursery rhyme was not about Mary at all. But somehow it stayed with me, and now it seems to have more truth than ever.

Mary—a contrary lady—certainly has been made into the image of opposites: mother, ever-virgin. Yet neither mother nor virgin as anyone else would experience those states of being. In statues and devotions she appeared ever young, holding her baby. She was often blond-haired and blue-eyed, dressed impeccably in blue and white, with tracings of silver and gold. She was distant, on a pedestal, floating on clouds, or held up by the hands of cherubs—Queen of Heaven, Star of the Sea, the Immaculate Conception. In the 1950s the Marian Year, the world was dedicated to her heart, and it seemed we were always praying for the conversion of Russia and saying rosaries for pagan babies and the souls in purgatory. For myself and many people she stayed that way and faded into a haze while history, politics, wars, revolutions, and distress among nations and individuals came to the forefront. She just wasn't much help in such situations.

But in Mexico and Latin America I met another Mary, the Virgin of Guadalupe, the staunch, fierce, determined woman, *comadre* of her people, a force to be reckoned with, faithful, enduring in solidarity with those who struggle to make her prophetic words in the Magnificat live in the midst of poverty, injustice, and violence. Now the images are of a poor woman, belonging to a land and a place, speaking the language of those in need of compassion and companionship, with her feet firmly on the ground and her heart and resources given freely to those who side with her forgotten and betrayed children. She is a dark virgin, a Madonna with muddy bare feet and bent back, carrying the burden of children, work, poverty, and oppression. She is partial to roses in December, pilgrims carrying crosses, and the stench of her children crowded in spaces where they gather away from the fear, the terror, and the disappearances of their beloved relatives and friends. She sings psalms of freedom and hope.

Back in my own land of wealth, violence, and individualism, the Scriptures opened up to me a realm of belief and a depth of perception that called for radical conversion, for discipleship, for community, for a church that was missionary, universal—catholic in its original sense, one in spirit and truth and holiness. In that study and struggle to integrate the Word with practice I was forced to reconcile the pre–Vatican II lady with the woman Mary, who believed that the Word of the Lord promised to her would be fulfilled, and who herself pondered and sought to understand the presence of her child as he grew into a prophet, healer, and dissenter.

This woman of the Scriptures slowly emerged as disciple, *comadre*, and sister-spirit. This woman lived in the shadow of the Spirit. She was overshadowed by the dark grace of the triune God, overshadowed as the prophets of old were when the Spirit was sent upon them, compelling them to denounce injustice, warn, cajole, preach, announce hope, and urge conversion.

She aged and lost the husband who had been her companion. She lived as a widow, growing older, cared for by a son whose soul was leading him not only away from his mother and home but into a world that she could not even imagine.

This woman was caught in history, in religion's grasp of power and sin, in evil's grip. She knew the horror of legal, though unjust, torture and execution. She was the mother of a criminal, a protester, a menace to the state, a threat to the nation's religious structures. She lived with the realization that her child did not belong primarily to her, but to the people, especially to those who waited in hope for the coming of Hope itself.

This Mary, a person in her own right, was called to conversion, belief, and the practice of the way of the cross and discipleship. She was asked to bear her share of the burden of the good news, as once she bore a child into the world. Mary, the mother of Jesus, was the model of discipleship in the early Christian community. She was obedient, a servant first, a prophet, a singer, a woman pregnant, unmarried, resourceful, intent on having her child come into this world. She was poor, seeking a way to survive and live in the political, economic, and religious reality that was to be altered radically by her assent to the will of God. She listened to an angel, but only once, and lived on the words, prayers, and actions of others around her: Joseph, the shepherds, Simeon, Anna, and finally and always her child, who became her teacher, master, rabbi, and Lord.

In John's Gospel, Mary is the church, and the mother of the church, the woman who is in relationship to the Word of God made flesh and dwelling among us. She is crucial to his hour of suffering and glory and to the revelation and birth of his community. She is given to his disciples and taken into their care. She becomes the church giving birth to the children of God, in obedience, service, forgiveness, and struggle with the forces of evil. She mourns not only her firstborn son's murder but the destruction of all the children of God by others in the family.

In the life of the church Mary becomes contemplative, mystic, the one who prays for wisdom and throws her cloak, her mantle of justice, over all those in need. There is a statue in Europe from the Middle Ages that shows Mary with her cloak opened wide. Inside, all crowded together, are people stacked on top of each other: nobles, kings, queens, and knights. But the ones closest to her heart and hands are the peasants, orphans, children, and the poor.

And now, after the year 2000, who is she? She is aging gracefully. Sometimes she seems middle-aged, reflective of the experiences, or contemplative, serving the will of God in the church. Her church is more like a small Christian community, intent on the Word. It calls for obedience to the needs of the poor and obedience to the prophetic imperatives of justice, nonviolent resistance to evil, the shadow of the cross, and an awareness of the world—the whole world.

And so Mary is the woman butchered in Rwanda, the Muslim woman raped and brutalized and left pregnant by soldiers, the single mother on welfare, working at subsistence wages, raising her children without help from the church or community or her ex-husband. She is all the women, one-third of the world's population, always on the move, fleeing starvation, war, and disasters of flood, earthquake, and drought. She is the woman who mourns the slaughter of the children, the executions of the state, the torture and disappearances of men and women. She is the shadow of the old ones battered or shunted aside, institutionalized or left on the streets to wander and scavenge for a living.

But Mary is also anyone who comforts, consoles, or speaks boldly on behalf of others. She is the one who says, "Do whatever he tells you to do." She is the obedient servant of all our brothers and sisters in the kingdom of God. She is the one who belongs to those who have no one else. She is the one who mourns injustice, violence, insensitivity, and selfishness. She is both victim and advocate. She is singer and crier for an end to evils and unnecessary hurt. She is the nonviolent resister to sin.

And she is single-hearted and single-minded, whole, all of a piece, devoted to the Word of her child and the will of her Father, obedient to the whim of the Spirit. She is virgin, mother, single parent, widow, growing old and becoming grandmother to a church, a world.

She is parent, with Joseph, who adopted her child, mother of a son named Jesus. She finds out as time passes she is mother to all his followers and friends, mother to communities, people, nations, a church. She is mother of the son of the living God, mother of the Son of Man, the judge of nations, the mother of the presence of the Son of Justice. She is a mother who expects her children to grow up and surprise her as her firstborn son most emphatically did. She is a mother who expects that the best of her will be found in the lives of her children and grandchildren on and on throughout time. She is a mother who expects to be taken in and cared for, as her dying son commanded his young beloved friend John to do. She expects us to become disciples of her child, as she did. She is a mother who expects us to leave home and do for others what she has long done for us—to make space in our hearts for all those who cry out, and open wide our mantles of justice and cloaks of consolation, gathering in our brothers and sisters and growing up to be mothers, fathers, grandparents, and friends to all.

Mary, Mary, how does your garden grow? These days her garden is in trouble through pollution, the devastation of war, bombs, stockpiled nuclear weapons, lands burned into desert by greed, economic systems that serve only to encourage consumerism, cities barely inhabitable, a thinning ozone layer, and waters and ground poisoned by chemicals and radioactivity. It is a garden that is fast losing some of its best plants and creatures, with ancient trees felled, and the escalating demise of endangered species. The children have forgotten how to be gardeners of food for survival (justice) and cultivators of beauty (mercy). The garden has need of children who know the ways of the winds and the waves, the mountain fastnesses, and the desert places as her child Jesus knew them. He too, it seems, has a fondness for gardens, where all tears will be wiped away and the sun will shine, everlastingly dispelling the shadows of death and evil. Mary knows the garden of Eden, the garden of Gethsemane, her own garden in Nazareth, and the gardens of Word, grace, and spirit everywhere that hint at the gardens of revelation that one day will perhaps be earth.

Mary is the virgin of the Eastern churches, who gazes at us with the future of her child in her mind's eye, carrying not just the child but the cross he bares, pondering the Word that will form her soul as surely as the bones were formed in her womb. This virgin mother is caressed by her child, with his arm around her neck, his cheek against hers, comforting her, tending to her heart. She is the woman dying, at the dormition, with her grown child bent over her.

Mary, Mary, quite contrary, how does your garden grow?

The Annunciation and "The Coming of the Light"

There is an ancient Native American legend called "The Coming of the Light." It is told in many different traditions; this version is closest to the Cherokee telling:

❧ *Once upon a time, long before any two-leggeds were in the world, the world was beautiful. But it was also pitch-black. The animals could not see their way around. They were always falling into ruts and running into trees and knocking each other over and getting into fights. Eventually they started meeting in small groups and talking with one another.*

"We can't go on living this way," they said. "This is not the way the Creator meant it to be. What we need is some light. What we need is some fire. We can't even see creation."

Finally all the fish, birds, and animals got together to talk over the situation (they could still all talk in those days). They all agreed they needed light.

"Does anyone know where the light is?" they asked.

Raven swooped in and said, "There is light a long way off in the east. Sometimes when I fly long and high, when I'm about exhausted, I can see the light just breaking in the east. Somebody has it—it's over there."

The animals talked about it and thought of sending a delega-

tion over to see about getting some of the light. But Fox broke in and said, "If they have the light and have had it all this time and haven't shared it, they are probably selfish and won't share it with us. I think we'll have to steal it."

The animals discussed this and decided that Fox was right. But who was to go and steal it? They immediately decided Buzzard should go. After all, Buzzard was strong and would last the journey. He wouldn't need to eat much along the way if he ate a lot before leaving. He could steal the light and bring it back.

Now, Buzzard didn't look as he does today. In fact, Buzzard was beautiful. He had a great head of feathers, huge ones that shot straight up in the air, covering his whole head with rich, vibrant colors. He could fly high and fast. So they all gathered around and sent Buzzard off into the east.

Buzzard flew higher and longer than he had ever flown before, and finally he saw the light in the east. He was tired, but he swooped down and grabbed a bit of fire and placed it on top of his head and headed off for the west and the waiting animals. As he flew, the wind fanned the flames. It grew really hot! By the time he swooped down to the animals waiting for him, the fire had gone out. And worse still, he had lost his beautiful head feathers. He was as bald and ugly as he is today.

All the animals felt terrible, not only because they didn't get the light but because Buzzard looked so awful. They realized how much he had lost on behalf of his community, and they tried to comfort him. Then they discussed whom to send next.

There was a murmur in the group, and Possum stepped forward, saying, "I'm not as stupid as Buzzard. I'll steal the light but I won't put it on my head. Besides, they'll be looking for someone now and watching the sky. I can go on the ground and blend in with the darkness and hide until the last minute."

So off they sent him.

Now, at that time Possum had a large, bushy, beautiful tail.

He headed east, found the light, grabbed a bit of it and placed it right in the middle of his great tail, and headed home as fast as he could. He moved fast, smelling smoke and feeling really hot. By the time he got back to the animals, the fire had gone out again, and poor Possum had lost forever his great bushy tail. They all gathered and comforted Possum, although Fox said, "Oh, it's a shame you lost your beautiful tail, but I thought you said you weren't as stupid as Buzzard."

The animals were trying to be solicitous, but they were also getting frustrated. They really needed fire and light. Finally a tiny little voice piped up and said, "I'll go."

Everyone looked around and said, "Who is that?"

It was Grandmother Spider.

She said again, "I'll go. After all, they're going to be on guard now, and I am so small and inconspicuous that they won't even notice me. I'll let out my spun thread on the way and then find my way back in the dark. I'll bring back the fire. Who knows? Maybe I was created to bring light into the world."

So they sent Grandmother Spider off to the east. She made her way very slowly, but as she went, she gathered a little bit of wet clay and formed it into a small pot, which she placed on her back. As she went into the east, it slowly dried and hardened. She continued along, leaving her trail of thread behind her.

Although they were waiting and watching for someone to steal their light, they weren't expecting someone so small and quiet. Grandmother Spider stole in, took just a little bit of fire, and put it into her pot. Then she followed her own trail back home, rolling in her thread as she went.

The animals all knew she was coming, because as she drew near, the light spread, coming from the east until dawn arrived, the first day, on Grandmother Spider's back. Soon the light spilled out of the bowl and filled the whole sky. The animals took the little clay pot and announced, "Grandmother, you have done what none of *us could do. You have brought the light, the fire, and warmth into the world. We are grateful and we will honor you. From now on, spiders will remind us of the Creator's presence. And anyone who weaves and makes pots brings light into the world and continues creation's journey. We will remember."*

And so it is today. Among Native Americans, anyone who weaves and makes pots works with the Creator to hold the world together. And God is a great Spider that weaves the web that holds us all together. They ask, "Have you been caught in the web of the Spider yet?"

This ancient story reveals belief in light, hope, the continuance of creation, and the intercommunion of all that is made, and the meaning of certain creatures in the world. This creation story says much about how things got to be the way they are: how Buzzard got so ugly, why Possum has such a bare-looking tail, and how light came into the world. It also explains the connection between weavers and potters and the Creator. It speaks of a progression, a long history of attempts to obtain what is necessary for life, culminating in Grandmother Spider's small powers doing what the more obvious powers of others could not.

What does this story have to do with Mary? For believers, all stories reveal the One Story, the coming of light into the world, who God is, who we are, how we are all connected, and why things are the way they are. All cultures and races and religions serve the one true God and reveal the Creator among us. Grandmother Spider says it clearly, simply, and quietly: "Maybe I was created to bring light into the world." She does so with her quiet, small power, unnoticed by others, with creativity and imagination, using all she touches to bring the fullness of life to her people and setting in motion a trail of tradition for all weavers and potters and storytellers. This close-to-the-ground power of humility is necessary for all the earth's growth.

Always light comes from the east, the place of resurrection. In ancient baptismal rituals we are asked to turn and face the light that is coming upon us; we are baptized and given the light to take into the world, as Jesus brought light into the world, and as Mary, the first believer, brought light into the world. When light comes, all is revealed.

In this story light comes from a grandmother—old, wise, and close to the earth. The grandmothers and grandfathers, the leaders of the community, sit on earth and make decisions, knowing their choices will affect the next generations.

Perhaps Mary is Grandmother Spider. This remarkably different relationship reveals Mary as one who brings light into the world and teaches us to grow up and do things for the larger community. She is grandmother of the earth and grandmother of the people of God. The Creator—and Mary—continue to weave the web that holds the world together. She expects us to do it as well.

According to tradition, Mary lived in the community at Ephesus until she was ninety-two years old. But grandmothers are more connected to a relationship than to a certain age. Grandmother implies wisdom, understanding, patience, fortitude, enduring grace. In Native American traditions it is a high honor to be a grandmother, and a grandmother need not be a biological relative. Perhaps this relationship reveals as much about Mary as being a mother, since this new family, this new community, is not based on biology, but on wisdom, love, knowledge, affection, commitment, growth, and support. Mary is great not because she is the physical mother of Jesus, but because she believes in Jesus.

The grandmother of the story is a spider! Spiders spin their webs out of the stuff of their own bodies. The web is there for catching unsuspecting creatures. Once in the web, the only way out is to get eaten by the spider or to tear a hole in the web. It seems the web of God works pretty much the same way.

Grandmother Spider's pot is made of earth, and it is earth that brings light into the world. We are made of earth, and with Mary, we are to bring light into the world. Grandmother Spider and Mary have known the truth of incarnation for a long, long time.

The Advent of Mary:
The Woman Hidden in the Shadows

Every year on the last Sunday before Christmas, just days before the birth of the child to Mary, the readings go backward in time, to the coming of the angel Gabriel to Mary and the description of how the birth came about (Matt. 1:18–24; Luke 1:26–38; Luke 1:39–45). The other readings go back even further: to Isaiah the prophet promising Ahaz a sign—a young virgin conceiving a child called Emmanuel; to the Second Book of Samuel, in which King David decides to build a house for God, and Nathan the prophet is sent to tell him what God thinks of the idea; and to the prophet Micah's words about the place Bethlehem, the House of Bread, least and greatest among the tribes and places. All these readings are overshadowed with peace—a respite from fighting and striving, a time when the poor are fed, the pastures rich, and there is breathing space for the people.

In one of the letters of Paul we are told that the gospel reveals the mystery hidden for so many ages but now manifested through the writings of the prophets (Rom. 16:25–26). The Jewish people believe that long, long ago, before time started, God was lonely and didn't have anyone to tell stories to, so God made us. The Jews believe that the history of the world is the stories of God coming true. As Christians we too believe that these stories proclaimed every Sunday morning are the stories of God, but sometimes we believe the stories and sometimes we don't. Sometimes we believe the stories when we're small, and then we don't believe them so much when we get older. But every year in Advent the old stories come round again and we are called to listen afresh, wide-eyed, hopeful. We are asked to become as children again—but this time aware, awakened—and believe in outrageous miracles that have happened in history and continue to happen.

The story of Christmas is the story that God has been trying to tell us since the very beginning of time. On the last Sunday before Christmas Day the church tries to help us remember and tells us to start believing in the stories again. The angel Gabriel tells Mary "nothing is impossible with God," so in the week before the birth of God in the world in a human child we have to practice believing that nothing is impossible.

Let's look at the story of David and Nathan (2 Samuel 7), for example. Nathan, the prophet, has the word of God in his mouth. His vocation is making David and the people remember—remember that we live God's story and that it is God who makes and uses history for God's ends. Nathan has to remind David—and us—that it is God who takes care of him. God intends to build a house that David can't even imagine.

We are a part of something much bigger than just our individual or small community lives. The story began with the annunciation. Soon we will celebrate its culmination. It's been nine months. Mary knows and a few other people know that God has been hiding in the world. Joseph knows. The angels know. There is a tradition from the Middle Ages that the angels started learning the song that they would sing at midnight on Christmas way back at the annunciation because it was such a strange song. It took them nine months to learn the words and the melody and to believe that its message was really coming true.

The angel came to a poor backwater place, Nazareth, to Mary, to the remnant of the people of David, who were very poor. But it was a place where the dreams and promises were not forgotten—as David forgot in his great wealthy palace. Mary is asked if she will build a house for God. God is about to make another piece of the story come true, in collusion with Mary and Joseph and a few others.

The prophets have always hinted that certain people know where God hides out. They talk about specific groups of people mentioned in the Holiness Code of the Jewish Torah: the widows, the orphans, the old, the illegal aliens in our midst, the migrants, the prisoners, the oppressed, and those bereft and alone. That is where God hides out. We lump them all together and call them "the poor." God hears their cry and bends down very close to them. God bends close to Mary, Joseph, and the shepherds, who are all very poor. If God is going to come this year, it probably won't be to the great and the mighty. God will go—as always—to the people who already know God is in the world.

The incarnation and annunciation say that God is hidden in us. Mary believes that part of the story, as unbelievable as it is. She believes too that Elizabeth, an old woman, is now pregnant. That's a little hard to believe. She believes that she, Mary, a virgin, has conceived a child. That's a little harder to believe. Her child is going to be human and the child of God too. That's still harder to believe. This child is going to be killed when he grows up for preaching good news to the poor ones of the earth, but he's going to be raised from the dead. That's even harder to believe. We are all invited into the relationship that her son will have with his Father-God, and we too live that resurrection life already, right now, because of our baptism. That's hard to believe too, but that's the way the story goes.

At Christmas we celebrate. We celebrate the fact that Mary said yes. We can almost imagine Mary looking at the angel Gabriel and saying, "Tell God I say yes." But we also celebrate the fact that every one of us said yes in our baptism. We said yes, we believe the story of incarnation, of God becoming human and dwelling among us, and we believe in hope and peace with justice here on earth for all. We tell God we'll obey; we've listened and we say yes. Like Mary, we say, "We are the servants of the Lord. Let it be done unto us according to your word." It makes an incredible difference in history that Mary said yes. It makes an incredible difference in this world that we say yes today and make the story keep coming true in our lives.

Oftentimes we think: What does my word mean? What does my life mean? I'm just one of millions and millions of people. There is a story, an old one, told among peacemakers, that can give us heart in the season of hope:

❀   *Once upon a time there were two birds sitting on a branch of a tree. One was a dove and one was a titmouse (a small gray bird, sort of like a sparrow). They were sitting and talking about all* the things that were going on in the world. They had heard stories from all over as they migrated and visited with other birds, and they were exchanging the news. Then, as was their habit, they began to discuss philosophy and theology and politics. But after a while they became bored with that.

Then it began to snow. It was the kind of snow that brought fat, fluffy flakes. The dove looked at the titmouse and asked, "Do you know how much a snowflake weighs?"

The titmouse thought about it a while and said, "No, I never thought about it."

"Well," said the dove, "I think it weighs nothing more than nothing. I mean, look at the snow floating down, these fat, soft, fluffy flakes."

The titmouse thought about it some more and said, "If you think a snowflake weighs nothing more than nothing, I have a little story to tell you. Once when I was sitting on a branch, just like this one, I didn't have anything to do. It started to snow, so I began counting snowflakes, fat and fluffy ones just like these. I counted a lot, a couple of hundred, a couple of thousand. I got up to one million, eight hundred and forty-six thousand, six hundred and twenty-two snowflakes, and then one snowflake—which you say weighs nothing more than nothing—floated down, landed on my branch, and cracked it straight through. The branch went falling to the ground, and I had to fly off."

With that, the titmouse flew off and left the dove sitting alone on the branch.

The dove, who has always been associated with peace, sat there trying to figure out the story. Suddenly it dawned on her. Of course. One snowflake, one person, when added to all the others, may be the one that makes all the difference in the world.

What if we, who are nothing alone, are the difference between the way the world is now and the coming of peace on earth? What if we are the difference between darkness pervading the world or light coming into the world? At Christmas we celebrate the fact that Mary said yes. Will we tell God that we too say yes? If we do, perhaps the story will come true in ways none of us ever thought about, and the world will know that nothing is impossible with God—and that God needs us to make all the stories come true.

The Visitation: The Greeting

The story of Mary's visit to Elizabeth begins abruptly: "Mary then set out for a town in the hills of Judah." This is the first of three journeys that Mary will make to Jerusalem, recounted in the first two chapters of Luke. In a sense, these chapters mirror the journeys of the soul and spirit that each believer makes in imitation of Jesus.

In this first trip Mary is pregnant and alone, traveling the ninety miles to the outskirts of Jerusalem. She will stay for three months, until the birth of John, and then return to Nazareth. Then she will go again to the outlying districts of Jerusalem, with Joseph, when she is much further along in her pregnancy, so that her child is born in Bethlehem. Third, she and Joseph will take Jesus to the Temple in Jerusalem for Jesus' appearance before the priests and elders when he is around twelve, at his bar mitzvah, his coming of age as a Jewish adult.

For the first journey Mary leaves immediately after the annunciation. The angel has given her one small piece of practical information: her relative Elizabeth is already six months along in her pregnancy, even though she was barren all these past years and is old, beyond the years of bearing a child. Elizabeth's house is ninety miles away, safe from prying eyes; besides, there is already talk of Elizabeth and Zechariah and what this child of theirs will be. So Mary goes. She acts on faith. She goes to serve her relative in need. She is moved by compassion and her own need, and she immediately responds. She will be a help to Elizabeth, but Elizabeth will be a help to her as well. Elizabeth will understand more than others that they are part of a larger piece of history and promise. They will be *con-spirators*, people who "breathe together" to bring something hidden into the world. So a young virgin who is pregnant and unmarried and an old, barren woman who is now pregnant will encounter one another and live together for a while as friends. This is the beginning of the story, strange enough to give us due warning that from here on out the story will grow more mysterious, a story of faith and belief, enacted in our own lives as much as in the lives of Mary and Elizabeth.

The first thing we note from the story of incarnation is that when the good news breaks into history, our life and relationships are deeply disturbed. Mary is great because she gives birth to and brings the Word to the world. But this is the vocation of every believer. The power of the Most High overshadows and the Spirit comes upon each one of us, sending us out into the world and history to bring the Word to life and flesh in us.

Like Mary, we begin by asking how. This is the catechumenate, the time of asking questions and receiving theological answers to wrap our practical life around. The questioning is about Mary's relationship to the Trinity, Father, the Most High, the Shadow of the Spirit, and her child, Jesus. Her response is theological: "I am the servant of the Lord." In Luke's Gospel, Jesus is the Suffering Servant of the Lord, and all references in the Gospel to the servants tell us about Mary and about ourselves. "So you also. When you have done all that you have been told to do, you must say: 'We are not more than servants; we have only done our duty' " (Luke 17:10). It is an attitude of worship, of service, of obedience, of belonging to entirely; our life is not our own. It is based on the word of the one who owns us.

Mary is the servant, prophet, virgin mother bearing the Word into the world, a very hostile world. To bear this child is to bear the cross and to bear her share of bringing the gospel into history. She is a disciple of Jesus, her child, the Son of the Most High. What God called Mary to be, we are called to be as well. We are called back again and again, ritually, sacramentally, and in the proclamation of the Word in our midst. The first part of the story is similar:

Mary then set out for a town in the hills of Judah. She entered the house of Zechariah and greeted Elizabeth. When Elizabeth heard Mary's greeting, the baby leapt in her womb. Elizabeth was filled with the Holy Spirit, and giving a loud cry, said, "You are most blessed among women and blessed is the fruit of your womb! How is it that the mother of my Lord comes to me? The moment your greeting sounded in my ears, the baby within me suddenly leapt for joy. Blessed are you who believe that the Lord's Word would come true!"

(LUKE 1:39–45)

Elizabeth recognizes her Lord and the mother of her Lord. She is in relationships to the Spirit in that moment of insight and knowledge. She blesses Mary because of the Lord God, and because she has believed that the Lord's word would come true. Elizabeth's relationship to Mary is based on belief and hope and their shared faith and waiting. Belief is expressed in action, in response to hearing the word. Elizabeth senses the truth about Mary, who brings with her the presence of God, and they are one in the Spirit.

Even as Mary greets Elizabeth, the sound of her voice and the force of her presence evoke joy, leaping, and dancing. Jesus, in John's Gospel, describes his own Spirit as "rivers of living water leaping up and flowing like a fountain from within him" (John 7:38). This Spirit of Jesus in Mary causes John, the child in Elizabeth's womb, to take notice and leap and kick. This is the one for whom he and all the prophets have been waiting. Two women's belief in the word has set in motion the re-creation of the world, the revolution of power and redemption.

In the Eastern church this feast of the Visitation is called the embrace or the Kiss, and the icons depict Mary and Elizabeth warmly, fondly embracing each other. Their faces and figures are radiant, the presence seeping out of their bodies into the air itself, uncontainable in their flesh. The Spirit in the early church was called the Kiss of the

Mouth of God, and these two believers kiss ecstatically and embrace one another. The mystery envelops them completely.

Mary goes to Elizabeth and is recognized as she truly is, as God sees her and relates to her. Elizabeth is friend to Mary, accepting her, recognizing her, affirming her, and blessing her. Mary can only sing!

The process of believing is shared and extensive. All of us are blessed likewise in not being alone in our belief, in having a friend or friends who give us the freedom to sing and proclaim the glory of God in us, others in whose presence we know we are loved and honored. Elizabeth is the first to honor Mary; all of us follow in her wake. We sing the praises of Mary as we sing the praises of God and rejoice that we are a part of that wonder, that mystery, of salvation unfolding. Mary's belief is acknowledged and strengthened by another's faith. We too grow in our awareness of who we are and who God is and what it means to obey. It is others who call us forth and give to us the occasion to pray aloud and worship God with them. Mary's visit, her going to serve another in need and to learn what she is soon to experience, is returned by hospitality and gracious praise and welcome. The journey is completed with prayer and prophecy.

Mary sings, but she does not sing only for herself. She sings for her people. She preaches in song and joy. She prophetically announces what is to come, what will take place in the future, and what is already beginning in her flesh and blood. She speaks of her child and the three turnings, the three revolutions, that he will set in motion in the world: the turning of the heart, the turning of politics and power, and the turning of hunger and economics.

In Elizabeth's presence Mary can sing, borrowing from the ancient traditions of Israel, the song of Hannah (from Samuel) and about what God does in history using simple folk who believe and hope. She is careful to begin:

> "My soul proclaims the greatness of the Lord, my spirit exults in
> God my savior!

He has looked upon his servant in her lowliness and people
   forever will call me blessed.
The Mighty One has done great things for me, Holy is his Name!
From age to age his mercy extends to those who live in his
   presence."

(LUKE 1:46–50)

She is great because God has taken notice of her. God thinks of her! She is not great because of anything she does or will do, but because God includes her in the marvelous work of salvation and wonders. And so she proclaims aloud the great works of God and what has been done for her, in her, and what God will do in her child for the rest of the world. She is prophet, and she comes right to the point: God has acted with power and done wonders, scattering the proud with their plans.

The Night of Birth: The Woman Who Ponders

Mary's part in the incarnation, the mystery of God becoming human flesh, is only two lines in the account of the birth of Jesus: "They were in Bethlehem when the time came for her to have her child, and she gave birth to a son, her firstborn. She wrapped him in swaddling clothes and laid him in the manger, because there was no place for them in the inn" (Luke 2:6–7).

She delivers her child away from home and relatives, away from security and familiarity. She is on her way in obedience to the state, to be counted in a census as a member of an oppressed people in the occupied territory of another empire. She gives birth alone, with Joseph as midwife, in a place where animals shelter from the cold. She has very little to offer her firstborn, just her life and love. She is like every other poor woman who gives birth in a world that is alien and threatening, divided into nations, races, and kingdoms.

But strange things begin to occur. The birth does not go unnoticed. The small family is visited by the poor, shepherds who come looking for the Messiah. Besides Mary and Elizabeth and the child John in Elizabeth's womb, the first to hear the good news of peace coming to earth in the person of God are shepherds, people of no worth. Gabriel, this time accompanied by heavenly choirs, comes to Bethlehem, and glory descends upon the lowly and the meek.

In El Salvador refugees flee the government troops, hiding in the jungle only a couple of thousand yards away from the troops that would kill them. The group stops long enough for a woman to give birth, in devastating silence and pain. The women around her hold her, willing her to make no sound. The child, once born, is passed from hand to hand, blessed, prayed over. Each person hopes that this child will be the one that will help to free the people and bring peace to their land. Then they move on, with new life to be celebrated at the first stop where it is safe to sing, to rejoice, to eat together, and give blessings to the mother.

Mary's child too was born into a world that was hostile and fearful of the children of the poor, especially Jewish children. Women of war-torn countries birth their children with Mary, intent on giving life to the earth in the face of hate, war, and death. The poor, the farmers, the peasants, and other refugees wait in hope for this child to grow up.

The text points us only to the child. The traditional Christmas carol repeats the question: "What child is this that lies sleeping on Mary's lap?" The good news is about the birth of this child, the Son of God. That is the miracle that the angels herald and announce to poor folk. The words are clear:

> "Don't be afraid: I am here to give you good news, great joy for all the peoples. Today a Savior has been born to you in David's town; he is the Messiah and the Lord. Let this be a sign to you: you will find a baby wrapped in swaddling clothes and lying in a manger . . . Glory to God in the highest: peace on earth for God is blessing humankind."

(LUKE 2:10–12, 14)

The night of Christmas belongs to the babe born in the place of sheep and lambs, wrapped in swaddling cloths, welcomed into the world by shepherds and animals. What child is this?

Mary's response to the birth of her child, as it was to the greeting of the angel, is to treasure all these messages and continually ponder them in her heart. This description of Mary is repeated again and again in Luke's account. It shows how her soul and mind absorbed the Word of God and the will of God as it was revealed daily in her life and history. She learns as she goes along. She said yes and took it from that point imaginatively and creatively in light of the prophecies and dreams of her people Israel. Her faith in many ways is like ours, based on Word and community, shared prayer and worship, life experience and the difficult painful process of making choices and living by them.

In some ways she is also the first one to stake her life on the Word. She takes enormous risks to birth her child and, with Joseph, to keep him alive. She probably thinks of her child in the terms of Davidic kings, prophets, and the texts of the Messiah's care for justice, peace, and the nurturing of the poor in the land. She ponders, seeks understanding, reflects, and prays over what is happening to her and her child and loved ones.

This pondering also includes fear, worry, sensitivity to events and relationships around her, possibilities of response and action. This was the way she lived and the way we Christians should live: pondering all things in our hearts. The Spirit within her stirred and was released in her words and greetings, as with Elizabeth, and dwelled within her daily, long after she bore her child into the world on that cold night in a cave, with Joseph attending her.

Mary is a believer, not a knower. She believes in her child, and through crises and events she seeks meaning and insight, the gifts of wisdom and understanding and knowledge. The book of Wisdom lyrically describes wisdom as a woman whose spirit is holy, unique, intelligent, moving, and graceful, "an aura of the might of God." She is the one who produces "friends of God and prophets and even takes precedence over the light." The woman Mary is such a spirit, "a pure effusion of the glory of the Almighty," "the refulgence of eternal light, the spotless mirror of the power of God, the image of his goodness "(see Wisd. 6:12–21, 7:22–30; quotations from the New American Bible). Throughout the early chapters of Luke, Mary is portrayed as "keeping these things in her heart" (Luke 2:51). She is a silent, reflective woman, seeking to understand and know her God and her child and God's will for her life from day to day. She treasures words, events, moments in her life, as revealing to her the power and might of God, as incarnating the presence of God as Father and Lord of her life. Simple, ordinary human occurrences are her path to knowledge. She experiences conversion, insight, and ever-deepening awareness and love of God by the way God deals with her, in her present reality.

In the Indian pueblos of the Southwest and the Indian villages of southern Mexico the women have rituals for grinding corn and making bread. They sing and chant ancient words and songs, and when the song is done, the corn is ground and the bread is made. It is their ritual of time filled, time to themselves, time to pray and chant and think as they ponder over the day and do their work. It is a time-honored tradition that gives sustenance and soul to their daily lives.

What Mary learned in her musings and prayer and silent work, she passed on to her child. We are told that he grew "in stature and strength and was filled with wisdom: the grace of God was upon him" (Luke 2:40). Jesus was taught, nourished, and formed by this woman who knew God with all her heart and soul and mind and strength in obedience to the command of the Torah. Mary is Jesus' mother, teacher, and first concrete image of the love of God, whom he will call Father. It is from her story of what she has known and experienced of God that Jesus will distill and refine the good news that God loves us, even when we are unaware of that love or our need for it. All her life she will wonder, ponder, and pray over how God deals with her, how God saves her and the world through the freedom and the acceptance of being the mother of God's son. She is friend to God, a servant to her child, and a disciple of the Lord.

This stance of "pondering and treasuring all these things in her heart," this way of living, seems to be the way of Mary's life. The long process of analysis and critical understanding of truth has begun and will not end. Reflection, contemplation upon events and relationships, analysis—these are the constant and systematic channels of insight and growth into adult faith for the first disciple and for all others. They extend and deepen Mary's awareness, and ours, of the world and the role each plays in the kingdom of God.

Joseph the Just

There is a story that begins immediately after the genealogy in chapter 1 of Matthew's Gospel. We begin there because the story is also about the man Joseph, who has the heart and soul of a child. Joseph is one of the just ones of God. He believes in God's dreams and surrenders his entire life and strength to making sure that the dream comes true in his life and family. We begin:

> Now this is how the birth of Jesus Christ came about. When his mother Mary was engaged to Joseph, but before they lived together, she was found with child through the power of the Holy Spirit. Joseph her husband, an upright man unwilling to expose her to the law, decided to divorce her quietly. Such was his intention when suddenly the angel of the Lord appeared in a dream and said to him: "Joseph, son of David, have no fear about taking Mary as your wife. It is by the Holy Spirit that she has conceived this child. She is to have a son and you are to name him Jesus because he will save his people from their sins." All this happened to fulfill what the Lord had said through the prophet: "The virgin shall be with child and give birth to a son,

and they shall call him Emmanuel," a name which means "God is with us." When Joseph awoke he did as the angel of the Lord had directed him and received her into his home as his wife. He had no relations with her at any time before she bore a son, whom he named Jesus.

(MATT. 1:18–25)

Most people react to this passage with questions about Joseph and his dreams. They show disbelief and wonder at the way Joseph learns of the incarnation and the presence of the Messiah in the world. They are stunned at how easily he adjusts his whole life to obey the angel's instructions. It doesn't make sense to most people today. But this Joseph is not like most modern people. And Joseph is facing a dilemma. He is an upright or just man, but he is also "unwilling to expose her to the law."

To be just means to be obedient to the law, to do what is required, to consider what is good for all concerned, to give others their due. Sometimes the elements of truthfulness, of care of the weak and poor, of charity, are included as well. Rarely does anyone remember that justice can also be tenderhearted mercy, *hesed,* as in the descriptions of God's justice in the Hebrew Scriptures. Joseph, being just and good, decides to divorce Mary or (in some translations) "put her away" quietly. The verb *put away* has overtones of hiding someone, of putting a situation under the rug, of covering up the facts—much as many people would do if they found out that a woman was pregnant and unmarried, even today. Have the child, but send the mother away to a distant place, with cousins or to a home, hush it up and don't talk about what is really going on! Is this what Joseph has in mind?

The law in the Jewish community was harsh in the matter of a woman being pregnant and not married—death by stoning so that her child was not born. Joseph truly is a compassionate man, not willing to have Mary executed, destroying both her and her child. If he divorces her quietly and separates himself from her, she and the child have a chance of life—but what kind of life? She would be a woman alone with a child, rejected, an outcast; the child would be essentially fatherless, carrying the shadow of illegitimacy forever. Still, it would be better than death.

What did Joseph feel? Was he betrayed, brokenhearted, ashamed, rejected, hurt, disheartened, angry, dejected, in despair? Remember, all his hopes and dreams of a life with Mary, of a future in the community, of happiness and the prospect of children and a family of his own are gone. All he can do is react or respond to the reality: Mary is with child and the child is not his child. And then he sleeps and dreams. The angel of the Lord comes to him and tells him not to fear to take Mary as his wife because it is by the Holy Spirit that she has conceived a child. This child is Jesus, the savior of his people, the Messiah. The child is the ful-fillment of the hopes of the people of Israel, the divine presence among God's people, the presence of justice, mercy, and peace. Like the child born to King David and Bathsheba generations before, this child is the gesture of peace that God extends to a wayward and sinful people. Like Solomon, this child will bring a kingdom of hope and peace, care for the poor, and save the people from their sins. When Joseph awoke, he obeyed the command of the angel.

Jungian analyst John Sanford, as well as many in the Jewish com-munity refer to dreams as the forgotten language of God. Dreams, espe-cially in Jewish understanding, are a way of communicating God's will to individuals. Dreamers are willing to stake their lives on the knowledge that is given in the dream, even though they are unable to explain why they act as they do to others. They dream, and the dream becomes knowledge born of hope, faith, and belief in God.

Joseph is a just man. He is a good Jew, a believer in the promises, a man steeped in the Psalms, the prophets, and the law. He is obedient to God, righteous and holy. His prayer, and his agonizing struggle over what to do with Mary and the child to be born, lead him, by the grace and strength of the Spirit, to break the law. He disregards the law and takes Mary into his home as his wife and takes the child as his own. He be-comes the husband and friend of Mary, the man who adopts God into his family, the protector of both, willing to orient his whole life toward hope, toward what this one child might become for his people.

His compassion, his love, and his belief in life compel him to accept Mary and the child and give them life. A just man, he breaks the law to save two lives. A just man, an upright man, he knows the child is not his, but he remembers and recognizes that *all* children are the children of God. He sustains the life of this child and believes, in hope, that this child will be the long-awaited one of Israel.

This man Joseph is remarkable because of his graceful and spirit-filled response to a difficult and dangerous situation. He thinks first of those who are weaker and in danger; he sides with them, enduring much to honor their lives and their right to existence and a home. No wonder that Jesus' awareness of God as his father is filled with mercy, love, forgiveness, tenderness, and compassion, care for the poor and weak, endurance in the face of hardship and all events that seek to break that bond. His earthly father is a man of justice, an upright and holy man, a true child of God.

What role does the Spirit play in all of this, in the conception of the child and in Joseph's awareness of the reality of who this child is? It seems from the rest of Matthew's chapter 1 and the next chapter, which include all the references we have to Joseph, that dreams are the pattern of his life, the primary way that Joseph discerns what to do, when, and why. Dreams are visions of reality that are able to encompass the personal details of people's lives and draw them into a new world of reality, to enable them to create a world when one does not yet exist, to include the loose and lost pieces that one grows to cherish and honor and love and wrap one's life around. Joseph, the dreamer par excellence, like his namesake in Genesis, dreams a better world, one that is more holy, more careful of the weak and the little ones, one that opens up possibilities of God's working among humankind in unbelievably kind ways. Joseph is like God: he believes in human beings and in life and in the promises given to his people over the ages. And like Mary, he is ready. He has been waiting all his life for the hope to be made manifest, for the Word of the Lord to once again interrupt history and reveal the power of the Lord. Joseph believes that God is revealing himself in Mary and in his own life and that God is counseling him. Like any prophet of old, he obeys, and life is radically altered forever.

This family of Mary, with child and unmarried, and Joseph, a just and upright man who takes her in and cares for her and the child of God, is a new image of family—bound not just by blood and marriage and sexual ties but by ties of faith, of need, and of compassion that serves life. It reflects the kingdom and will of God, who fathers and births us all. It is Joseph who will hold this family together in the face of history's callousness, Herod's fear and agitation, and the hardships of being poor and Jewish in an occupied territory that belongs to the Romans.

The Christmas Story

There is a story I like to tell around Christmastime. It is about salvation and how God uses the small of the earth to confound the great and mighty. I first heard this story in northern New Mexico from an old woman descended from a Jewish family that had converted to Christianity but still practiced the old ways of the Marrano Jews.

✻   *Once upon a time there was a spider. She was an ordinary spider, but she was a bit slow. She just couldn't seem to spin a web right. Hers slipped, had huge holes in them, tore at the slightest pull, and wouldn't hold a fly. She was discouraged and worn out trying. Finally she decided to stay in a cave and make a huge web, slowly and painstakingly, and do it right. If she could just make one right, then she'd have it down and could go from there. She vowed that no matter what, she wouldn't come out until she was done.*

It was December, late in the month, cold, crisp, and clear, and she had been working on the web. It was coming together! She was

getting the hang of it! It was coming out right finally! Then one afternoon as the shadows lengthened, the animals, birds, and insects,
large and small, began filing past the cave chattering and talking,
urging her to take a break from her work and come with them. It
was the night, the long-awaited night when the child would be
born. Come away! Come and worship the Creator-King-Child!
The angels, the trees, and the wind all were whispering what was
coming. But the spider refused. After all, there had been rumors
before and it hadn't been the right night, so why tonight? No, she
must stay and finish her web. She'd come later. And so the animals
went on to Bethlehem and the spider spun her web.

Morning came and the web was finished! It was spectacular,
beautiful, huge. Finally she had gotten it right. She was a real spider, and now she could live like the other spiders, spinning webs
and catching flies. She was exhausted and spent but so happy at
last. Then the animals came by the web shining in the morning
light and dew, and the light of the dawn was shining in their eyes.
They were star-struck, in awe, silent, overwhelmed. When they got
to the cave, they began to talk reverently of the child born in a cave
and wrapped in swaddling clothes and lying in a manger, sung to
by angels and animals. They were all a part of it—too bad that the
spider hadn't come. She had missed the magic and the moment of
glory given to those in attendance.

The poor spider was crushed. What good was it to spin webs
if she had missed out on the birth of the Creator, come in flesh and
blood to earth? The spider hid in the cave and wouldn't come out.
Her friends and all who heard came and begged and pleaded and
consoled her, but she wouldn't budge. Her life was terrible, disastrous, a loss. Nothing would drag her out of the cave, and eventually they left her alone.

One day there was a terrible noise, full of sickness and fear,
screams and horror, the clank of swords, horses' hooves, and soldiers' laughter and cursing. Late in the afternoon a young couple,

a trembling woman of no more than fifteen and her young husband, and their very young child crawled into the cave, shaking in fear. The man was protective yet fearful, hovering over the woman and child, wrapping them in his cloak. She was weeping and the child whimpered softly. They stayed all night, huddled together, their arms wrapped around each other for warmth and comfort. The spider listened and heard the horror—the slaughter of the children, the wailing of the mothers and fathers, the wrenching fear. What could she do?

She did the only thing she knew how to do: she spun webs to comfort them with silken beauty. She recognized the child—it was one of the stars and angels, the Creator of the universe, the maker of spiders. It must be saved. She spun, working feverishly all night long, swinging far and wide, over and under, overlapping, thick and sticky. When morning came with dew and dawn light, the webs shone with shining glory. It was impressive, lovely—but would it work?

With the morning light came the soldiers, climbing the hills behind Bethlehem of Judah, searching for runaways, those who had thought to escape the slaughter of the day before. From cave to cave they went, systematically combing the caves in search of mothers and children. They came to the cave where the young family was hidden, barely breathing. A soldier yelled, "I'll check this cave, sir." And the answer came: "No, don't bother. Look at all those spider webs! No one has been in there in ages. Try some of the others." And they moved on.

All day the family hid in the cave. When darkness came again, they gathered their few possessions and set off into the night on their long journey away from the violence and terror. Before they left, Joseph gathered all of the webs together from the entrance to the cave, wadding them up into a ball, and gave it to the child to hold and play with. The spider decided to go with them and hid *herself in the fold of the lady's garment. They traveled for weeks, and then stayed years in Egypt, a foreign land far from the terror.*

But the lady never forgot. Every night after putting the child to bed and singing a lullaby to him, she would sit by the window of her small house and weep, tears streaming down her face, keening and praying for the children, for their mothers and fathers and sisters and brothers and the memories. And she wept in fear. They had wanted her child. When they came again, would they get him? Was it a question of time? And so the spider would seek to comfort her. Each night she would stay up all night and spin a web, intricate or simple, but each night a different pattern and shape, trying to delight the woman when she arose early in the morning and sat by the window to pray. And she always did notice and talked to the spider like an old friend, a sister in exile.

The spider, of course, died eventually, but she passed on the work and the story to her children. And even today the spider's grandchildren spin their webs in honor of the weeping lady and their ancestor who saved the child from death.

But the spiders also add a terrible reminder: "Remember, that was just the first time. They did get her child later, and her heart broke again and again and she wept unceasingly that long night." But in the morning a sister spider had spun her a web to keep her company in her grief, and on the third morning he came again, ducking under the night's web, to wipe the tears from her eyes and smile upon her as the sun of justice and the dawn of unending hope. And there were pieces of the web in his hair!

From the Revelation Story

It happened in 1976 in Chiapas, Mexico. I had been invited to a refugee camp to visit with some of the people who worked there. The refugees were Guatemalan Indians in exile, tired and beaten but still proud and dignified, waiting to go home, yet trying to build a small area where they could live in the meantime. The camps were huge, seventy or eighty miles inside the Mexican border, and the church was their protector from the soldiers.

I arrived in July, and it was hot and muggy. There was one water spigot for forty thousand people, and it was a good long walk and a longer wait to get two buckets of water. In the family I stayed with, as with others, much of the talk revolved around who was going to go get the water that day. Going was hard, but coming back was harder because of the temptation to drink the water.

I had been there a few days, and my shoes had disappeared, a brand-new pair of Reeboks. I had been given another pair, a spare pair, but they didn't fit well. They were too tight, had no laces, and were already well worn. But shoes are shoes.

My turn at the water spigot came about every three or four days. So my turn came again, and off I went. By the time I got there my feet were raw and blistered. I was limping. When I got to the line waiting for a turn at the spigot, my biggest question was whether to take off the shoes and let my feet rest awhile or just moan and groan and try to ignore my screaming feet. There were sixty or seventy people waiting in line, and it moved slowly. Most of the women didn't speak much Spanish; they were more at ease in their own native tongues. I spoke a little Spanish—together we probably knew the same amount. So we didn't talk much.

This day, and each time I went to get the water, there was one woman who cut into the line and changed the atmosphere totally. She was very tiny, about four feet five inches, and dressed in black from head to toe. I thought how incredibly hot she must be. She would come up to the line, and all conversations would stop abruptly. Everybody would move out of the way and let her go to the tap and get her water. She would very slowly fill up her one bucket and then leave. There was absolute silence when she was around. Nothing was said to her or about her.

I was intrigued and began to ask around about her. The only answer I got was—she's a little crazy, out of it. She thinks she's the Virgin Mary, *la Madre*. I wondered if she was the one by the church most days. There was a small adobe church and a large cross out in front. This woman would lean up against the cross for hours on end, just standing there. No one seemed to know where she lived, but they knew that her husband and all her children were dead, brutally murdered, and all her sisters and brothers had been disappeared or tortured to death. They would say sadly, "She thinks she's the Virgin. She goes every day and stands at the foot of the cross and thinks Jesus is being killed. Everyone treats her with respect and leaves her in her grief, but she is touched."

The day my feet were bleeding, I was about twenty people away from the water tap when the woman in black came. Everyone moved aside to let her in, and she filled her bucket. There was silence. But this time she didn't go away. This time she walked down the line and stopped right in front of me. I was nervous. I will never forget her face. She had an old, old face, but her eyes were bright, full of fire. She looked at me, and then she bent down and poured precious water on my feet and started washing my feet with the bottom of her dress. She patted my feet dry and dug some muslin out of her pockets. She wrapped my feet with great care and then helped me put my shoes back on. Then she stood up in front of me, almost smiled, and said very quietly, "Adios, mi hija"—"Go with God, my daughter." Then she went back down the line, filled her bucket again, and left.

The silence after she had gone was much longer this time. Then one of the older women put her arm around me and repeated the other woman's greeting: "Bienvenidos, mi hija." From then on, everyone spoke to me, even if I didn't understand their language, and they brought me small gifts of food and cloth. I was accepted.

I don't think the old woman was "touched." I think she was the Virgin. Everywhere I go I wonder where she is today. She is always in the place where there is welcome and tender regard even in the midst of horror. There is a certain amount of reverence toward her, but nobody really knows her. Maybe people think she is a little bit "touched." Perhaps we all need to be a little bit "touched" that way. The woman still lives in the desert and has the wings of the eagle and eyes of fire. She has soft, healing balm, especially for the poor, those in pain, and those who are outsiders.

From Rites of Justice:
The Sacraments and Liturgy as Ethical Imperatives

Confirmation: The Choice of the
Cross and Truth-Telling

The Spirit is given in confirmation to individual believers to sustain them in faith, to build up the church, and to witness to the world the death and resurrection of Jesus. The closing prayer of the sacramental celebration says it simply.

> *God our Father,*
> *complete the work you have begun*
> *and keep the gifts of your Holy Spirit*
> *active in the hearts of your people.*
> *Make them ready to live this gospel*
> *and eager to do his will.*
> *May they never be ashamed*
> *to proclaim to all the world Christ crucified*
> *living and reigning for ever and ever. Amen.*
>
> (NO. 33)

The sacrament of confirmation is a sacrament for in-between times—in between the future fullness of the kingdom and now, ordinary

time. There is a story by Madeleine L'Engle that reminds us why we need
the Spirit.

> ❧   *There's a story of a small village . . . where there lived an old
> clockmaker and repairer. When anything was wrong with any of
> the clocks or watches in the village, he was able to fix them, to get
> them working properly again. When he died, leaving no children
> and no apprentices, there was no one left in the village who could
> fix clocks. Soon various watches began to break down. Those
> whose continued to run often lost or gained time, so they were of
> little use. A clock might strike midnight or three in the afternoon.
> So many of the villagers abandoned their timepieces.*
>
> *One day a renowned clockmaker and repairer came through
> that village and the people crowded around him and begged him
> to fix their broken clocks and watches. He spent many hours look-
> ing at all the faulty time pieces and at last announced that he
> could repair only those whose owners had kept them wound, be-
> cause they were the only ones which would be able to remember
> how to keep time.*
>
> *So we must keep things wound: that is, we must pray when
> prayer seems dry as dust; we must write when we are physically
> tired, when our hearts are heavy, when our bodies are in pain. We
> may not always be able to make our clock run correctly, but at least
> we can keep it wound, so that it will not forget.* (Walking on Wa-
> ter: Reflections on Faith & Art ([Wheaton, Ill.: Shaw Publishing]
> 1980, p. 96)

The Spirit in the sacrament of confirmation is given to us so that we
will remember who we are, learn to endure, and steadfastly grow, as Jesus did, "in wisdom, age and grace before the world" (Luke 2).

The Spirit is first of all a teacher. What do we learn from the Spirit?
The Spirit teaches that the most important thing is the struggle to be
holy. Dorothy Day wrote: "We live in a time of gigantic evil. It is hopeless

to think of combating it by any other means than that of sanctity. To think of overcoming such evil by material means, by alleviations, by changes in the social order only—all this is utterly hopeless." And what does that holiness consist in? "Common sense in religion is rare, and we are too often trying to be heroic instead of just ordinarily good and kind. . . . On the one hand, we have to change the social order in order that men might lead decent Christian lives, and on the other hand, we must remake ourselves" (*The Catholic Worker*, early 1962).

What is sanctity? Thomas Merton quotes Georges Bernanos:

> *The saints are not resigned, at least in the sense that the world thinks. If they suffer in silence those injustices which upset the mediocre, it is in order better to turn against injustice, against its face of brass, all the strength of their great souls. Angers, daughters of despair, creep and twist like worms. Prayer is, all things considered, the only form of revolt that stays standing up.*

Merton comments on these words.

> *There may be a touch of stoicism in Bernanos' wording here, but that does not matter. A little more stoic strength would not hurt us, and would not necessarily get in the way of grace.* (Conjectures of a Guilty Bystander *[New York: Doubleday] 1968, p. 165*)

Merton prays in his journal, struggling with his place and times:

> *Father, I beg you to keep me in this silence so that I may learn from it the word of your peace and the word of your mercy and the word of your gentleness to the world; and that through me perhaps your word of peace may make itself heard where it has not been possible for anyone to hear it for a long time.*
>
> *To study truth here and learn here to suffer for truth.*

✳   *Life is, or should be, nothing but a struggle to seek truth: yet what we seek is really the truth that we already possess. Truth is mine in the reality of life as it is given to me to live; yet to take life thoughtlessly, passively as it comes, is to renounce the struggle and purification which are necessary.*

I think I will have to become a Christian. (Ibid., pp. 178, 184, 348.)

The Spirit gives us the courage to become Christians. We must keep at it, endure. We must pray like the Yokut Indians in their death-song: "All my life I have been seeking, seeking, seeking." And we must learn to take the struggle lightly, and laugh at ourselves. I recall an anecdote from a short book on parables written by Bishop Anthony Bloom. The martyr Hermas is being cheered up by his guardian angel, who tells him: "Be of good cheer, Hermas. God will not abandon you before he breaks either your heart or your bones." The other translation for the word *martyr* is "witness," and the Spirit helps us to be witnesses. A card from Vatican II carried this quotation by Cardinal Suenens: "To be a witness does not consist in engaging in propaganda, not even in stirring people up, but in being a living mystery. It means to live in such a way that one's life would not make sense if God did not exist."

What are we to witness to? First—to courage and hope. The word *hope* in Hebrew means to "twist, to twine around," like strands to braid a rope. We need to tie each other together, to haul each other up out of danger, to throw each other lifelines, to give support and courage to those who need it. We need to witness to justice, encourage others to work for justice, and help victims of injustice survive with gracefulness and some joy instead of despair. Why? Because by raising Jesus from the dead, God not only brought about an invincible hope in the ultimate victory of the divine kingdom but also identified with this poor man from Nazareth, who died in godforsakenness as a condemned blasphemer and thorn in the side of the government and the religious institution. To live resisting injustice and identifying with the poor and the powerless is to shout hope and resurrection; it is to continue the mission of Jesus. The Spirit proceeds from the cross and resurrection, and the Spirit sides with the destitute, the forgotten, the lost, the spurned and alienated, those persecuted for justice's sake, the downtrodden, and those broken in spirit. It is the Spirit who continues to move in protest against injustice, sin, and the world's ways of power and contempt. This Spirit is dangerous. This Spirit is prophetic.

Abraham Heschel describes the character of the prophet:

※ *To us a single act of injustice—cheating in business, exploitation of the poor—is slight; to the prophets a disaster. To us injustice is injurious to the welfare of the people; to the prophets it's a death-blow to existence: to us, an episode, to them, a catastrophe, a threat to the world. Their breathless impatience with injustice may strike us as hysteria. . . . to the prophets even a minor injustice assumes cosmic proportions.* (The Prophets [New York: Harper & Row; Philadelphia: The Jewish Publication Society of America], 1962, p. 4)

Elie Wiesel makes the link among prophets, martyrs, and witnesses in our society. "A witness is a link. A link between the event and the other person who has not participated in it. A witness is a link between past and present, between man and God, between man and Man." The Spirit witnesses to Jesus. We also are told to witness to his death and resurrection. We witness for the world's sake. This witness is desperately needed. Dom Helder Camara, a former archbishop of Recife, Brazil, prays:

Come Lord. Do not smile and say you are already with us. Millions do not know you, and to us who do, What is the difference? What is the point of your presence if our lives do not alter? Change our lives, shatter our complacency. Make your word flesh of our flesh, blood of our blood and our life's purpose. Take away the quietness of a clear conscience. Press us uncomfortably. For only thus that other peace is made—your peace.

The Spirit teaches us to tell the truth. The place where everything is laid bare, exposed, and the truth that rules all other truths is told is in the cross. It is here that Christians learn that, as Emily Dickinson wrote, "power is only pain, disciplined." What is the meaning of the cross? It certainly isn't a glorification of suffering or even a way to tread on the edges of God's mysterious presence and ways among us. It is to remind us to uncrucify the earth in living persons—to take them all down from their crosses and set them free. We are to acknowledge their human dignity, care for them, embrace them, be compassionate with them. The meaning of the cross is to undo injustice, hatred, poverty, and war.

The cross is a word of judgment against our priorities, projects, and lifestyles. It is a word of hope and mercy for the poor, the powerless, and the unimportant. It sets us at odds, draws the sword of distinction more surely than any other interpretation of scripture, tradition, and spirituality. Jesus died on a garbage heap, reminiscent of Job on his dunghill. Why? There is no simple answer. What is important is that this subversive memory of Jesus is kept alive in words and in deeds. Dan Berrigan reminds those who speak out on justice and peace issues: "If you're going to get involved with justice, you'd better look good on wood!"

The Spirit urges us to speak out courageously for others, in compassion. This speaking on behalf of the truth is never easy. But Roger Schutz, the prior of Taizé, tells us what happens when people do speak.

During the darkest periods of history, quite often a small number of men and women, scattered through the world, have been able to reverse the course of historical evolutions. This was only possible because they hoped beyond all hope. What had been bound for disintegration then entered into the current of a new dynamism.

Not to speak is a sin, a crime against humanity, against the Spirit of God. Pastor Martin Niemoller of Germany reminds us of our excuses and their consequences in the world:

> In Germany they first came for the Communists and I didn't speak up because I wasn't a Communist. Then they came for the Jews, and I didn't speak up because I wasn't a Jew. Then they came for the trade unionists, and I didn't speak up because I wasn't a trade unionist. Then they came for the Catholics, and I didn't speak up because I was a Protestant. Then they came for me—and by that time no one was left to speak up.

Those who are confronted or caught in the web of injustice often have to ask themselves difficult questions and decide how to live or die. Nadezhda Mandelstam in her book *Hope Against Hope: A Memoir* recalls her terror when her husband was jailed and sent into exile. She was not to learn what happened to him for over thirty years.

> ❧ *Later I often wondered whether it is right to scream when you are being beaten and trampled underfoot. Isn't it better to face one's tormentors in a stance of satanic pride, answering them with contemptuous silence? I decided that it is better to scream. This pitiful sound, which sometimes, goodness knows how, reaches into the remotest prison cell, is a concentrated expression of the last vestiges of human dignity. It is a human's way of leaving a trace, of telling people how you lived and died. By one's screams, one asserts his right to live, sends a message to the outside world demanding help and calling for resistance. Silence is the real crime against humanity.* (Hope Against Hope: A Memoir [New York: Macmillan] 1967, pp. 42–43)

As Christians we need to learn to speak and break our silence long before it reaches such a level of anguish if we are to tell the truth, obey

the commands of Jesus and witness to the power of the cross and resurrection in the world. We need to speak out and remind the world of the
presence of the gospel of Jesus long before it reaches the brink of persecution and martyrdom.

The role of the Spirit today is protest, resistance that is nonviolent
and imaginative, and the making of peace and unity among peoples. It is
in the arena of racial differences, the political process, and getting people to face their national and religious separations and forge harmony out
of them. It is in places like the Middle East, Ireland, South America, the
ghettos of the first-world countries, and Africa. The Spirit calls us from
Native American reservations, the castes of India, and the classes of people in every country. The real prophets of the Spirit, ones who tell us the
truth, sometimes forcefully, are the real heroines and heroes of holiness.
We are church; we must learn to *conspire* together, to breathe together,
to share life together. In the words of Nikos Kazantzakis:

> ⁂   *And I strive to discover how to signal my companions . . . to*
> *say in time a simple word, a password, like conspirators, let us*
> *unite, let us hold each other tightly, let us merge our hearts, let us*
> *create for earth a brain and heart, let us give a human meaning to*
> *the superhuman struggle.*

It is this struggle in the world that saves us and brings to fruition our
baptism. Merton prays: "The world without storms and our lives without
agony would give us nothing to grow on. Make us glad for stormy
weather."

At the very beginning of the Second Vatican Council John XXIII received the diplomats in the Sistine Chapel, pointed up to Michelangelo's
scene of the Last Judgment on the ceiling, and said, "Well, gentlemen
and ladies, what will it be?" The choice still lies before us.

The Eucharist: Part I, The Choice for Shared
Bread and Solidarity

Jesus was vitally concerned with the poor, with the question of bread for the hungry. As he went about his ministry he often met great numbers of hungry people. And he fed them, four or five thousand at a time, not even counting the women and the children. But his disciples failed to see any deeper meaning in these events. For them, the bread was bread, fish was fish, something for an empty stomach that would get empty again. Nothing more. When Jesus warns the disciples to be on their guard against the leaven of the Pharisees and the yeast of Herod, all they can think of is their own scarcity of bread—one loaf. In Jesus' reply to them he sounds irritated.

> Aware of this, Jesus asked them, "Why are you talking about the loaves you are short of? Do you not see or understand? Are your minds closed? Have you eyes that don't see and ears that don't hear? And do you not remember when I broke the five loaves among five thousand? How many baskets full of leftovers did you collect?" They answered: "Twelve." "And having seven loaves for the four thousand, how many wicker baskets of leftovers did you collect?" They answered: "Seven." Then Jesus said to them: "Do you still not understand?"
>
> (MARK 8:17–21).

And of course, they don't. They must have looked at each other, embarrassed. They remembered every detail of the events but did not grasp their meaning.

Memory of the past does not necessarily help us to understand the meaning of the present; sometimes it actually gets in the way of understanding or believing. Yahweh had fed the people in Moses' time—"It is the bread that Yahweh has given you to eat" (Exod. 16:15)—and the chosen people had not understood.

C. S. Song comments on the disciples' misunderstanding of Jesus' actions.

✤ *Imprisonment in the memory of the past causes a chain reaction. It leads to this: "blindness" is "deafness" is "hardness of heart" is "misunderstanding." The disciples were blind and deaf to the deeper meaning of Jesus' feeding five thousand and four thousand persons: namely, that God loves and cares about these hungry crowds. In the disciples' minds, daily bread and God's salvation could not become connected. They saw the bread distributed to the hungry, but did not see God's promise to feed the hungry realized by their ministration. They heard the excitement of the hungry gathering around the food, but they did not hear Jesus' good news for them. To see God's promise fulfilled in others, to hear Jesus' good news for them, the disciples needed "the seeing-hearing-understanding heart." But they were not to have this kind of heart until the dark night of the cross was over and the bright morning of the resurrection had dawned.* (Tell Us Our Names: Story Theology from an Asian Perspective, [Mary Knoll, NY: Orvis], 1984, pp. 41–42)

It is often poets and singers who make the connections between symbol and theology, between food and God.

Those who struggle to worship in spirit and in truth while living lives of hope and meaning often see the connections among worship, food, and God's concern for those who hunger, whether for bread or justice. Rabindranath Tagore writes:

The Hidden God

Leave this chanting and singing and telling of beads.
Whom do you worship in this lonely dark corner of the temple
    with all the doors shut?
Open your eyes and see that God is not in front of you.

He is there where the farmer is tilling the hard ground and
  where the laborer is breaking stones.
He is with them in the sun and the rain and his garment is
  covered with dust.
Put off your holy cloak and like him come down on to the dusty
  soil.
Deliverance?
Where will you find deliverance?
Our master himself has joyfully taken on the bonds of creation;
  he is bound with us forever.
Come out of your meditations and leave aside the flowers and
  the incense;
What harm is there if your clothes become tattered and stained?
Meet him and stand by him in toil and in the sweat of your
  brow.

([DOSTER, BERKELEY, CALIF.: BLACK OAK BOOKS], P. TK)

Mary, the mother of Jesus, heralds the wonders of what her child will do for the earth in echoes of Hannah's (mother of Samuel) song: "He has acted with power and done wonders, and scattered the proud with their plans. He has put down the mighty from their thrones and lifted up those who are downtrodden. He has filled the hungry with good things but has sent the rich away empty" (Luke 1:51–53).

Jesus in Mark's gospel seems to echo her feelings: "Beware the leaven of the Pharisees and the yeast of Herod," he says, referring to the arrogant elite and the monarch of his day. God, not those in positions of power, is the one concerned about the poor, the hungry, the masses of people in the world.

We are human. We are always hungry. Food occupies a great deal of our thoughts and reveals much about our priorities. "Things are getting worse, please send chocolate," says a contemporary greeting card. Food and families are intimately tied together. TV commercials promote fast food restaurants, make suggestions on what to serve at a party, and tell us where to get the best deals on food. Yet it is only in a few countries that people enjoy the luxury of a wide choice of food, the reality of a supermarket. The experience of bringing foreign visitors into a first-world grocery store and watching them weep uncontrollably at the display of fresh fruit and vegetables is a sobering experience. So is the experience of bargaining for food each day in a country where prices fluctuate drastically, or standing in line for rationed staples and bread.

Food has played a huge role in the tradition of spirituality, prayer, and worship. A few quotations from various times remind us of its centrality.

✿ *I've suddenly discovered that the exploitation of men by men and undernourishment relegate luxuries like metaphysical ills to the background. Hunger is a real evil. I've been getting through a long apprenticeship to reality. I've seen children die of hunger. What does literature mean in a hungry world? Literature like morality needs to be universal. A writer has to take sides with the majority, with the hungry—otherwise he is just serving a privileged class. (Jean-Paul Sartre, 1905–1980)*

We may be misled in many ways by worldly peace. For instance—some people have all they require for their needs, besides a large sum of money shut up in their safe as well, but as they avoid mortal sin, they think they have done their duty. They enjoy their riches and give an occasional alms, never consider that their property is not their own, but that God has entrusted it to them as His stewards for the good of the poor, and that they will have to render a strict account of the time they kept it shut up in their money chests, if the poor have suffered from want on account of their hoards and delay. (St. Teresa of Avila)

You will find out that charity is a heavy burden to carry, heavier than the bowl of soup and the full basket. But you will keep your gentleness and your smile. It is not enough to give soup and bread. This the rich can do. You are the servant of the poor, always smiling and always good humored. They are your masters, terrible, sensitive and exacting masters, as you will soon see. The uglier and dirtier they will be, the more unjust and insulting, the more love you must give them. It is only for your love alone, that the poor will forgive you the bread you give them. (St. Vincent de Paul)

Bread is given to us not that we eat it alone but that others who are indigent might be participants. When we eat bread acquired unjustly, we eat not only our own bread but another's—for nothing that we have unjustly is ours. (Meister Eckhart)

You are not making a gift of your possessions to the poor person. You are handing over to him what is his. For what has been given in common for the use of all, you have arrogated to yourself. The world is given to all, and not only to the rich. (St. Ambrose)

Those who make private property of the gifts of God pretend in vain to be innocent, for in thus retaining the subsistence of the poor, they are the murderers of those who die every day for want of it. (St. Gregory the Great)

What is a man if he is not a thief who openly charges as much as he can for the goods he sells? (Gandhi)

Share everything with your brother and sister. Do not say, "It is private property." If you share what is everlasting, you should be that much more willing to share things which do not last. (Didache)

We are human. We are always hungry. Everyone is always hungry. We remind ourselves daily as we pray: "Give us this day our daily bread." This is eucharist. This is our life.

✼   *The obvious contradiction between the waste involved in the overproduction of military devices and the extent of unsatisfied vital needs is in itself an act of aggression which amounts to a crime, for even when they are not used, by their costs alone, armaments kill the poor by causing them to starve. (Pope Paul VI, speech at the United Nations)*

All these connections come from the stories of Jesus and the consequences of meaning that are the basis for our liturgical celebrations. In John's Gospel a simple story is told. It will be repeated many times throughout the Gospel and in history:

Then lifting up his eyes, Jesus saw the crowds that were coming to him and said to Philip: "Where shall we buy bread so that these people may eat?" He said this to test Philip, for he himself knew what he was going to do. Philip answered him, "Two hundred silver coins would not buy enough bread for each of them to have a piece."

Then one of the disciples spoke to Jesus. Andrew, Simon Peter's brother, said: "There is a boy here who has five barley loaves and two fish; but what good are these for so many?"

Jesus said, "Make the people sit down." There was plenty of grass there so the people, about five thousand men, sat down to rest. Jesus then took the loaves, gave thanks and distributed them to those who were seated. He did the same with the fish and gave them as much as they wanted. And when they had eaten enough, he told his disciples, "Gather up the pieces left over, that nothing may be lost."

So they gathered them up and filled twelve baskets with bread, that is with the pieces of the five barley loaves left by those who had eaten.

(JOHN 6:5–13)

It is here in John's gospel that we are told something very specific: there were five *barley* loaves and some fish. In Israel, barley is the bread of the poor; it symbolizes obduracy. The dough is heavy and requires a strong yeast before it will rise properly. There are three stories of barley in the Hebrew scriptures, all intertwining elements of stubbornness, hunger, and generosity. The first is found in Judges 7:13–14, where Gideon is threshing his grain in hiding. God is patient with stubborn, slow, and unbelieving Gideon, who after three signs of God's presence and power is told to go and overhear a dream. The dream is about a barley cake that flattens the camp of his enemies.

The second is the story of Ruth, who comes to Bethlehem ("House of Bread") at the beginning of the barley harvest and goes gleaning in the barley fields, where grain is left for the poor. There she meets her future husband, Boaz, and he gives her six measures of barley in gratitude for finding a wife in the fields of the poor.

The last story, found in Ezekiel 4:12–17, is harsh. Ezekiel prepares a special barley cake dough at the request of Yahweh, bakes it on human dung, and eats it, an exact measure each day, as the foretelling of the punishment and hunger of Jerusalem, terrible words of deprivation but a deserved punishment for their insensitivity to the poor and their unfaithfulness to God.

And Jesus, in John's Gospel, feeds the people barley loaves that belong to the hungry, the poor, his own people. He himself will become finest wheat ground for Israel's eating, his peoples' Bread of Life. Jesus' life will be forfeit in society because he aligns himself with the poor and seeks to respond to their hunger with the good news of God's presence with them in his own person, in his life and death.

We are given a memorial of Jesus' life, passion, death, and resurrection in the eucharist. At the Last Supper Jesus gives a sign, a symbol, a way of being present to us through our own identification with the poor and the suffering in solidarity with him. He shares his liberation and new life with his followers and tells them to share it with others. He shares his last meal with his friends, giving himself to them before he suffers and dies. He tells them: "I shall not eat it again until it is fulfilled in the kingdom of God" (Luke 22:16). It is fulfilled in the cross and resurrection and in the lives and belief of his friends, the church, which celebrates his life and truth until the end of time. Each Christian's first communion is meant to be celebrated along with baptism, the promise to "put on Christ." Communion, thanksgiving, sharing life, food, and hope are the gifts given to those who follow Jesus' way of having pity and compassion on the crowds of poor and needy people. The simple, central action of eucharist is the sharing of food—not only eating but sharing. Our capacity for hunger is parallel to our capacity to know compassion and to hunger and thirst for justice. Sharing reminds us and lets us experience the need of always being hungry and never satisfied. Hunger brings into focus our human dependency on other human beings. We do not live by bread alone, but we must begin with bread. The very gesture of sharing bread does more than alleviate.

The Eucharist: Part II, The Choice for Shared Bread and Solidarity

Nicolai Berdyaev has said: "Bread for others is always a spiritual question." It is always a question of love. Most of us are sure we love. In James's letter to his community he warns that there is no meaning in love for the hungry person which leaves that person hungry, love for one who is cold and without shelter that does not supply the necessary clothing, fuel, and housing. Jesus' message is good news, hope for the poor that their suffering is to be alleviated. It is to be alleviated in the kingdom, by those who follow his ways and share. As the feeding stories attest, there is always more than enough to go around when we share and when we remember to gather up what is left over so that it does not go to waste. Ministry begins with these leftovers. The community is gathered in the act of sharing.

The early Christians saw this as a reality in history and took it upon themselves to ease the hardships of the poor and excluded. This led to large-scale social change that has historically worked toward eliminating certain forms of suffering—slavery; abandonment of lepers, the sick poor, and orphans; education for women; and more. Community was expressed in concern for the poor of other churches, the concern that none should go hungry while any had wealth to share, even in collections sent from one local church to another to relieve need. The Acts of the Apostles reveals that no one should be in need and that Christian society should be structured so that the needs of all are amply taken care of without embarrassment or the need to beg. This behavior toward others is the act of doing "this in memory of me," as Jesus commanded. It often means standing in opposition to the values of the world and can put oneself and one's family at risk, even within the larger church. Our message and good news as Christians is communicated in how we relate to others, by who we are, by our lifestyle, concerns, priorities, affiliations, and by the real difference we attempt to make in any situation. In the world of despair we have bread, abundant life, and the love of our God to share.

Jesus is sometimes sung about as the "Lord of the Dance," dancing forever in the presence of God, leading us in the dance of resurrection that cannot be stopped or turned aside from its ecstasy. Eucharist teaches us to dance in trying situations, in the face of a world that has forgotten Jesus' dance of glory, and with others who have never learned to dance. The meaning of the dance, the meaning of the eucharist, is the doing of it. First, we invite others to share it with us, and only then are we able to speak about it, to theologize. The more we seek to be eucharist, as Jesus is, the more we will understand our calling as Christians. There is an ancient prayer of the church that is apropos here. It was sung and danced during the resurrection cycle of liturgies.

Grace makes the dance
I will make the music
and we shall all dance in a ring. Alleluia.

Glory to thee, Father
Glory to thee, Word
Glory to thee, Grace
Glory to thee, Spirit

Glory to thee, Holy One
Glory to thy Glory.
We praise thee, Father
We praise thee, O Light
We praise thee, in whom there is no darkness.

A lamp I am to thee, beholding me
A mirror am I to thee, perceiving me
A door I am to thee, knocking
A way I am to thee, a traveler.

Join now in my dancing
Alleluia Alleluia.

Eucharist is described by a story that was told in many immigrant communities of Irish, people who left their homeland in droves hoping for a better life, and knowing that most likely they would never return to those they left behind. Always such leaving was a desperate measure, an act of risk, a chance at freedom and dignity.

Once upon a time there was a man who agonized about taking his family to the new world. He scrimped, saved, sold, and borrowed money until he had the price of the tickets. They would have only the clothes on their backs and a few coins; nothing else was left. They would start from scratch after the long sea journey.

The night before they left, their neighbors, relations, and friends came to sing and weep and send them off. It was a party to remember during the long days and nights on board ship. As they set off the next morning, tight-lipped, faces betraying their fear and loss, they were met along the road by their neighbors again, this time with bags of bread and bits of cheese and potatoes. They were reminded that the trip was long and arduous, and this was the best gift they could give them: food. It truly was their best gift, for they would go hungry in the days to come. The family was filled with gratitude and tears. They set off with the love of their community.

Once on board ship they found themselves on the lowest deck: the grandmother, mother and six children, father, and three cousins. The father was frantic, gathering them about him and exhorting them to be careful, stay close, and not to get lost. He especially eyed one of his younger children, a boy of about six, who was forever going off to discover things. The trip dragged on, day after day. They soon ate much of the bread and cheese and even the now-moldy potatoes. The food was being doled out by the grandmother, a piece or two here, more for the younger ones. They were always hungry, dreaming and talking endlessly of what they would eat when they got to America. The last few days of the trip were the hardest. After months at sea they were tired, afraid, near starving.

Then one morning, as he did every morning, the youngest boy pleaded with his mother for something fresh and good to eat. This time, however, he kept at it, whining, pleading, begging until the mother was near her wits' end. They had those few pennies, coins saved in case of emergency when they arrived. She looked at her husband, pleading with her eyes, and finally spoke softly: "We can buy one or two oranges to share among us. Let him go and get them, and we can celebrate that we only have a few more days until we land."

The father took a few of the precious coins out of his bag. He handed them to the young boy, who by now knew every corner of the great ship, and told him to go and get two oranges up on one of the higher decks. It should only take fifteen minutes or so if he didn't tarry. So off the boy ran, bursting with expectation and thrilled with being given permission to go to the upper decks.

He was gone longer than fifteen minutes. The mother and grandmother began to worry. What could have happened to him? The father calmed them. It was a long way up the decks and perhaps he had trouble finding the fruit vendor. Half an hour went by, and both parents were frantic with worry. It was such a huge ship, and there were so many things that could happen to a youngster. After another ten minutes the father climbed to the upper decks himself, looking for his lost son. Deck after deck he searched for him, more fearful and praying more to the Virgin for his safety.

Finally, painstakingly going from room to room, he reached the top deck, which was crowded with people. At last he found his son sitting at a table in a huge sprawling dining room, eating everything in sight! He grabbed him by the collar and hauled him out of the chair, sputtering in anger. "How could you worry your mother and grandmother, frighten them so? And how can you do this, eat so much? You will destroy us. We have no money to pay for all this food." The boy sputtered, trying to talk with his mouth full. "Papa! Papa! You don't understand. The food is free. The food is ours. It came with the price of the ticket!"

Stunned, the father turned, and the steward nodded affirmatively. The young boy was sent below to bring his grandmother, mother, cousins, and brothers and sisters up to eat. They ate in silence, thankful, thinking of the past weeks of being hungry, below decks, fearful of speaking to anyone, doling out their neighbors' bread and parting gifts. The words kept thundering, pounding in their heads: *The food is free. The food is free. It came with the price of the ticket!* If only they had spoken to someone, shared their food, reached out to others. That night, below deck again, full for the first time in weeks, they promised that in their new life they would share, they would trust, they would reach out to others, they would speak to all around them and not live in fear and scarcity.

The food is free. It comes with the price of the ticket. Baptism draws us into the body of Christ where the food is free, the hope is lavish, the possibilities of sharing limitless, and there are always leftovers, more than enough to go around. The price was paid ages ago in the life, love, death, and resurrection of Jesus, shared with us all now in eucharist and in our commitment to feed the world on the bread of justice, the bread of hope, the bread of life. We feast on the word, bread, and wine of the Lord so that the world can feast on our faith, hope, and love shared freely, with great gratitude. How long it takes us to learn the basics, the simple things!

Rites: What If . . . ? Theological Options for the Near Future

What If the Word of God Were a Sacrament?

Much of our reflection has been rooted in the words of Jesus: "Do this and remember me." It is in this process of remembering that the Scriptures reveal what we as Christians are to do and who we are to become. The Scriptures provide a framework of meaning, a progression of the acts of God in history, a narrative of saving grace, a tradition of our ancestors in faith, and an account of the presence of the Spirit weaving through the lives of all. The Scriptures testify to the covenants and give us perspective on being believers in a community that belongs to God.

Our unity, our life, and the quality of our relationships together are based on our telling the story of Jesus and living it with our own words and acts in this portion of history. Our identities as believers and as church are derived from the word of God that we celebrate in the sacraments and liturgy, in our ethical decisions, in our communities, and in our personal lives. We differ from the world around us by rendering our memories in the choices we make in our communities. The Scriptures tell us who we are: sinners, forgiven and forgiving. We are the children of God, intimate with the Holy, nonviolently resisting evil while bringing the kingdom of justice, lasting peace, and the possibility of mercy to the world. We are commanded to go forth with this news, to tell the stories of hope that are already true because of the incarnation, crucifixion, death, and resurrection of Jesus. We conspire with the Spirit of God to draw the world into the arms of the Father. We remember what sin and evil have done and can do, and stand under the word, intent on repairing the world and atoning for all sin. The Scriptures make us people who continue to believe and to make the story come true in our own lives.

The community tells the story and becomes the story just as Jesus became the message. Ethics are prior to actions and serve as the basis for answering practical questions. What shall we do? is the core of the church's response to the message and life of Jesus as well as the individual's response to baptism. In relation to the world, Paul VI wrote in 1971:

> In the face of such widely varying situations it is difficult for us to utter a unified message and to put forward a solution which has universal validity. Such is not our ambition, nor is it our mission. It is up to the Christian communities to analyze with objectivity the situation which is proper to their own country, to shed on it the light of the Gospel's unalterable words, and to draw principles of reflection, norms of judgment and directives for action from the social teaching of the church. (*Octogesmia Adreniens*, cited in Richard Gula, *What Are They Saying About Moral Norms?*
>
> [NEW YORK: PAULIST PRESS] 1982, P. 43)

Ethical decision-making entails the community, Scripture, history, tradition, and the magisterium of the church, the witness and testimony of the prophets, and the personal conscience of the believers. We are called to be disciples, to change our hearts, and to live alternatives of hope in history, in our communities. This is fundamental to our identities. We are followers of the Way, the way of life rather than the way of death, the way of the Spirit in the world. This is what we celebrate in liturgy and in the sacraments, because this is what we practice in our lives. Without living the Way, the rites of justice, and the life of the Spirit, our liturgy and sacraments are hollow or, worse, hypocritical.

Jesus' own words vividly describe who we are and how we are to live: "I solemnly assure you, the one who has faith in me will do the works that I do, and greater far than these" (John 14:12). Our times call for a response of Spirit and grace to the crying needs of individuals and the world. We must begin with ourselves, our parishes, and our communities with the words of Jesus: Repent, reform, change your lives, bend your hearts. There is a story told of a German woman who hid Jews during the Second World War. When her friends found out what she was doing, they said: "Don't you realize that if you are discovered you yourself will be imprisoned, perhaps even executed?" The woman said evenly: "Yes, I know that." "Then why in heaven's name," they asked, "are you doing it?" And she replied simply: "Because the time is now and I am here."

The time is now and we are here—the future of the church depends on each of us, each of our communities, responding in the power of the Spirit, under the challenge of the Scripture, with the support of other communities, to the realities of our times. No less is asked of us, and no more. Our liturgy and our sacraments have within them the power and possibility for mystery, holiness, and righteousness. What we do or do not do in the immediate future will say a great deal to our children and to the earth. We must have something hopeful and freeing to say to them. We must offer ethical responses to the demands of our day. If we are to follow Jesus so that others can see and take heart, we must begin again at the beginning, as novices, new Christians, followers of the Way.

The Scriptures describe us, teach us, exhort us, reform us, announce forgiveness and good news, and reveal to us the meaning of the sacraments and liturgy.

It is not ourselves we preach, but Christ Jesus as Lord; and for Jesus' sake we became your servants. God who said: "Let the light shine out of darkness," has also made the light shine in our hearts to radiate and to make known the Glory of God, as it shines in the face of Christ.

However, we carry this treasure in vessels of clay, so that this all-surpassing power may not be seen as ours but as God's. Trials of every sort come to us, but we are not discouraged. We are left without answer, but do not despair; persecuted but not abandoned, knocked down but not crushed. We carry everywhere in our person the death of Jesus, so that the life of Jesus may also be manifested in us. For we, the living, are given up continually to death for the sake of Jesus, so that the life of Jesus may appear in our mortal existence. And as death is at work in us, life comes to you.

We have received the same spirit of faith referred to in Scripture that says: "I believed and so I spoke." We also believe and so we speak: We know that He who raised the Lord Jesus will also raise us with Jesus and bring us, with you, into his presence. Finally, everything is for your good, so that grace will come more abundantly upon you and great will be the thanksgiving for the glory of God.

(2 COR 4:5–15)

We are called to be no less than the glory of God shining on the face of Christ. We are called to celebrate in our sacraments, liturgy, behavior, persons, and communities the injunction of the prophet Micah: "Do justice, love tenderly and walk humbly with your God" (Mic. 6:8). The only way we can do this is to approach the Scriptures as reverently as the eucharist; to gather around the Word in community, to search its meaning, and to allow it to resound in our minds and in our lives. The Word is core to all the sacraments, to the celebration of the liturgy, and to our daily lives as believers.

The universal church over the last forty or more years has been drawn to the study of the Word in small groups, listening to it for conversion of heart and conversion of life, both individually and as communities of justice and mercy. Such groups are called base Christian communities, ecclesial Christian communities, and their leaders are called delegates of the Word. Perhaps the Spirit is urging the church to acknowledge the power of the Word in these communities of believers, its strength as lifeline and source of hope for Christians when it is proclaimed aloud and taken to heart together. The word of God to the poor is a sacrament that should be celebrated and honored not only in the context of the sacraments and liturgy, but as a sacrament as powerful and revelatory as the body of Christ. We break open the Word and chew on it and we break the bread of eucharist and chew on it to become in word and flesh the body of Christ for the world.

> Once upon a time a sculptor was chipping away at a huge block of marble. Two young children, a boy and a girl, watched him work for many weeks. They stood silently and were amazed when finally a magnificent lion emerged from the stone and stood towering over them. They ran to him excitedly, their eyes wide with wonder and asked: "How did you know that there was a lion hidden in that rock?"
>
> The sculptor laughed and thought to himself, How do I tell them that I had to know the lion before I knew the marble stone and what it hid? But he looked at the children and said: "I was very quiet when I first started and listened to the stone and I heard the lion roaring inside. Then I chipped away at everything that wasn't the lion and set him free!"

The Scriptures tell us of the Lion of Judah, and that we are all the lion's children, but the Word makes us remember who we are and reminds us how to roar, sets us free, and shows us how we can bring wide-eyed wonder to the world we dwell in. We must know the Word and be known by it. It must be in our mouths, in our communities, before it can be let loose in the world. It must chip away at all that is not of God and form us daily. It is the undergirding of all the sacraments and liturgy. The word of the Lord is the sacrament of the Word, Jesus; it is good news to the poor, the body of Christ. If we are to be this Word enfleshed, if it is to shine radiantly on our faces and be the source of conversion in our communities, we must celebrate it and take it to heart as food for our minds, hearts, and souls. "Remember" sends us first back into the Scriptures and then, after listening and being "re-membered," we are sent into the world to preach the Word, to be good news, and to practice the ethic of Jesus that is now incarnated in our flesh. Then when others see us, they too can remember, catching an echo and a glimpse of the Word, which is both a two-edged sword and as sweet as honey on the tongue of believers.

We end as we have begun, with the word of the Lord: You have been told, O children of the earth, what is good and what Yahweh requires of you: to do justice, to love mercy, and to walk humbly with your God.

The Liturgy: Do Justice in Word and Bread

There are, at root, five elements that are needed for liturgy. In the order of importance and meaning they are the people, the bread and wine, the Word, a collection for the poor, and a priest. Liturgy, the worship of our God, is the work of the people, our primary work all week, which culminates on Sunday when we gather. We sign ourselves with the cross and welcome one another with peace and begin by telling the stories of the presence of Jesus the Christ with us, risen and glorious, and of the great acts the Spirit continues to do in those who believe. We break open the Word and break open our lives, break open our communities in reflection, song, and exhortation. We ask for forgiveness and recommit ourselves to the word of hope, the good news, as the substance of our living alone and together. Then we stand on our words of belief in the creed and offer our words, lives, bodies and souls, hearts and dreams, communities, resources, and even our lacks and sins as gifts to be transformed and given back to us by God. Then we tell the story again, the story of what the Father has done for us in Jesus through the power of the Spirit, and we call down that Spirit on our gifts of bread and wine and our offering for the poor. We break our bread and share our wine, and we break open our lives so that God can rush in with forgiveness, peace, hope, and life. Then the doors are broken open and we rush out to be Word to others, to tell the story and let it come true in us, to be the bread, to be the wine, to be the body of Christ for a hungry, yearning world—to do justice and walk humbly with our God. We "do this and remember." We remember God, who we are, what we promised in our baptism, and God's covenant with us. We remember and make Jesus present in the community that gathers, in the Word proclaimed, in the offerings and gifts given for the needy, in the bread and wine and eucharist, which is the gift returned to us. The liturgy overflows with the presence of the risen Lord, and we seep out into the world like leaven in bread, like balm for all pain and sorrow, like abiding peace with justice, like glory's radiant reflection.

The liturgy reminds us that we are known by the stories we tell and the company we keep. The word *company* is that used to describe those who became disciples of Jesus, "going off in his company." It is a rich and dense word, with the root meaning "to break bread together," "to share and eat together." But in our society and culture it also is an economic term. We are known by those we eat with, what we do with our money, and the stories we tell that come true in our lives, relationships, and structures. This storytelling and sharing of a meal reconcile us and forgive us, heal us and strengthen us. Among those who pass the cup and the bread, and share the Word, there can be no divisions, only communion, only walking together again. We grasp hold of hope in the word of God and in the bread handed to us. We eat it, become it, and take it outside to share. It is the bread of justice that makes restitution and restores the world and our own lives, broken by sin and evil and injustice.

There are many images of eucharist. One that recurs is that of the beggar. We are all beggars in the presence of God, and so beggars are to be treated with special care and tenderness. Charles Peguy says: "Oh, if only we'd remember that before God we are all equal—begging with empty bowls." Those who went home from Jesus' feeding of the four and five thousand went home filled. The disciples picked up the leftovers. What did they do with them? Who got them? Did children, the old, the sick, and people who had never met each other before take them? Leftovers—the food of the poor.

We are the leftovers of God's feasting. We are a meal shared, bread blessed and broken, and wine drunk together, passed around. We become what we eat, and others feed on us, just as we feed on God. Liturgy is a celebration of resurrection, of the presence of the risen Lord, and a hint of God's coming in glory again. It is service, another way of washing feet, of bending before one another, of committing ourselves to the practice of the corporal works of mercy, of suffering with and for one another. It is memory—"Do this." Like the woman in the gospel, we too will be remembered for what we do for the poor, for those facing suffering and death, for God. It is thanksgiving. Eucharist means gratitude poured out, given away, yet it always is returned to us, a lifestyle of bending before God and one another because of the Incarnation and all that God does for us. It makes the story come true. It is the telling of the truth that constitutes who we are and our relationships in the Trinity and in community; it reconstitutes us in forgiveness and mercy.

The liturgy is full of words and full of stories, invitations, petitions and prayers. But it is also silence, what is between the words. Its attitudes and gestures speak volumes. Just as in John's Gospel, the Word is presented most clearly by acting it out, by Jesus presenting himself as a slave before his disciples, kneeling before them and washing their feet. Liturgy is a "feet-first" way of life. It is anonymous service, with bent head and shoulders, concentrating on the feet of others. It is giving because of others' need and our own gratitude for what has been shared so fully with us. This is our worship: doing for and with others what we would like to do for God, because God keeps doing marvelous things for us. It is the place too where God hungers for us, where Jesus reminds us how to hunger and thirst for justice. The liturgy makes community. We need others to tell the stories, to listen with, to make dreams flesh, to pass the Word on to. As Paul said, "I pass on to you exactly what I heard and was given" (1 Cor. 11:23).

The words of Jesus, these words of our tradition, remake the world and refashion us in the image of the crucified and risen One, the compassionate One, son of God, our brother. This is our family, and we feed on dreams, eat together, and become what we proclaim, so that others may come to gather with us. There is always room at the table for more, and God comes in the guise of the stranger, the poor, the outcast, the forgotten, the beggar, the prophet. The way we eat at liturgy and the way we eat daily reveal who we are and how we worship. Our liturgical ritual only extends what is already happening. When we gather, God rests with us and listens to us tell God's stories and our own, and God remembers us and puts the world back together as it was in the beginning, is becoming now, and will be forever. This is what puts flesh and blood on our bones and breathes spirit and life into us, so we can get up from the table and go forth together, sent into the world by Jesus, as the Father sent him to us, spirited, fed, at peace, and in communion.

An old story from India tells it well:

※   *Once upon a time there was a good man. He was a hunter and good at it. He fed his family, his relations, and many poor and needy people, and sometimes he sold the leftovers in the market so that he could get other things for his family. One day when he was out hunting he saw something most unusual. He came upon a fox with only two legs. He had heard of foxes like this one, and he wondered how it had managed to survive. It could barely drag itself around. How could it hunt? Was it alone? The stories told of foxes that loved their freedom so dearly that if they were caught in a steel trap they would chew their leg off to get free. He stood and watched this fox, amazed. It had chewed itself free twice and was still alive.*

As the hunter mused over the determination of the fox, he was startled to see a tiger come out of the forest into the clearing. It was dragging a half-eaten carcass of a deer. It had obviously eaten its fill and now left the carcass for the fox to eat. The hunter had never seen anything like this before in his life. Were the animals so careful of each other that they tended to the needs of the weaker and the lame? The fox ate its fill and dragged himself off, leaving the rest of the carcass for the smaller animals to finish. Nothing was wasted. The man thought about this for a long time.

Even when he went home, it weighed on his mind. He was a very religious man and was sure that God was trying to tell him something. He went back to the forest the next day and hid, looking for the fox and the tiger to see if it would happen once again. He learned over days and weeks that it did, but only as needed, only when the fox was hungry. He was sure now that God was teaching him a great wisdom and truth. He prayed and thought and finally decided that he must learn the ways of the animals, especially of the fox: how to trust a natural enemy; how to trust that God would take care of him; how to wait for another to give to him. It was very hard. It did not come easily to the man.

He stopped hunting. No longer did he bring food home to his family and relations, his neighbors and the poor. He became poorer, along with his family and others. His wife begged him to go hunting, and he looked at her sadly, knowing that he couldn't and thinking that he couldn't explain to her what he saw in the forest. She would never believe him, yet he knew from his reflection and prayer that God was teaching him. Eventually his wife and children left him so that they could find something to eat, a way to live without him. Others shied away from him, wondering what had happened to him.

He grew weaker and weaker without food and prayed earnestly to know what to do. He worked at trust and being open to what others might bring. He came close to death. At the very end an angel came to him. He was overjoyed and heartened to see this presence of light before him. The angel looked at him long and hard and said: "Why are you so stupid? Why aren't you hunting and taking care of others? You were given a vision of what you were doing and should do, that all should do. Get up and stop thinking of yourself as the fox. Remember: you are the tiger!"

The liturgy reminds us to stop thinking of ourselves as the needy ones but to see we are the tigers! It reminds us to feed the lame and lost, the suffering, those aching for freedom and a life lived with others. God provides for us with lavish gifts; the body and blood of Jesus. We, children of this God who remains with us as food, are to do the same and let others feed on us. We are all tigers for the foxes and the folk of the world. Remember! "Do this and remember me!"

From keepers of the Story: Oral Traditions in Literature

A Word about Words and Sounds

Even your silence holds a sort of prayer.

—APACHE

Earth with her thousand voices praises God.

—SAMUEL TAYLOR COLERIDGE

There is an ancient story that keeps reappearing in each age:

❊   *Once upon a time it was that Tibetan monks spent their entire lives chanting the names of the Holy One, God. They believed that, when they had finished the chanting and the naming, all would be said and done. It would be finished and earth would have reached its end time. For time begins with God's voice, God's words, and so time will end with our sounding, chanting the names of the Holy, the unspeakable: God.*

Two men, visitors to the ancient roof of the world high in the Himalayas, had heard of this theory and stopped a monk on his journey to inquire about this idea. They stood in the wind, prayer flags snapping in the stiff breeze, and asked him if this was actu-

ally what monks believed and did. He looked at them intently and in the silence they could hear the chanting, droning coming from the monastery walls. He didn't answer immediately and so, while waiting for his response, they began a discussion of the theory. Soon they were laughing at the idea, even with a hint of contempt for the very thought of it. But the chanting continued in the background and, as they spoke, the earth began to disappear, to be erased: grains of sand, soil, leaves, rocks, animals, birds, the prayer flags shredded and torn, even the clothing on the men as they spoke. The air thinned out even more, the sky emptied, the world turned in upon itself, and the shining eyes of the monk spoke softly: it is happening even now. We are reaching the end of the names, of what can be said.

It is said by old ones in every generation that the names of God are like the names of the stars. All words, all sounds spun from small atoms, from the alphabets of imagination, whether stuttering or magnificent, are expressions of the Creator. Each one is a fragile, tiny incarnation—an a-ha. The scientists claim we are made of stardust, nondescript dust mites, but together saying something spectacular and meaningful. And of course, we are not just talking about stars, or sounds, or even just about us. We are talking about the Holy, about communions and correspondences, about the universe. The ancient Hindu Scriptures (Vedas) of India tell of the generation of the material universe out of the "full void," an emptiness of infinite intelligence that makes everything out of silences and sounds, the fundamental energetic vibrations of divine thought. Only in recent years has Western science begun to catch up to this fundamental metaphysics of creation through the advances of quantum physics and mind-body medicine.

The stars are in motion. They are moveable feasts—like words, like notes in music, like us. We are all of a piece, one piece of the uni-verse, one unending piece of poetry, rhyme, rhythm and heart beat. Whether we are made of stardust and the music of the spheres or of skins stretched across frames to make drums or of quivering flesh and blood and bone, we are singing. Whether our words stick in our throats or move into our stomachs like butterflies, we are about saying something, expressing ourselves and connecting with others.

Even before there are words, sounds and silences already tell stories. Those stories lurk in everything: the creak of a rocking chair, footsteps on stairs, the breathing of our sisters or brothers in the same bed, snow falling, the gasps and moans of a fever of 105, whispers between parents, the crack of a bat and a ball thudding into a glove, the land being dug for a tree planting, the amaryllis sitting in the closet waiting to rebloom, the refusals to speak or looks that "could stop a clock." They are endless: the owl's cry before swift descent, the grasp and the kill and the mouse's pounding heart throbbing in fear before the claws close around its body. Or a comet visible for weeks as it moves—eventually out of range into the vast silence of the universe. If we were out "there" we would be dumb, mute, speechless, without words.

When I was young I was fascinated by stars. I would lay in the grass as it grew wet and damp and watch them come out. Pinpricks, tiny eye-holes where perhaps others and/or angels peered through at us here below. The first time I stood on a chair and telephone book and looked through a keyhole in the double-bolted door I was sure that was what it was like from the other side of night. I was sure there was another space-place out there beyond the stars. I longed to look back or to see earth the way it might look from there. When I first saw El Greco's pictures with their slanted perspectives and elongated objects I wondered, did he hear sound like that—stretched out, tensing the silence? For eyes are connected to ears, seeing to hearing, looking to listening.

What do our silences sound like? What are the colors of our sounds? And the sound of my own voice? Angels sing; do they hear? Do the tremors that show in our voices and so subtly reveal us to others entertain God? Some *koans* (loaded questions, usually encapsulated in one line) to play with: What is the sound of one hand clapping? What is the sound of a soul praying in agony? What is the sound of a heart beating?

What is the sound of one person contemplating sin? What is the sound of evil looming? What is the sound of hope erased? What is the sound of a child born dead? What is the sound of waking in a tomb and being summoned to resurrection and home, at last? The first sound, the sound of God creating, does it still echo in the universe and has it seeped into every stone, tree root and piece of skin?

This isn't as strange or even as imaginative as it may seem. There is an ancient tradition among the Jews that when YHWH (certain words you do not speak aloud or even write down) spoke and gave the law on Mt. Sinai, the words were heard not just by all who were present; the words have echoed down through the ages and every human being can hear them. In fact, it's impossible not to hear them.

We have our stories in the Christian tradition that are filled with underlying sounds, past words. Lazarus was in the tomb (John 11) and Jesus cried out, summoning him forth from death, from the tomb. That voice, the Word made flesh, commands even flesh that has been rotting in a tomb for four days to surge forth, fresh, with bones knit together. What did that voice sound like? Did Lazarus ever hear anything the same way again? Or we are told that John, the child of Elizabeth and Zachary, leapt in his mother's womb and danced for joy at the sound of Mary's voice already laced with the Word made flesh (Luke 1). Did John spend all his life waiting for that voice again? This God is behind all our words. We pray repeatedly, borrowing another's words: "O Lord, I am not worthy, only say the word and I shall be healed" (sprung from the story of a man seeking healing for his son). And the holy ones of our traditions tell us that in the presence of the Holy it is we who are sounded, like tuning forks, and read, entered and sung through to glory or to endless mourning.

All stories are made of words. It is surprising how many creation stories from far-flung civilizations and geographies share a fascination with words, sounds and breath as the beginning, as that from which air, light and water have sprung, as though all were the same "stuff" rearranged in different patterns. Emily Dickinson even describes the resurrection as "a strange slant of light." And "in the beginning," even according to the astronomers, was a time of light. There are about one hundred atomic elements, the "stuff" of the universe. We have twenty-six letters in our alphabet as the "stuff" that we work with and a score of sounds to accompany our matter. The mix of matter and spirit seems to issue forth in sounds and words.

The universe is expanding, we are told. In religious or theological terms, God, the maker and keeper of all creation, breathes, sighs, expands. Everything, it seems, swells like a child in a womb. And all these words are about one thing: revelation—the uncovering and unveiling of what's already there. When we talk about stars we say they shed mass (they die). The sun has a solar wind (it breathes) and stars burn out and give birth. Matter is indestructible, though never at a standstill.

A Jewish rabbi once said: God is always revealing himself to the soul, but, like sunrises and sunsets, he never repeats. Stars fall or become shooting stars and we treasure the story of the star that rose in the east to herald the birth of the newborn king of peace, the star that led astrologers on a journey to wisdom. We count stars and live with our heads in the sky (like Galileo). And yet scientists tell us that we know only about 3 percent of the stuff in the universe! That other 97 percent—ahhhhh. And storytellers, beginning with my Nana, tell me that stars don't really fall or go shooting across the sky at random: they decide! They choose death so that someone on earth can choose life and goodness and they hurl themselves across the sky, throwing their soul and life away, siding with the weak so that they may live. In scientific terms they cast off matter.

It is all about revelation, whether we are peering through telescopes and counting stars or being accosted by burning bushes on holy ground. It is we who cannot stand the intensity of such burning light, such purity. Scientifically it is hydrogen, carbon and oxygen, but the spirit hovering, moving and stirring with something like the wings of a dove or tongues of fire, reminds us that we too are the stars of the universe, made of old molecules of stardust, and we return, we live, and pass it on some-

where. Words, matter and spirit, we ourselves exist to take the veils away
from what is.

We are told:

> In the beginning, when God began to create the heavens and
> the earth, the earth had no form and was void; darkness was
> over the deep and the Spirit of God hovered over the waters.
>
> God said, "Let there be light"; and there was light. God saw
> that the light was good and he separated the light from the dark-
> ness. God called the light 'Day' and the darkness 'Night.' There
> was evening and there was morning: the first day.
>
> (GEN. 1:1–5)

Five lines and the universe is set in motion. (Notice: God *began* to
create, so it must still be happening!) But in these few lines and equally
few words there is light, history, the beginning of time, geography, naming, separation, and goodness. There is form and something now in the
void. It is all beginning.

Opening Your Mouth:
Utterance and the Unspeakable

No more words. Hear only the voice within.

—RUMI

*The rhythm of my own heart is the birth and death of all that are
alive.*

—THICH NHAT HANH

※   *Once upon a time, when the earth was still covered by great
forests, there lived in an ancient wood a simple woodcutter. He had
lived there all his life, like his father and grandfathers before him,
marking trees for the axman. He was good at his living, being care-*

ful to search out the split trees, those struck by lightning, or rotting from disease, or just broken from old age. If birds had nested in an old pine or a family of squirrels or woodmice had chosen a sagging tree for a comfortable home, he silently crossed these trees off his list. They no longer belonged to the woodcutter, but to the forest.

For years he had lived this way, every day, marking out the trees. Every day, that is, but one. One day each year he singled out the best tree in the forest and sacrificed it. From the very heart of the tree, he took the finest wood and made a musical instrument. Each year he made just one, and a different one each year. He had been doing it now for over a decade, in the tradition of his family. And all year long, he took the instrument with him into the woods at evening to play and to make music for the forest trees and creatures to hear—since they had given the best of their own in order to make the gift. He had fashioned a cello (named Hilary), a flute, an oboe, a piano, an organ, a violin—all the woodwinds. Each was more precise and purer in tone than the one he had made before.

This year, though, he just couldn't seem to find the right tree. He spent many hours looking for the tree. And, as the day approached, he grew sad. No tree would give up its heart, the heart he needed to make the music this year.

On the very eve of the great day, as he walked through the still woods, seeing the night falling softly and the sky turning slate blue, he was ready to admit that there would be no new music this year. And then—just as he was about to go home to sleep—he saw the tree, standing in the waning light, shadowing the ground. He couldn't understand it. Why hadn't he noticed it before? He walked up close to the tree and in the gathering darkness he could barely make out the outline of the young girl who slept, curled up against the trunk of the tree.

She looked so peaceful that he didn't want to wake her up, so he crossed over and sat down under an oak opposite her to wait. Time passed and he slept. Then, as the night sounds grew louder, he awoke to find her wide-eyed and watching him intently. She didn't seem surprised to see him, and it was almost as if she had been the one waiting for him, rather than the other way around. It was she who spoke first.

"I am the spirit of the wood. I have come to put a question to you, and you have until morning to give me an answer. Every year you have taken the heart of my best trees to make your music. Who are you to do such a thing? Why do you take them? What price are you willing to pay for your music and our hearts?"

Stunned, the woodsman was silent. After a while, he got up and went off to walk in his woods again, so unsure now, so troubled at the wood spirit's questioning.

All night he walked, sometimes weeping, pondering her words. "Why?" Why had he taken the wood? He had always thought it belonged to him. He had been careful to return the music to the forest and to go each evening to play for the trees.

As the light began to slide its winding way through the lines of trees, he still had no answer for the girl. His heart was raw—like the open wound a saw might make in the trunk of a tree. He understood the girl's question but still had no answer for her. All he had was his own suffering, his longing for his music in the forest, and his tears for all the trees of the past—the ones given for music and the ones that went for fires to provide warmth, or for homes to provide shelter from the night and storms.

She stood waiting for him by the tree, which was more magnificent in the sunlight than it had been in the shadows. And he spoke finally, stuttering over the words: "I took as a gift to give as a gift. I have nothing as repayment."

"Yes, you do," she spoke, almost laughing. "Your heart—it does make the most precious music, you know." And then, smiling, she handed him his ax.

As he cut the tree down he sang, knowing that his heart was no longer his, but all the wood of the forest was his, and there was *music enough for a lifetime of giving away. He knew, now, the reason for her questions, and the reason for his living, "that when you have nothing left to give, then perhaps you have begun to live with gracefulness." The day began gloriously, as it always does, and the music of his ax and a song of his heart rang through the woods like bells on a clear, bright September day. (Written for Paul, on his diaconate ordination, Sept. 1979)*

All languages begin with sounds, utterances, tones—in a word, music. Originally stories, like prayers, were sung. The breath, the air, and the spirit were intimates. Where I live in New Mexico, the state itself is referred to by the natives as "the land of enchantment." And within an hour of where I live there is a place called Enchanted Mesa. I climb it at least once or twice a year to hear the ones who dwell up there, high above the desert floor, tell the story of what happened to their ancestors in that place.

✻   *Once all the people lived on top of the mesa. It was a good life. They were safe from their enemies below and could easily guard the few steep ways up. They relied on the winds, the Spirits, for water. They lived close to the sky and in harmony with the seasons, following the old ways, the rituals, prayers, and dances that so delighted the Spirits of the place. Because it was a good life, there were some (and as time passed more and more) people who gradually fell away from the old ways. They took for granted the goodness of rain, thunder and lightning, and water, the coming of spring and winter. They neglected to pray, to be thankful, and to acknowledge what was given as gift.*

And the Great Spirit was not pleased. Warnings were given— less water, too much water, harsh winters and equally harsh summers—but few heeded the signs. One year it was worse: there were only a few old ones willing to do the dances and tell the stories and offer corn to the Great Spirit in thanksgiving for harvest and in hope of good plantings. There were not enough people to do these things with respect. That night there was a terrible storm and all the paths up to the mesa were destroyed. There was much destruction of homes and carefully preserved water. In the morning when the sun appeared, the people realized to their horror that they were trapped on top of the mesa with no way down.

The days and weeks passed. There was no rain. There was less and less food and finally no water. The people prayed. They sang. They danced, but the sky was unresponsive. It would thunder and clouds would gather and approach but no water would fall from the skies. The people cried out, pleading and moaning. In time there was only silence above, except for the sound of the Spirits singing in the night, faint echoes of a people that once was strong.

The mesa is inhabited again by families that honor the old ways and keep the steep steps up toward the sky passable. And they show visitors around their pueblo and tell the stories, emphasizing the need to remember, to sing, to pray, and to be grateful for all.

The word "enchant" means to cast a spell over, to delight, to charm greatly. It comes from the Latin, *incantare*, meaning to sing or chant magical words or sounds over, to entice within. There has always been a sense of power associated with specified verbal formulas, spoken or sung aloud, repeated, or intoned silently within. And those who could sing had power, had the presence of another—of the Spirit—within them. In the first book of Samuel we hear the story of the Spirit with David as he heals and calms Saul's tormented soul.

✻   Samuel then took the horn of oil and anointed him in his brothers' presence. From that day onwards, Yahweh's Spirit took hold of David. Then Samuel left for Ramah.

The spirit of Yahweh had left Saul and an evil spirit sent by Yahweh tormented him. Saul's servants said to him, "We know that an evil spirit sent by God is tormenting you. If you so wish, your *servants who stand before you will look for someone who can play the lyre so when the evil spirit from God comes over you, he will play and you will feel better."*

So Saul answered them, "Get someone who can play the lyre well." One of them said, "A son of Jesse, the Bethlehemite, plays very well. He is, moreover, a courageous man, intelligent and pleasant to talk with and Yahweh is with him."

So Saul sent messengers to Jesse and asked for his son David who tended the sheep. Jesse loaded an ass with bread, a wineskin and a kid and had David take all these to Saul. David then left and entered Saul's service. Saul grew very fond of David and made him his armor-bearer. Then he sent word to Jesse, saying, "Let David remain in my service for I am very pleased with him."

So, whenever the evil spirit from God overpowered Saul, David would play on the lyre and Saul would feel better for the evil spirit would leave him. (1 Sam. 16:13–23)

The Spirit of Yahweh is wedded to sound, to music. It is as if the Spirit has a voice in the body of another person, one chosen by God. This voice of God sounded in Moses' mind and heart but all the people of Israel heard it in the desert wilderness of Sinai. In Deuteronomy we are told the story of the children of Yahweh in the presence of God at Mount Horeb when God spoke to them:

✻   *"Gather the people before me that they may hear my words. Thus they will fear me as long as they live in that land and will teach these words to their children."*

Then you came nearer and stood at the foot of the mountain. It was burning in flames reaching up to heaven amid the dense fog and the dark clouds. And Yahweh spoke to you from the midst of the fire. You heard the sound of words but did not see any figure; you only heard a voice. And Yahweh spoke to you that you might know his Covenant by which he commanded you to keep his ten

commandments, which he had written on two slabs of stone.
(Deut. 4:10–13)

"You heard the sound of words but did not see any figure; you only heard a voice." That voice of God remains in the world and the people of Yahweh are exhorted continuously throughout their history to listen to that voice, to attend to it and to know its sound and timbre. To listen is a command of God to the people. The God of the Israelites is close to them, and he listens whenever they call out to him (Deut 4:7).

This voice of the Holy One reveals mercy, attentiveness, and expectation. The voice is near, waiting to be summoned, to be heard and obeyed. The Rule of St. Benedict begins with the word: *Ausculta*—listen! And St. Bernard of Clairvaux said: "If you wish to see; listen." It is said that the word *listen* can just as easily be translated as *obey*—the meanings are so close. The world of the spirit, the realm of the holy, is encountered and entered into by listening and obeying.

So, then, who are we listening to? What are we listening for? The voice of God is singular and yet it can sound through others, like Moses, or Joshua, or Miriam, or David. It can sound through the prophets who speak the voice of God entreating the people to hear, to remember and to obey again.

This voice, this Spirit of God moves; it comes and goes; it visits, stays, and leaves. One of the ancient marks of the presence of the Spirit of God with a person is found in that person's ability to sing, to make music, to tell stories which not only enchant, ease, and heal but also enthrall with warning, with power, and with destructive possibility. The voice breathes life and takes it away.

Tell Me a Story

In his book for children, *Crow and Weasel*, Barry Lopez describes the journey of two friends seeking wisdom for their people as they learn from animals and seasons and places. "Remember only this one thing," said

Badger. "The stories people tell have a way of taking care of them. If stories come to you, care for them. And learn to give them away when they are needed. Sometimes a person needs a story more than food to stay alive. That is why we put these stories in each other's memory. This is how people care for themselves." This is wisdom.

The stories in our traditions are life-lines, life-blood for people. They are a necessity of life and we must tell them. Many cultures and peoples believe that when poets, storytellers and singers (all artists) are lacking in a society, then that people is becoming extinct and beginning to act inhumanly. It is a dangerous time for a people when there are few truth tellers and proclaimers of the ancient wisdom, few left who practice the old ways of living.

There is a story told of the great rabbi Menachem Mendel of Kotzk. When his disciples asked him how he became a follower of the Hasidic movement, he was swift in answering. "There was a man in my town, an old man, and he told stories. Those stories persuaded me."

The answer surprised many of his disciples, and one said, "Oh, that man—he must have been an amazing storyteller, a great preacher and teacher or rabbi."

"No," said Rabbi Menachem, "he was a simple storyteller. But he told what he knew and I heard what I needed."

In the Jewish tradition, as well as in the Christian and other traditions, the primary prerequisite for a story, if it is to be true and to be worth telling, is that it be lived. The story is given to be transformed into an experience, into reality, into something that has power to transform people. Rabbi Carlebach says that the story is real in the moment of the telling and it strives for the "holy shiver" effect that reaches the soul. The story told and heard is another way of knowing, a mystical way of knowing. Elie Wiesel has said, "What does mysticism really mean? It means the way to attain knowledge. It's close to philosophy; except in philosophy you go horizontally while in mysticism you go vertically."

The soul has its own reality and stories take us there, into the deepest places, some of which have become blurred or misted over. Stories put us in touch with knowledge that we already know, but don't know we know, or have forgotten how to use. Words are passed on by word of mouth, from one person to another. The people are often carefully chosen, like Elijah and Elisha, Jesus and his disciples, the mullah and his followers, the shaman and her initiates, the storyteller and those who love the stories and are caught in the web. Once chosen, you realize that though you begin by listening to the word of another, eventually the stories are spun out of your very soul and being. You can't tell a story that you don't believe or that hasn't claimed you already, one that you don't practice. Ancient teachers in many traditions say that God hides in the stories; stories are where God takes refuge from the world that has become, hoping that someone will uncover and dream another more truly human world, closer to God's dreams.

The act of telling a story is a ritual. It seeks to transmit knowledge and pass on secrets of the heart and soul cherished by a community of people. It opens those who hear, who copy the stories and try to tell them, interpreting the secrets of the God that this community believes in and follows. And finally the story calls us to obey, to respond by making the story come true, through living it, through making the words take flesh in us. In the very down-to-earth words of Daniel Berrigan, "Faith is where your ass is" (not your head or your heart). It's where your words take you and where they make you stand. Each story you choose to tell defines and reveals. This is why we must choose our words with care, and our stories with even greater care. For those of us who claim to believe in the Word made flesh, our words are our truth. We will be judged on our words in practice, on how we have identified ourselves with the Word of God among us.

The story is told. After it is spoken aloud it is written down, annotated, put into other forms. Then inevitably it is interpreted, defined, codified, illustrated, put to music and shifted, sifted through other hearers and tellers. But whether it develops into a written word, a printed word, bytes on a computer, another language that crosses boundaries, cultures, religions—still, the story is in us. We are hieroglyphs, pictographs, and as the story moves through us it becomes altered, it becomes us and we become the stories we tell, the words we honor.

A closing story about the power of words, of ancient oral commands and power (all words and stories are really about power). It is called, simply, "The Druid."

She was tall and tousled and the color of dusk settled about her face and the sort of light that comes from shooting stars dwelled in her eyes. But it was her hair that caught you: the raven blue-black of night and the richness of it, flying in the evening air like the birds going home, luring you to follow her there.

She was one of the old ones, a druid, and was more at her ease among the trees than among the children of earth, for the trees were known to be kind and mild, faithful, reaching for the highest points, and there was always a soft singing hidden in their leaves.

Here in the forest places she did not want for companionship, even of her own kind, and here she was immortal, deathless and undying. She did not know fear or terror or even loneliness, for she did not know love, a weakness that belongs only to those who will someday die.

One day it came to pass that another wandered lost into the land of oak and fir and evergreen and she looked upon the shadow that followed wherever this one went. She looked and gazed again, for she had never known shadows—she cast none as she crossed the ground whether in grand sunlight or in shade. She was not bound to earth, only to time.

She knew the laws intimately. To speak with one of these, an outsider, a stranger to her own kind, was to court death, to invite all the remnants of that outer world inside her. And so she walked silently behind, but kept her distance.

The stranger was hungry. She touched the trees and ate. She was thirsty, and she looked for a stream. There she bowed low with her face to the water's edge and an image emerged. The stranger

gazed into her own eyes, eyes that were familiar reflecting back
from the stream, and she laughed aloud.

Fascinated, the druid too drew near. She had never seen her
own face—but having no shadow, she had no reflection either. She
stood forlorn and orphaned on the water's edge.

She had forgotten one of the laws—never to show herself to an
outsider. The other spoke and asked directions. What was this
place, and how could she find her way out?

The druid knew that here, now, if she did not speak, the
stranger would enter her world. Unbound by time, the stranger
would become like her, deathless and undying. But too, she would
lose her shadow and her reflection. Then she knew terror, sadness,
desire—or was it care or love? Wavering, she spoke and the
stranger disappeared before her eyes.

Bewildered, she looked around and down into the stream. She
saw her eyes like falling stars sparkling and saw too the shadow ly-
ing behind her on the ground. And then she knew . . . she had
stepped over the boundary into time: the stranger dwelled within
and the druid would die.

Always in the story is "the thing not named," the thing that is evoked piece by piece, slowly, given soul and tempting you into it, forcing you to hear, to wonder, to interpret, to decide. Willa Cather says: "Whatever is felt upon the page without being specifically named there—that, one might say, is created. It is the inexplicable presence of the thing not named, of the overtone divined by the ear but not heard by it, the verbal mood, the emotional aura of the fact of the thing or the deed, that gives high quality to the novel or the drama, as well as to the poetry itself." In more theological or religious terms it is the Midrash, the underlying truth, the inspired layers that are hinted at, that invite but do not force themselves upon us. They must be searched out, struggled with and taken to heart. It is, at root, the mystery that makes the story memorable, worth telling over and over again, and staking your life on.

Storytelling and Community

Vaclav Havel, the president of Czechoslovakia, reminded a Western audience in 1989 that any struggle for freedom and dignity must begin with the effort to reclaim and redeem the language, restoring true meanings to words corrupted by abusive regimes.

> At the beginning of everything is the word. It is a miracle to which we owe the fact that we are human. But at the same time it is a pitfall and a test, a snare and a trial. More so, perhaps, than it might appear to you who have had enormous freedom of speech, and might therefore assume that words are not so important. They are. They are important everywhere. The same word can be humble at one moment and arrogant the next . . . It is not hard to demonstrate that all the main threats confronting the world today, from atomic war and ecological disaster to a catastrophic collapse of society and civilization . . . have hidden deep within them a single root cause: the imperceptible transformation of what was originally a humble message into an arrogant one . . . Having learned from all this, we should all fight together against arrogant words and keep a weather eye out for any insidious germs of arrogance in words that are seemingly humble. Obviously this is not just a linguistic task. Responsibility for and toward words is a task which is intrinsically ethical.

In this area, oral traditions and written traditions are one. Words can be dangerous and destructive, curative and encouraging, demeaning and insulting, nurturing and wise, or stupid and murderous. It is not just the content and meaning of the words; it is also their sound, their tone, and their placement with other words. We are responsible for the words we use, the stories we pass on, the tales that make us more human or less so, that repair breaches or tear apart relationships. Just as the world came forth in a word from the Holy, our words either create or kill. There are no neutral words or stories. There are words and stories that glorify evil, war, violence, hatred, nationalism, racism, oppression, injustice, or insensitivity toward the suffering of others; such words and stories must be shunned and exiled. There are stories worth telling over and over again and stories that should never be heard or put into the air, and it is in the telling that the difference is learned. In every storyteller there is a streak of the prophet who seeks to defend and be the voice of the ones forgotten, those who are weak, infirm, old, too young to speak or without access to the dominant forms of communication. The strongest stories are those that come from below, from underneath, from those who are considered foreign or strange or different.

There is a Cheyenne story that someone once gave me. It was written on a sheet of paper and copied and passed along to me in Oklahoma by a Cherokee woman, so I do not know its source. It's short and startling. It's called "How the World Will End."

The earth is held up by a tall, tall tree trunk. This tree trunk is like a sacred dance pole. The spirits of all living creatures swirl around it in a beautiful rhythmic dance. Great Beaver is slowly gnawing at the pole. When he is displeased, he gnaws faster and the pole gets weaker.

We displease Great Beaver when we interfere with the rhythm of the dance. Great Beaver knows and gnaws faster and the pole tips a little. If Great Beaver gnaws through the pole, the earth will fall.

That is why all creatures, especially people, must keep the earth in balance.

So as not to anger Great Beaver.

A warning. A telling of an old truth. A story that catches our modern way of looking at the world and history and relationships and puts them in simple terms that can be used to alter our ways of being in the world. The story is a reminder that we have to remember the ancient truths if we are all going to live together and have a world to pass onto our children and our children's children.

The stories of indigenous peoples, Afro-Americans and many in the Americas and around the world are intent on keeping earth and sky, birds, fish, two-leggeds and four-leggeds in harmony, caring for each other and working together so that all can live as the Creator meant us to live, in peace, growing old like great trees left standing in old-growth forests.

To end, two very young stories that hopefully speak the same truth, first about earth's creatures, and then about humankind. The first is called "A Secret of the Trees." It was the first story I ever wrote, sitting up against a tree and watching the trees opposite me, in a soft rain shower in western Louisiana. I swear the trees told me the story and I wrote it on a piece of scratch paper I had in my pocket, word for word as it appears. I have never changed a thing, but knew I had to honor the gift as given on that spring day more than twenty years ago.

✻   *Once, in the days following the very beginnings of all things, there lived a tree. It was old as trees go—piney, well-lined and scarred from time and heat and random blows from skies handing out rain and lightning touches.*

Each year the tree made its meaning, ritually shedding its needles till a thick bed covered its feet and softened its stretching out into the space about it a few fingers at a time. It looked like all the other trees in the mild wood—except for one small thing. In the insides of the tree lived a fox.

Now, foxes usually live in hollow places in the ground. But when the tree was young it had been hit by another tree falling and had a good piece of its insides laid bare. It had taken years to cover over the hole and the tree had felt bad about its emptiness. It was always afraid of someday being cut off from the ground.

But the fox had discovered the hole one day and for some reason always returned to just that hole in that tree, and eventually he had moved in. He had been there so long that the tree had come to believe that it was natural for other creatures to live in one's hollow empty spaces.

More and more, with time, the tree wondered what the fox would do for a home when the tree fell due to the weakness of its internal structure. Before that came to pass, the tree decided it had to find a home for its houseguest the fox.

Now there was a tree that lived next door. It was a thin, fragile tree, that turned only light green in spring and nearly died each summer. It wasn't suited to housing anyone. It could hardly stand up by itself. But the trees had been close for years and one day the pine tree shared its concern over the fox's home with its thin friend.

Now the tree was thin, but it was young (as trees go) and it was still growing quickly. It hit upon an idea. Why don't I just shift a bit and start growing among your roots, right up alongside your old scar. It will strengthen your base, and still leave the fox a place to live in for a long time to come. And I might even live awhile longer myself, since I don't do too well alone when the seasons change and my thin covering begins to crack and tremble.

So, it was agreed. The young tree crept over and the old tree learned to accommodate its nearness to its insides, and the fox was happy too. In fact, all the other trees were so impressed at the strength and length of time the trees lasted together after that, that ever since then, if you walk in a forest—any forest—you will notice that all the roots run together and the trees fall over each other, living so closely that if one needs to bend or lean, there's another near enough to hold it up. And, if you listen, you'll hear in the silent woods the secret of the trees that stand against time: Leaning can make you live forever and your weakest places can be someone else's home.

Opening Your Mouth and Coming True

The word is carried on the welcoming wind of breath, sigh, song, silence, and articulation that creates as powerfully as it did at the moment of creation. The voice is in reality more permanent than the written word, for it is the voice that brings the story to life, using the power of the moment, the presence of the listeners, and the need that draws us together to hear.

There are precise and demanding rules of telling, but it is the voice's imagination and skill that carry the Spirit's message and intent, as God comes sounding through us. Each human being is the best gift, the best story each can tell, the only response to God's sigh and breath pouring into us and bringing us to life. We hasten the coming of Truth, the fulfillment of the promises spoken and clung to and of the dreams sketched on scrolls whenever we take a deep breath and begin: "Once upon a time . . ." Inherent in that beginning is the prayer and fervent blessing: "May you come true and may there be life everlasting where all creation lives happily ever after. Amen."

Jon Sobrino once said there are two kinds of people in the world: the ones who take life for granted and the ones who don't. Crucifixion is the image, he continued, of those who can't take life for granted. Perhaps there are only two kinds of people who tell stories: those who take words for granted and those who can't or won't because they believe and proclaim that The Word dwells among us. They believe that we stand on our words and, in a world where there is so much that is an affront to life, they pledge to resist, to brace themselves with stories and sign themselves, crossing word and flesh again and again, responding amen to every story told that nurtures truth and life in the world.

If God rests on the Sabbath to listen to our stories, then perhaps heaven is nothing more than the place and the time where all the stories are told. They are sung, honored, and delighted in so that their truth echoes throughout the universe, and is woven in and out of the stars— perhaps.

The stories must make us look at and face all the ragged edges of life as well as attend to the details of loveliness, for the truth embraces both sides of the hand. Long ago, I wrote the next two stories.

✻   *I knew a man once. No one seemed to remember his name. He had just always been there. He sold balloons on a street corner in Washington, D.C., mostly at night. In the snow and rain and on windy days he stood there under his splotches of color, holding onto them, keeping them close to the earth. He didn't talk much and never asked you if you wanted one. He just stood there like he was reminding you of something even he couldn't remember well enough to put into words. Tall and black, white-haired and alone, the man belonged on that corner. During the day when he was of-ten absent, the corner looked bleak and empty—crying out for his presence and his colors. The corner lived only at night. You weren't aware of it until there was nothing there to look at or to look for when you passed by.*

   And now, the man comes no more to the corner. Someone said he died over the holidays. But when I come to the corner, he's still there. I remember. I see and know he still waits for someone to buy his balloons. And I wonder if there's any place that my presence fills up and makes whole, or whether I move so fast that there is no space that is touched so intimately and thoroughly by me that it is truly mine. And you—where's your space?

Years later I still remember and wonder about such things. Some-times it is a small piece of reality standing out starkly that arrests atten-tion and becomes a kernel of truth that becomes a question, then a story that questions. Other times it arrives in a dream, in a phrase overheard, or in thoughts that drift through while one is attending to something that is gloriously mundane. Out of myriad of sunbeams and dust motes, a few become shafts of insight and memory.

❧   *Once upon a time I dreamed. In my dream I came to a planet of darkness. It didn't look like earth. It was full of music and laughter like chimes and air that carried echoes in the background all around me, a background of shadows and immense stars.*

Two children, a boy and a girl, were playing. Their arms, hands, legs, feet, all the skin of their bodies was etched and streaked with traces and intricate patterns of light that made them move like dancers, will-o-the-wisps in the twilight. They were playing—with stars and streaks of light. I watched, half-hidden, fascinated and wanting so desperately to play. They threw, faster and faster: the shafts and orbs and stars multiplying.

Unknowingly I stepped out. Great laughter. I was included in the game. Quick, in both directions, light, fire, delight. Then I dropped one, a lightning bolt, and it went right through my foot and pinned me to the ground. Incredible pain, terror, horror. They ran to me. "Forgive us. We are sorry. We forgot you were of earth." They took out the light and a scar formed white and silvery where it had entered my foot.

A realization: All those traces on their bodies, scars of light.

I spoke, "You are all so scarred."

"Yes. When we were young we dropped the stars a lot and couldn't hold onto the light. It's better now, reflexive, more natural."

"When you were young?" I asked. "How old are you?"

They laughed so easily, completely, freely. "We are only apprentices," they said, "That is all we can tell you about us. But we can share with you these three truths: Angels recognize the children of light from their scars. Stars don't fall, they are thrown in delight. And remember, light is always more powerful and dangerous than the dark, though light loves the dark. Remember."

I awoke, expecting to see a scar, a trace of light where I had dropped a flash of lightning on my foot. There was nothing, unless you looked really closely. Now the stars are my friends. And I re-

member and wonder . . . every time a star falls, lightning flashes, a
scar on skin is noticed, a light falls on a face in a certain way . . .

Much later, I realized that my first gift from an Indian tribe had been a lightning bracelet, a gift for storytelling, the symbol of tellers in that native tradition. Since then, I have always wondered.

In the end, our stories must do so much more than give meaning, or hope or enduring grace in the face of life and death. They must make community, make amends, redeem and endear every human face to us. They must make us true and turn our bodies into quickened flesh that begins to tremble with resurrection even now in the midst of the tearing of severed hearts. Our stories must heed the Presence that hides in every breath, in every word and sound and silence, waiting to be found out and brought home. Our stories must ask the ancient question once again: Do you believe? We answer and so we tell stories, all our stories, saying simply "Yes!"

From Blessings and Woes: The Beatitudes and the Sermon on the Plain in the Gospel of Luke

Blessings

A blessing is the visible, perceptible, effective proximity of God. A blessing demands to be passed on—it communicates itself to other people. To be blessed is to be oneself a blessing.

—DIETRICH BONHOEFFER

In the musical *Fiddler on the Roof*, the Russian Jewish peasant Tevya sings of life—glorious, hard, demanding, ordinary life—using the image of the fiddler dancing and playing on the steep roof of a village house. He must remember to keep his balance, to keep playing and, of course, to remember the tune. It isn't easy, but sometimes the music carries and lifts him. He is something to behold, this fiddler on the roof, this Jew in the world. And in the course of the song, Tevea sings a blessing on his family, on his neighbors, even on the tsar—that the tsar be kept far away from the village! It is a moment of laughter in a serious presentation of life, a lighthearted prayer in the midst of beseeching the Holy One's blessings on the world, on the Jews, and on all that rubs shoulders with them, good and not-so-good. And his prayer too is a blessing: a blessing of God, a giving thanks for life and all that life entails, both what is easily grasped as worthwhile and what is harder to take hold of with gratitude.

Many of the ancient Jewish psalms begin with this image of blessing, of being blessed, and of praising someone who is a blessing. Psalm 34 (33) begins with such exaltation:

> *I will bless the Lord all my days;*
> *his praise will be ever on my lips.*
> *My soul makes its boast in the Lord;*
> *let the lowly hear and rejoice.*
> *Oh, let us magnify the Lord,*
> *together let us glorify his name!*
> *I sought the Lord, and he answered me;*
> *from all my fears he delivered me.*
> *They who look to him are radiant with joy,*
> *their faces never clouded with shame.*

(PS. 34:1–6)

This psalm and so many others sing of relationship and of the intimate care and high expectations of one who is blessed by God and so blesses in return. The source of the blessings overflows and the one who receives gives back from the plentitude.

This sense of blessing extends into many cultures. The Celtic Isles are rich with blessings: for travelers, friends, the dead, guests, cows, the hearth, the coming of dawn and dusk, the stars, one's family, just about everything and everyone. Here is one that I have heard and received often on greeting cards and even had sung to me after a few pints in a pub:

An Irish Blessing

May you have many friends
And may they be as mature in taste and health
and color

and sought after
as the contents of this glass.
May you have warm words on a cold evening
A full moon on a dark night
And the road downhill all the way to your door.
May every hair on your head turn into a candle
To light your way to heaven,
And may God and his Holy Mother
Take the harm of the years away from you.
And may you have no frost on your spuds
no worms on your cabbage.
May your goat give plenty of milk
And if you should buy a donkey
Please, God, she be pregnant!

Again, the blessing mixes the frivolous and the near irreverent with the sublime and the pure, drawing heaven and earth close and magnifying the simple graces of life alongside the eternal hopes of hereafter. I have no goat, nor need of a donkey, pregnant or otherwise, but the sentiments are clear enough. May my life be amply rich and blessed with excess of what really makes for a life—a blessing.

A blessing: a beatitude, a prayer, a cry of joy, a description of reality present and to be fervently expected, an expression of life that at its fullest is a startling reminder of eternity, an acknowledgment of innate goodness and well-being, an affirmation that draws us into a charmed and intimate circle of people, the telling of a truth that honors our deepest realities. Even Jesus is blessed in such a manner. In the very first chapter of Mark we are told the story:

At that time Jesus came from Nazareth, a town of Galilee, and was baptized by John in the Jordan. And the moment he came up out of the water, Heaven opened before him and he saw the Spirit coming down on him like a dove. And these words were heard from Heaven, "You are my Son, the Beloved, the One I have chosen."

(MARK 1:9–11)

Many other translations say: "This is my Beloved, on whom my favor rests." It is clear that this is a blessing, a testimony to love and to an existing relationship, an affirmation of belonging, the telling of a deep-seated truth that reveals the essence and meaning of who this person really is.

The word blessing comes from the Latin root word *benedicere,* to speak well of, but this means more than just a compliment or a kind-hearted word. It points back to the source, to the ultimate goodness of the one who made us and keeps us all in existence, re-creating us moment to moment, keeping us in mind and heart. In our tradition, that takes us back to Genesis, to the stories of our beginnings and the meaning encapsulated in God's words repeated at the end of each day's work: "God saw all that he had made, and it was very good" (Gen. 1:31). It is also expressed in the favor of God that Mary knew in the announcement of Gabriel and that Jesus heard from the mouth of God: "You are my Beloved, on you my favor rests." This is a blessing, a speaking well of, a delight in, a pronouncement of goodness.

Blessing is almost second nature to many of us. Every liturgy, many prayers, and times of departing from family and friends end with the simple, profound words "I bless you in the name of the Father, and of the Son, and of the Holy Spirit." We trace or have had traced and etched upon us the sign of the cross, the marking of the presence and blessing of God upon our lives, our bodies, and our journeys. We pass on the blessing, and we carry with us the holiness and care of God, the love of others, and the remembrance of who we most truly are. The blessing tells the truth about us and we bend to it deep within. It is a gesture and prayer that respects our natures, our essences, and what we are to become as creations of the Holy One.

There is an Islamic story told of Hazrati Ali, a close friend and companion of Muhammad. He was a Sufi, one of the friends of God, intimate with the Beloved and with those who followed the path of ecstatic love of God. It is a custom among the Sufi to kiss the tea glass from which they drink and the hem of garments in which they dance, to show respect as often and as graciously as they can to all creation.

✿   *Once upon a time Hazrati Ali's friend Muhammad was about to begin the prayers. He was anxiously looking about for his friend Ali, who hadn't yet come. It was very unlike his friend to be late, so devoted to the prayers as he was. Muhammad fidgeted about but then knew he must start.*

Just then, the Angel Gabriel appeared and held him back, asking him to wait just a little bit longer—his friend would soon arrive. Ali, who had been hurrying to get to the mosque on time had fallen in behind an old Jewish man, moving very slowly, crippled and bent. Out of respect for the old man, Ali did not want to pass him up on the street. And Allah, the Most Compassionate One, did not want Ali to miss the first blessing and prostration of the day, so he sent the Archangel Gabriel to delay the beginning of the prayers.

This short story is full of blessings: Ali blessing the old man whom he followed in respect and humility, the first prayers and prostrations of the day, and the coming of the angel on behalf of another's soul, acknowledging that one blessing is rewarded by another, and another, and another. There are, it seems, no limits to blessings.

Blessed Are the Poor for the
Kingdom of God Is Theirs

Abundance is seeking the beggars and the poor, just as beauty seeks a mirror. Beggars, then, are the mirrors of God's abundance, and they that are with God are united with Absolute Abundance.

—RUMI

"Blessed are you who are poor, the kingdom of God is yours." These words are staggering for modern North Americans and residents of many countries of the world. In many of the workshops and retreats that served as the foundation for this book, getting past this one line was nearly impossible. The reactions of revulsion, anger, and outright rejection were often overwhelming, and ended up short-circuiting any further look at the rest of the Beatitudes. Sometimes the whole weekend retreat dealt with understanding the resistance this one sentence evoked. However, when this line is pronounced in poor areas of the countries I visit, the reaction is different. First there is disbelief. Then quickly, as awareness dawns, there is rejoicing and a sense of powerful hope based on God's closeness and involvement in human history and the affairs of the poor. In a sense, it almost makes being poor a bit easier to deal with, knowing and believing that God's kingdom is here now and that it can be grasped firmly in the situation of being poor, of being the *anawim*, as the poor are called in the Scriptures.

This introduction to the Beatitudes operates like a one-line parable, an upending of reality. It is like cold water in your face, or an oriental *koan* that must be pondered and struggled with before there can be any true understanding of experience.

Herman Hendrickx, in his superb book on the Beatitudes, *The Sermon on the Mount: Studies in the Synoptic Gospels* (London: Geoffrey Chapman, 1984) puts the first beatitude in the context of the kingdom of God.

The kingdom of God means, then, to be with and to identify with people, especially the threatened, the oppressed and the downtrodden; to give life to those who have none; to remove all oppressive relationships of one person over another, or one nation over another, to bring them to mutual solidarity; to liberate people from any kind of fear; not to condemn people, not to nail them to their sinful past or negative experiences, but to give them in all circumstances a new future, and hope that brings life; to love people without distinction, without selection, without limits; to oppose what is untrue, what is no longer relevant and has no future, a legalistic mentality which overlooks the actual person and promotes only uninspired conformity, and prayer that is not in spirit and truth but mere routine. In short, Jesus' words and deeds reveal the kingdom of God as God's rule concerned with the radical well-being and humaneness of man.

(INTRODUCTION, PP. 2–3)

The Beatitudes are indispensable to the faith of the Christian community and, at the same time, they are a sword thrust straight to our hearts. The words and concepts are so strange to our cultures and sensitivities and fears. No matter how many times we hear or read or meditate on these words, they leave us uneasy, for they reveal a God whose concerns do not mirror ours and a world that is out of sync with the Holy Mystery. They do not put our minds and souls at ease. However, they are linchpins for the kingdom of God, this kingdom that has been promised since the beginning of our religious history to one day become a vibrant reality that will transform the world. We believe that the kingdom arrived with the birth, life, and death of Jesus and that, since the resurrection, the kingdom is wherever Jesus is found. The Son of Justice lights the way of the kingdom as it spreads out across the earth like the rays of the sun. The kingdom is about internal attitudes (be-attitudes), but it is just as surely about economics, politics, and social relations. It is about history redeemed and it is found first in the poor of the earth, the poor who seem to be everywhere.

This first beatitude and the last (the fourth in Luke) are both in the present tense, while the others are in the future, the not-yet-a-reality tense, and perhaps that is the real source of the tension. The kingdom of God is present in a group of people, masses of human beings that are "stark reminder of our failures. They are a model of faith for us. They call us to look radically at our priorities. And they are vivid signs of the times for us. Here are two questions for those who would be disciples of Jesus: Living as we do under the pervading and domineering influence of our secular and materialistic societies, can we still read such signs of the times? And if so, are we willing to do something about them?" (Donald McQuade, M.M., in " 'Anawim'—Beloved of God," *America*, May 11, 1996)

These people, the unnamed and faceless and forgotten of the world, pose living questions to us, as they always have. In Israel's history the poor, the *anawim*, were touchstones of faith. The quality of liturgy, faith, and life in the community was revealed in the way the poor, the widow, the orphan, the illegal alien, and the stranger were treated. When lack of care for these people reached a critical point then the prophets were sent to hound the people, to help them remember that the Holy One had led them out of bondage and slavery, giving them the law on Sinai so that no one in Israel would ever know indignity and suffering again. As God's people the Israelites were to reveal to the nations that God is a God of life and freedom and hope for all, especially those the world wishes to forget. All the prophets cried out against the basic inhumanity of people who ignored their neighbor's need or worse, made a profit off the suffering of others, all the while proclaiming to honor and worship God. Amos spoke to his people about the God who defends the rights of the poor because no one else will, but the words apply to every country and every generation of people.

> ✵   *Hear this, you who trample on the needy to do away with the weak of the land. You who say, "When will the new moon or the*

sabbath feast be over that we may open the store and sell our grain? Let us lower the measure and raise the price; let us cheat and tamper with the scales, and even sell the refuse with the whole grain. We will buy up the poor for money and the needy for a pair of sandals."

Yahweh, the pride of Jacob, has sworn by himself, "I shall never forget their deeds." (Amos 8:4–7)

Not only does God never forget the deeds of injustice, but God remembers the poor, those who have been cast aside and dishonored, as God and his law have been cast aside and dishonored. If God truly exists and is in relationship with human beings, then what transpires on earth has ramifications in heaven. We coexist both with God and with one another, and the two are inseparable. By the time the prophet speaks, God is thundering at our callousness and cruelty, our ability to ignore and disdain the pain of others. God is a comfort and a security only to those who live with integrity; to use God as a comfort when practicing injustice is an insolence and insult to God. As Abraham Heschel (1907–1972) said: "God is a challenge, an incessant demand. God is compassion, not compromise; justice though not inclemency. The prophet's predictions can always be proven wrong by a change in man's conduct, but never the certainty that God is full of compassion" (*The Prophets: An Introduction,* Vol. 1 [New York: Harper Collins], 1962).

The poor are all those without power, without influence, without rights, those falling through the cracks in society. The poor are welfare recipients and immigrants, all those who are blamed for the economic problems of the day. They are the victims and casualties of violence, those caught in political cross-fires, made homeless, landless, nationless. Afterwards they are caught in the web of economic injustices that result from war, racial and ethnic hatreds, and religious conflict. They are those who must rely on God's providence and care, for *we* have abandoned them. They must trust God because they know from experience that they cannot trust us, even those of us who call ourselves faithful believers in

God, the God who became human and dwells among us in flesh and blood. And the poor, those blessed in the Scriptures, hardly know that blessing consciously. More often they are completely unaware of being beloved of God.

I am always struck by a simple devastating memory when I bless the food I am about to eat. One day a couple of years ago when I was on vacation in southern Mexico near the Chiapas border I had spent the morning with some youngsters talking about the rebels and church, about Bishop Ru.z and the gospel for the following Sunday. I bought lunch for a half dozen of these street urchins, as most people would call them, and one of them said grace. It was a direct hit: God is great. God is good. God lives in this neighborhood. I have never forgotten that experience, and when I eat in so many places around the world, I wonder: does God live so clearly in this neighborhood, in my neighborhood?

Blessed Are You Who Are Hungry Now

The kingdom of heaven is possessed by the poor and it is in the presence of the poor themselves that the kingdom is most accessible and most easily recognized and entered. Among the poor, the kingdom is there for the taking! Those who mourn will find comfort and the oil of gladness, for God delights in his people. Isaiah again offers consolation:

> No more will the sun give you light by day,
> nor the moon shine on you by night.
> For Yahweh will be your everlasting light
> and your God will be your glory.
> No more will your sun go down,
> never will your moon wane,
> For Yahweh will be your everlasting light,
> and your days of mourning will come to an end.
> Your people will be upright;
> forever they will possess the land—

they the shoot of my planting,
the work of my hand—
in them I shall be glorified.
The least of them will become a clan,
the smallest a mighty nation.
I, Yahweh, will do this,
swiftly, in due time.

(ISA. 60:19–22)

Consolation is an act of God, begun in the presence of Jesus among us and extended by all who believe in him, in their relationships and work with the poor and those who mourn, who do without and are in need. Simone Weil wrote: "Human beings are so made that the ones who do the crushing feel nothing; it is the person crushed who feels what is happening. Unless one has placed oneself on the side of the oppressed, to feel with them, one cannot understand." The suffering of the world is undeniable and religion is never to be a source of insulation from this suffering. In fact, true religion that ties and binds us all together in the presence of God makes us ever more aware of suffering and opens our hearts to the heart of the world. Real religion and faith, along with true worship and prayer, make us able to feel the world's suffering and other peoples' pain—even the pain of strangers and enemies—without being drowned by it or crushed by its power. Jesus taught us to see that being servants of the poor, the sick, those who mourn, those who are hungry makes us more human and holy and transforms us into the image of God. To live is to uncrucify, to alleviate others' sufferings, to bear one another's burdens, and to be a refuge for those who are in pain. Those who suffer because of injustice and others' sin and evil teach us what perhaps can be called prophetic mourning, in solidarity with them, raging against what is and should not be, was never meant to be.

Our mourning, our prophetic rage must propel us into movement, into action on a personal level and as communities of believers. So much poverty, so much suffering, so much exploitation, so much evil and sin, personal and communal, cannot be abided. We, as Christians, have no choice but to revolt, to subvert any order that tolerates this situation, let alone encourages it or makes profit from it and increases it. What this prophetic mourning cries out is: the poor must come first. Those who suffer must be listened to first and attended to first. The priorities of the hungry, the sick, those dying because of violence, injustice, disasters brought on by economic exploitation and pollution of the earth and those caught in the vise of greed and avarice come first. Óscar Romero once preached on this option for the poor, this over-riding demand that the poor be listened to, now! He compared it to a fire in an apartment building. A crowd is watching. People are pointing at the people in the windows, talking and discussing, even asking if anyone has called the fire department and rescue squads and then someone yells: your sister is trapped in there! Or, your child is in there! And suddenly all theory and conversation ends abruptly. You move. You have to. It is imperative, even if all you can do is organize people into a water brigade, make telephone calls, or clear a space so that rescue workers can get through. The poor, the mourning, and the hungry come first. They are people who, like us, feel, hope, laugh and cry, dream and desire to live with their loved ones. There are prophets and martyrs who run into the building, searching for those trapped to rescue them, but all of us must put out the fire and root out the causes of the fires, the overcrowding in the buildings and the neglect and dismal conditions that create tinder-boxes that can be set off by a spark or even just too much sun. And we begin by listening to and watching the poor, and by being evangelized by them, opening ourselves to their ideas and dreams and coming to repentance through them and becoming their friends and servants, struggling with them.

There is a story about hunger that is fraught with mourning and yet brings tears that could be those of repentance and rejoicing at what human beings are capable of even in the face of misery and pain. It is about a photographer who watched the world through a camera lens yet never took the most arresting picture of his life.

❧   Once upon a time there was a photographer working on a book of black and white photographs of people caught in large world catastrophes and war, starvation, ethnic cleansing, and misery. He found himself in Ecuador in the late 1980s. The U.S. was pressuring the Latin American governments to pay their debts and to keep up their enormous interest payments while threatening to cut aid and investment. In response, and at the suggestion of the U.S., the government heavily taxed cooking and heating oil as a broad way to increase monies. This served to beggar an already struggling mass of people: the poor, the indigenous, and day laborers. Then the country was hit by a cholera epidemic of huge proportions. Then there were torrential rainfalls and land and mudslides that destroyed crops and brought devastation to whole villages and cities. The United Nations and Catholic Relief Services responded by bringing plane loads and truck loads of food into the devastated areas. They came with supplies of corn, soybean products, powdered milk, fruit, tortillas, rice and beans.

The photographer took up a position on a main street, crowded with refugees and people wandering about, lost, tired, injured, sick and hungry. They had lost their homes, their possessions, even, in some cases, relatives and entire families. He was struck by one young girl, about nine or ten, it was hard to tell. She was thin and scraggly, hair matted and clothes torn. She waited on line along with hundreds of others for food. The photographer noticed that while she waited patiently on line, she seemed to be looking out for three younger children huddled under a large bush that gave them some slight protection from the hot sun. Two boys, about five and seven, held between them a little girl of about three. Her attention was divided between watching them and keeping her place on the long line moving slowly toward the trucks of food.

He had been trained to see small details and developing situations. It was what made him a world-class photographer and what he noticed was dismaying: they were running out of food. The aid *workers were becoming visibly distraught and anxious because the line was endless and the supplies were not. But the young girl hadn't noticed. She only watched her charges from a distance. The photographer's heart was pounding. His cameras were slung around his neck, at the ready.*

After hours in the sun, the young girl finally got to the front of the line. All she was given was a banana. One banana. But her re-action stunned him and paralyzed him and brought him to tears. First her face lit up in a beautiful smile. She took the banana and bowed to the aid worker. Then she ran to the three children under the bushes and ever so carefully peeled the banana, split it evenly into three pieces and, almost reverently, put one piece into the palm of each child. Together they bowed their heads and said a blessing! They ate their pieces of banana, chewing slowly, while she sucked on the peel.

The photographer lost it altogether. First he wept uncontrol-lably, forgot all about his cameras and what he was there for. Then he began to question, not only himself and what he was doing and why, but also everything he took for granted and assumed the world was. He watched the girl and said later that in that moment he saw the face of God, shining. He had been given a glimpse of the king-dom of heaven in the face and actions of a poor street child rich in love, care for others, generosity, and such beauty in spite of poverty, hunger, international exploitation, the politics of greed and profit and human indifference. He never did take a picture of the young girl or her sister and brothers, if that is who they were, but her face and her smile are etched forever in his memory and his soul.

Rabbi Abraham Heschel once said: "It takes three things to attain a sense of significant being: God. A soul. A moment. And the three are al-ways there. Just to be is a blessing. Just to live is holy." And Rumi, the great Sufi mystic and poet, would tell his followers: "Look carefully around and recognize the luminosity of souls. Sit beside those who draw

you to that." We are exhorted to sit beside the poor, to sit at table with
them, to share our plenty, to walk with them and live with them and recognize the luminosity of their souls and to remember and make sure that
for all peoples just to be is a blessing. Just to live is holy.

Jesus speaks only the truth: Fortunate are you who are hungry now,
for you will be filled. Fortunate are you who weep now, for you will laugh.
Alas, if we never see the truth in so many of the poor, the hungry, and
those who weep around us. Alas, if we never realize that poverty, hunger,
and mourning are the result of oppression. All of us are sinners, but there
are some who are the sinned-against and their faces can be described as
poor, as hungry, as weeping now, because they are the oppressed and captive of the land, those to whom we are blind in our injustice. The first
three beatitudes in Luke proclaim Jubilee, a year of favor and God's
mercy, and Jesus' words come true when we hear them and put them into
practice. But it is God who is doing this marvelous work in Jesus, and until he comes again, in us. Blessed will we be if we accept the invitation
to God's kingdom now.

The Last Blessings: Other Blessings in Luke

The last separation, the final distillation of blessings and woes, comes on
the cross, with Jesus hung between two thieves. The story is familiar:

> One of the criminals hanging with Jesus insulted him, "So you
> are the Messiah? Save yourself and us as well!" But the other
> rebuked him, saying, "Have you no fear of God, you who re-
> ceived the same sentence as he did? For us it is just: this is pay-
> ment for what we have done. But this man has done nothing
> wrong." Turning to Jesus he said, "Jesus, remember me when
> you come into your kingdom." Jesus replied, "Truly you will be
> with me today in paradise."
>
> (LUKE 23:39–43)

These are the last words of blessing before Jesus hands his life over to his Father, entrusting him now with his own body and the kingdom that has been planted, in the form of a mustard seed and in hard ground, but planted nonetheless. The word is spoken and the blessing is breathed out, sighed out upon the world and cried out in the death of Jesus, the Blessing of God that will not be stilled or broken or destroyed. The sign of the cross has become our blessing, our experience of mercy and the judgment of God's justice on the world. What remains is the blossoming, the emergence of the blessing in resurrection, in freedom, and in the kingdom of God firmly planted in all those who hear the Word of God and endeavor to put it into practice. The blessings are many and strong among those who remember the Word of God and bend before everyone on earth and say: "Blessed are you," *"Namaste,"* "I greet the God in you." Blessed are you poor. Blessed are you who mourn and weep. Blessed are you who are hungry now. Blessed are you who are persecuted, rejected, ignored, and demeaned. Blessed are you who preach the Good News to the poor, who do the will of God and believe it with all your heart and soul and mind and strength. Blessed are you who have been brushed by the mercy of God in forgiveness, healing, and hope and pass on that blessing indiscriminately, kneading it into the hard bread of the world.

The blessing first rooted in the body of Mary cannot be held by the womb of the earth. It will push out from there too into the light and declare the goodness of God whose mercies are without end and must be sung of, danced with, and recognized especially in the poor and those cursed and cast off by the world. The ultimate blessing of God is Jesus' resurrection and our own. Blessed are those who believe that the Word of God that has come to us will come true.

Luke's Gospel ends with the last instructions of Jesus to go and be witnesses to the kingdom of God, to the words of the prophets and psalms and the Law that were written about Jesus. "He opened their minds to understand the Scriptures" (Luke 24:45). The word, the blessing is found in the Scriptures, in the memory of a community and in the minds and hearts of those who hear it, reflect upon it, take it to heart, and practice it. Luke ends with Jesus saying:

❧   *And he went on, "You see what was written: the Messiah had to suffer and on the third day rise from the dead. Then repentance and forgiveness in his name would be proclaimed to all the nations, beginning from Jerusalem. Now you shall be witnesses to this. And this is why I will send you what my Father promised. So remain in the city until you are invested with power from above."*

Jesus led them almost as far as Bethany; then he lifted up his hands and blessed them. And as he blessed them, he withdrew. (Luke 24:46–51)

The last blessing is just another form of the promise to send the Spirit, the Blessing of God who breathes and lives among us still. And he is blessing us still. He has only withdrawn for a while; he will return. Are we ready, we who are his servants, his faithful friends and close kin in the kingdom of his Father? Will he find us waiting, our aprons on, the fields plowed and the sheep tended? Will he find the kingdom of God among us as a shelter for all the poor who have found blessing among us, as we have found blessing in the heart of God? The kingdom of God blossoms first among the poor, then in those who serve them, defend them, and hunger for the justice of God to be a fuller reality in this world. The poor count for something with God and when they count for something with us then the blessing of God blossoms in us and the kingdom grows strong, until it comes in fullness.

In the meantime, with Mary, we can only cry out, Bless the Lord, my soul, and all that is within me, bless his Holy Name. His mercy endures forever. We have heard his Word and his Word is true. O God, may we be a blessing upon the earth. Our Father, blessed be your Name. May your kingdom come among us and be honored in those you seek out and bend before: the poor and your faithful servants. You wait on us and serve us. What can we do but turn in blessing, for so much has been given. We bend before you and sign ourselves in your power: in the name of the Father and of the Son and of the Holy Spirit. Amen. Mercy visits us from on high and seeks us out. Mercy blesses us all. Mercy sings in our midst still.

From Prophets: Words of Fire

Introduction

It's not the earthquake that controls the advent of a different life
But storms of generosity and visions of incandescent souls.
—BORIS PASTERNAK

There is a succinct story told by Jewish rabbis and teachers, this by David Wolpe, that should be kept in mind when reading this book:

> Once upon a time a man approached the rabbi who was learned and wise, saying: "Rabbi, I don't want to boast but I consider myself a devout and learned Jew. I have been through the Talmud three times in my studies!" The Rabbi smiled back at him, nodding, and said: "Admirable. Admirable. But my friend, I have a question for you. How much of the Talmud has been through you?"
>
> (*THE HEALER OF SHATTERED HEARTS A JEWISH VIEW OF GOD*
> [NEW YORK: PENGUIN], 1991, P. 100)

Prophets are difficult to talk about because they are not like us at all. They suffer terribly. They live on the outskirts. They live as strangers even to those they love most dearly. They cause dissension. They are intent on making us see the truth about ourselves, which can result in our feeling humiliated and shamed. We slink away from such a glaring eye or are enraged beyond words, thinking only how to silence that person forever.

Their styles are unique and diversified, yet they all attack with a similar intensity. They never let up until we change, or until we make a choice, or until we attack back, or until what they say comes to pass on us—or until they disappear or die. When they denounce, they go after everyone indiscriminately, but especially governments, the economy, the military, leaders, priests, other prophets, other countries. Then they turn on us as a people and on each of us as individuals—there is no escape or rationalizing. Their words sting us—as individuals and a people—into a recognition that we are the absolute worst of the lot and should know better. They remind us over and over again by their presence that their prophetic word comes out of our sin, our evil, our injustice, our collusion with systems and authority that do harm, our insensitivities, our absorption with ourselves. They lay our lives bare, down to bone, marrow, and soul. They try to break through our well-planned and smoothly functioning worlds to say that we are the problem. We're the product of our systems. We're immersed in their values. We typify the systems that grind down the majority of the world. We are self-righteous and without religious sensibility, either in relation to God or morally in relation to one another, especially those who are brutalized by our injustice and lack of concern.

Prophets don't just go after the system or the politicians or the rich and powerful—they go after us all. Either we are among the poor—those who, while money is being wasted, cry out, are hungry for food, decency, and shelter, who are caught in cycles of violence, and who suffer for lack of medicine—or we are among those who are profiting from the system and the labor and suffering of the poor. The problem is not the government or the church—it's us! And one is only a prophet when one is cast off, outside the system, hidden among the voices of the silent, the mute, and those stunned by evil. Many of us in the church today would be seen and revealed as armchair critics, whiners, individuals and groups set on bettering our own positions in society and church, who are paid for praying, teaching, going on retreats, seeking spiritual direction, theologizing, and so on, making sure the system continues to function and making sure that knowledge and information do not convert, cut to the heart, and move us out of our safe positions to stand over there—there where every word burns, where every word tells the truth, and where every word puts us further outside what is acceptable and allowable. Yet the Jewish tradition that birthed prophets as wild offspring would say that life is never so full as when you stake your life on it, even if you lose your life doing it.

The prophets ached over injustice and were torn to shreds by it. They had *no* life but God's honor—which was the only hope of the poor. They were reminders in the flesh of that honor—painful, angry truthtellers who knew what was wrong. They made people nervous, sick to their stomachs, vicious, and self-righteous. Or worse, after all the reactions, the prophets were ignored—the people didn't change, didn't convert. And then the prophets' words came to pass: the warnings, the threats, and the punishments that were the natural consequences of people's behavior came about. The prophets were, after all was said and done, people who knew the truth, who spoke it, and who effected it in their worlds. They had to speak, whether people responded to them or not. An old Zen story puts it clearly:

Once upon a time an old Buddhist monk went to the town square every day to cry out for peace with justice and for an end to hostility and anger. His cries went unheeded and unheard and had absolutely no effect on his country's war-making or his own neighbors' hatred and petty selfish lives. After awhile even his own monks were embarrassed for him and sent a delegation pleading with him to stop, saying that he was having no effect and that people thought him senile or crazy. They did not want to be associated with him anymore. They begged, pleaded, and

rationalized with him to stop. They told him, "No one cares
what you say. They don't even listen to you anymore. Everyone
in the country has gone insane with fear and war, selfishness,
greed and killing. Why go on?" His answer was given directly,
looking his own monks right in the eye: "I cry out for peace and
justice so that I will not go insane!"

This too is the prophet. The prophets' vocation is to cry out—to God,
to the air, to any open heart; they cry out on behalf of God and on behalf
of the poor because no one is listening except God. They cry out for
those no one heeds, except maybe in passing in lip service. There have
always been three kinds of prophets: the individual chosen, sent, and
compelled to speak; the scripture that is the word of God; and the poor.
In contemporary theology one of the people who made this most clear
was Ignacio Ellacuría, a theologian and prophet of El Salvador who both
lived and ministered with the poorest and was also an articulate
spokesman on human rights, a professor at a university, a Jesuit, and, in
the end, a martyred prophet. He wrote:

> Among so many signs that always exist, some calling for atten-
> tion and others barely perceptible, there is in every time one
> which is the principal one, by whose light the others should be
> discerned and interpreted. This sign is always the historically
> *crucified* people, which joins to its permanence the always dis-
> tinctive historical form of its crucifixion.
>
> ("DISCERNIER 'EL SIGNO 'DE LOSTIEMPOS,"
>
> *DIAKONIA 17* [JAN.–APRIL 1981], 57–59)

This book is about prophets, the prophets of the Jewish tradition,
and it will be quickly apparent that The Prophet, Jesus of Nazareth,
seems to be missing. In Luke's resurrection account, simply referred to
as the Emmaus story, we overhear a conversation between two disciples
running away from Jerusalem who are intercepted by Jesus, although

they do not recognize him. They describe what their exalted notions of
Jesus had been before those ideas were dashed by his bloody crucifixion
and death: "Jesus of Nazareth. He was a prophet, you know, mighty in
word and in deed before God and the people. But the chief priests and
our rulers sentenced him to death. They handed him over and he was
crucified. Yet we had hoped that he would redeem Israel" (Luke
24:19b–21). In older translations that last line read: "Oh, we had so
hoped that he would be the one who set Israel free!" And they go on, talking about what happened around the empty tomb, and then they fall
silent, in their dashed dreams and lost hopes, in their despair. And then
it is Jesus' turn. We can almost see him take a deep breath—he has had
to do this many times before, and they never hear. They do not see. They
do not listen or obey or remember. The story tells us:

> "How dull you are, how slow of understanding! You fail to be-
> lieve the message of the prophets. Is it not written that the
> Christ should suffer all this and then enter his glory?" Then
> starting with Moses and going through the prophets, he ex-
> plained to them everything in the Scripture concerning himself.
>
> (LUKE 24:25–27)

The present book, after a first chapter on the nature of a prophet,
begins with Moses and continues through all the Old Testament
prophets. It is meant to be read backwards—from where we stand now
back through the person of Jesus Christ, the prophet of Nazareth, the
crucified and risen one, back through the history of Christianity and of
Israel, our ancestor. And it's meant to be read forward—through the history of those called the chosen people of God, through those called to the
Kingdom of God, as the brothers and sisters of the prophet Jesus up
through our own day—and on into our as yet unknown futures. So in a
sense this is a book about Jesus as the word of God made flesh, the passion of God made manifest beyond anything the prophets could have
imagined, though Jesus is only mentioned by name a few times.

In conjunction with the words above of Ignacio Ellacuría, it is also a book about the crucified one, the Body of Christ, the crucified people of the world, the poor, and it should be heard and read while standing with them. Ellacuría wrote about Jesus the Christ with a vitally new and demanding perspective that I have sought to incorporate throughout this book. He turned to the figure of the Suffering Servant from Second Isaiah "on which the primitive Christian community fastened in order to understand Jesus' death." And then he argues that "this entitles us to use the image to offer a christological interpretation not only of 'the death of Jesus,' but of the 'crucified people,' " which he defines as that "vast portion of humankind which is literally and actually crucified by natural, . . . historical, and personal oppressions." Ellacuría also reminds us of the disturbing fact that the ongoing crucifixion of the poor and oppressed has been a defining aspect of "the reality of the world in which the church has existed for almost two thousand years, [literally] since Jesus announced the approach of the Reign of God" ("The Crucified People," in *Mysterium Liberations,* [Mary Knoll, New York: Orbis], 1993), pp. 592, 580–604).

In a sense, from the very beginning of time, every prophet stood at the foot of the cross, watching those crucified and crying out on their behalf; they spoke and wept and raged in its shadow. Ellacuría's good friend Jon Sobrino adds to this image of Christ what this means for the majority of the world's people and for the rest of us today: "The crucified peoples—shows us what we are; we tend to ignore it, cover it up, or distort it, because it simply terrifies us" (*The Principle of Mercy: Taking the Crucified People from the Cross* [Mary Knoll, New York: Orbis Books], 1994, p. 49). Today the prophets speak on behalf of hundreds of millions of people, rather than just a small, insignificant nation centuries before the coming of Christ. If these people are, as the theologians of the Third World call them, "the presence of the crucified in history," then all theology is radically altered by positing them at the center of reflection, of interpretation of the scriptures, and of moral responses within the parameters of worshiping as a community of believers. We are to become a single people, universally the people of God, who worship in truth and who live in justice and peace—a clarion call and a light to the nations of the sanctity of God's name for all the earth.

Today, if the poor of the world are prophets by their lives and their dying, then there are far more prophets than we have previously imagined. Leonardo Boff has written that there is a significant analogy between the innocent death of these crucified people and the martyrdom of Jesus. Just as Jesus was a martyr for the Kingdom of God, so these people are martyrs of the kingdom, prophets by their presence and their lives and their deaths. Sobrino builds on this idea, extending who these prophets and martyrs of today are to all those who "lay down their lives for love." Not only are they the outspoken ones—catechists, priests, religious community members, peasants, journalists, students, delegates of the word, doctors, and lawyers who were hunted down because of their service to the people—but the people themselves are prophets, witnesses, and martyrs to the truth:

> Finally, there are the masses who are innocently and anonymously murdered, even though they have not used any explicit form of violence, even verbal. They do not actively lay down their lives to defend the faith, or even, directly, to defend God's Kingdom. They are the peasants, children, women, and old people, above all who died slowly day after day, and die violently with incredible cruelty and totally unprotected.

> (JESUS THE LIBERATOR: A HISTORICAL-THEOLGOICAL VIEW
> [NEW YORK: ORBIS], 1993, P. 270)

These are the people who seek justice and peace for themselves and their communities—what the prophets of old cried out for as central to the worship of Yahweh, the God of those who cried out from Egypt's bondage. They struggle simply to live, and their suffering reveals the presence of Jesus who, in the tradition of the Suffering Servant, was "crushed by sin." They bear the burden of all the world's actions, and—

even if they are unaware of their religious meaning—they seek to break the hold of injustice and proclaim once again that those who seek the truth become the light to the nations. Their presence in the world reveals the lie that is the life we lead, the lie the world seeks to conceal. All theology, all spirituality, all ethics, all prayer, and all ritual must be done at the foot of the cross, at the foot of their cross, with them as prophets and with all the prophets who have gone before us in faith:

> At the hour of truth, unless we profoundly accept the truth of the crucified peoples and the fundamental responsibility of successive empires for their crucifixion, we will miss the main fact. That is, that in this world there is still enormous sin. Sin is what killed the servant—the Son of God—and sin is what continues to kill God's children. And this sin is inflicted by some upon others.
>
> (SOBRINO, *PRINCIPLE OF MERCY*, P. 53)

There are few enough individual prophets in every generation. Fortunately, the poor and the crucified of the world confront us with truth, holding up a mirror to our lives and values, our sin, and our collusion with the systems of the world that destroy other human beings as a matter of course. Their existence, their shortened lives, their sufferings, and their premature and violent deaths cry out for mercy and for people to join their struggle. The spirituality of the prophets, if you can speak of such a thing, is based on three principles: *prophecy*—the message and the honor of the name of God through justice and peace; *their presence as God's witnesses* in the world for truth and against those who disobey the word of God; and *pity*—the overflowing of compassion and mercy.

The prophets can seem harsh, unbending in their righteousness, tedious in their repetitions, and scurrilous in their denunciations, but we must remember that their words and actions are born of God's pity, God's compassion, and God's truthfulness. Their very existence is birthed in God's horror at what we do and in God's terrible dismay at our refusal to be made in the divine image—God's people of justice and peace. A story about Elijah told by Rabbi Jose (ca. 135 C.E.) reminds us poignantly of how closely God is bound through the prophets not only to Israel's existence and future but over time to all the peoples of the world:

⁂   *Once I was walking through the city of Jerusalem at the time of evening prayer. I slipped off the main street and into a side street that held ruins of the devastated city. I entered one of the ruins, leaned against a crumbling wall, and prayed, quietly chanting the old words. As I prayed I sensed the presence of another and turned to see the prophet Elijah standing close by the wall. He waited until I finished and he greeted me with peace, bowing with extended hands. I returned his greeting, wondering why he had once again come to visit me. It was he who asked the questions: "My child, what are you doing here?" I thought, wasn't it obvious that I was praying?*

I answered, "I came inside to pray."

"But why inside?" he asked. "Couldn't you pray on the streets as easily?"

"No, I was sure to be distracted, or interrupted." He looked at me intently and asked another question: "What was it like to pray among the ruins? Was there anything different than the usual? Did you hear or sense anything? Did your prayer change?"

I was surprised but remembered Elijah's role of teacher, the one who reminds and enlightens, and so I answered him truthfully. "Yes, my master and teacher, it was different. It was hard. It was lonely. It was like praying and having an echo of sorrow come back upon me. And I kept hearing something—the cry, the call, the moan of a dove, but it was not of this world. I thought it kept trying to say something to me. It too was praying."

Elijah pushed me, his hands on my shoulders: "Remember! Think! What was it saying?"

I closed my eyes and the cry came back, so full of sadness and loss: *"My children, my temple, my people, my land . . . all is broken, all is in ruins, and my children are in exile, scattered like seed on the wind among the nations. . . . My children, my children, my children . . ."*

"Yes" was the prophet's response. *"That lament, that prayer, rises three times a day from everywhere in what was God's city, God's dwelling place among the people, but so few, so few, have ears or hearts to hear."*

Woven throughout the tradition of the prophets, and of the rabbis of Israel, is the idea that God mourns, that God shares the sufferings of the people, that God is so wed to those he has chosen that his faithfulness brings him intensely close to those who suffer, even when their sin and injustice bring terrible ruin upon them. It is this God who searches out the prophets and seizes their hearts, their words, and drives them unceasingly into the midst of the people, hoping that this time the people will hear, will heed and come home to obedience and to justice, and so to peace with their God.

Interlaced in the long prophetic tradition is the move from God's concern with one people to concern for other nations and tribes, even the enemies of Israel, and then in the later prophets to all the nations, all the earth, and the promise, the hope, and the demand that Jerusalem be the city for all and that God's name be known everywhere.

We move backward and forward in time, for all is present for the Holy One. After the disciples on the road recognize Jesus the prophet, the crucified and risen one, in the breaking of the bread, they remember. They remember and exclaim to one another, "Were not our hearts filled with ardent yearning when he was talking to us on the road and explaining the Scriptures?" (Luke 24:32). Again an older translation is better, more poetic, and more to the point: "Were not our hearts burning . . . or on fire as he opened our minds to the Scriptures?"

The word of God in the Scriptures, in the mouth of a prophet, in the crucified peoples of the world, or in the person of Jesus the crucified one risen and among us, sets our hearts on fire and instills in us those seeds of fire that can be stirred into flame again and again—the flame of hope, of justice, of zeal for the honor of God, and of righteous rage against evil, insensitivity to others' pain, and the hypocrisy of religious people.

The Jewish rabbis teach that the Torah, the words of God, are "black fire written on white fire." The words of the prophets, on the page and in our covenant written on our hearts and on the faces of our brothers and sisters, are "black fire on white fire." May these words on this paper make our hearts burn as the Scriptures are opened to us and the message of the prophets echoes in our minds and ears. May we remember that these words are born in the furnace of God's heart and that these words of fire are but breaths and intimations of God's own love for all of us.

There is now one word of fire, one word, one prophet, one hope, one people, and one God. A Hindu saying repeats the theme: "Call God what you will, God's name is Truth." May this book make us all words of truth, words that honor the name of the Holy One, words that lift the burden from the poor and crucified of the earth, and words that set afire a new creation, a new century with people who "do justice, love with mercy, and walk humbly with one another and with their God of peace on earth." May it be so. Amen. Amen. Amen.

The Prophet

What in the world is a prophet? What manner of beast? Often the prophet is imaged as a ragged creature, disheveled, living in wild places, apart from humankind and civilization, fanatical in dress and behavior, threatening and uncouth in ways and words. Jewish scholar Rabbi Abraham Joshua Heschel begins *The Prophets: An Introduction* with the words: "This book is about some of the most disturbing people who have ever lived: the men whose inspiration brought the Bible into being—the men whose image is our refuge in distress, and whose voice and vision sustain our faith" ([New York: Harper and Row], 1962, ix). These men and women capture our imagination at the same time that they repulse us. There is something about them that we sense as radical, as disruptive, as too intense for more than a few moments of conversation or meeting. A short dose of their presence seems to be more than enough, thank you!

A Jewish story can perhaps bring us to the heart of what it means to be a prophet. I have seen a one-line version of this tale attributed to Rabbi Nachman in a collection of his sayings called *The Empty Chair*, but this is the way I heard it once and the way I tell it.

※   *Once upon a time there was a great rabbi who had many disciples. Parents would go hungry and endure hardships to save money so that their children could go and sit at the master teacher's feet for even a few months, or a year or two. His wisdom was very highly valued and his mere presence led to changes and transformations. One day the rabbi was working on his Torah portion, pouring over his books and praying, and the other students were gathered at another table, supposedly engaged in the same work.*

They were studying the Torah portion and doing some research, but they were also talking about what was going on in their own lives in between more serious appropriation of the text. One of them said, "I just can't concentrate. You don't know how bad my life has been. I just can't pay attention to these readings. My mother is visiting and my wife—she is fine when my mother is not around. But my mother's very presence does terrible things to my wife and my life is so bad, I just don't know what to do."

Another of the students looked up from the Torah portion and said: "You think you have troubles! I have visitors, so many of my relatives I don't know what to do. There are maybe eight or nine of them, and we are trying to feed them on what we usually have to stretch just for ourselves. I'm frantic and exhausted. I don't know what to do next."

Another chimed in before the other had barely finished with his tale of woe: "You haven't seen anything like what I'm going

*through—I have all these relatives visiting me, but they're all sick!
I don't want to leave the study house. I'm more than happy just to
stay here and study the Torah. I dread having to go home. It is so
bad."*

*Everyone had something to say about their particular troubles,
putting in their two cents. It seemed that everyone's life was bad.
Another interrupted with the words: "Bad! You haven't heard bad!
Wait until you hear my life!"*

*Suddenly, the rabbi slammed his fist down on the table, send-
ing the books scattering. He stood up and looked at his students
hard and shouted at them: "Stop! Be careful! The Almighty, the
Holy One, listens to every word you say! And he, Blessed be his
Name, has been listening to you in your conversation, and he is sitting back there thinking: 'Bad! Bad! I'll show you bad!'"*

*The rabbi went on: "But God also listens if you say: 'Morning!
Ah, blessed be the God of Heaven. God is good. Earth is good! I
heard the birds awake the morning. Life is so good!' And God
would have heard you just now if you'd said: 'My children wrapped
their arms around my legs this morning and wouldn't let me go off
to the study house! Life is good.' God would have sat back and said
quietly: 'Good! Good! Now I'll show you good!' So be careful! God
is listening to every word you say! And the future is yours!"*

The reaction to the rabbi's words is a gasp, a murmur that runs
through the group. The seemingly simple story has massive insights, insights that are devastating for believers. The story, like a prophet, affords
an insight, a momentary glimpse into the mind of God, as it were, altering reality forever after.

The story rattles attitudes we have toward life, toward church,
toward people, toward good and evil. Our attitudes have power, and God,
it seems, takes personally even our attitudes! The story posits that God,
the Holy, is intimate with each one of us, with each situation of our lives.
The creation that develops between God and us is an ongoing work. Of-

ten people don't like the story once they begin to talk about it. They derogatorily label it as "Old Testament," meaning that *our* God doesn't act like that—*our* God is interested in showing us love, not the "bad." That's the reaction until I change the words a bit and ask, What if the conversation were about politics and economics in the United States? What if God overheard our conversations about politics and money and our own self-serving ideas of justice? Mightn't God say: "You think you are one just nation under God? You think you know justice? I'll show you justice!" Do we think we know how to live the good life? "Hmmm," God might say, "so you think you understand what a good life is? Forget that and listen to me. I'll show you a good life." And suddenly, when I say these things, there is quiet in the room, a gulping kind of quiet followed by admissions of guilt, or at least a move to question our priorities and ways of living.

The story reveals that we see the world and one another the way we choose to see them, not the way God sees them. And so it hints that we might also see God the way we are and not the way God is. The prophet interrupts, intervenes, and jolts us into uncertainty or doubt and then turns and points directly at us and says: "What is wrong with the world is wrong with you!" Like the rabbi, the prophet is intent on stopping history—reality as it is—because the reality insults both human beings and God. This story is a prophetic moment that indicates what a prophet does and how it is done. This is the prophet's entire life—eating, sleeping, and drinking God's horror at what we are doing. The prophet is intent only on stopping us, if only momentarily, so that God's word can censure us, threaten us, and call us to repentance and transformation.

We have a tendency to think of a message as only words. And yet in Hebrew the term for "word" is *dabar,* which can mean word, gesture, action, presence, pattern of repetition, or liturgy. The prophet exists for one thing only—to tell God's truth, God's revelation to this people at this time. The Hebrew word for "prophet" is *navi* (in the plural, *n'vi-im*), which means "to speak for someone else." That is why the prophets' calling card, or their most often used expression to introduce a prophecy, is

"Thus says the Lord." That is why they speak in the first person, using words such as "I the Lord, your God, say this . . ."

The validation of their words is utterly simple and undeniable. Those who listen to them either change in response to their pronouncements or resist them and attempt to kill them for their words. There is no middle ground. The prophets' presence is about choice, about standing in the right place, about commitment, and about obedience to God now. Those who listen must be converted, or else. As a result, prophets are very creative at capturing attention and keeping it while denouncing offensive behaviors and intentions. Those who are not converted will persecute the prophets relentlessly and without mercy and, in many cases, drive them into exile or kill them. For the prophets, the word of God is their spirituality. It defines both their response in life and their understanding of who God is. And so it should be for all of us, for the word of God reveals who we are and who God is and what constitutes the responsibilities and promises of that relationship.

At the beginning of this century and millennium we, the people of God, seem interested in every form of spirituality except the word of God. We seem to have forgotten that most of the ancient and more traditional spiritualities, though lived in a specific historical epoch, were originally derived from the Scriptures. For instance, there is much interest in the spirituality of the medieval mystics such as Julian of Norwich. Yet Julian most likely lived sealed up in a wall of a church, studying the Scriptures, while the world outside her anchorage was living and dying through the horror of the bubonic plague. The experiences that affected her most were isolation, visitations by strangers she never saw but only heard, and the backdrop of the black death that probably wiped out more than a third of the population of Europe. Julian's words were crafted and birthed out of terrible suffering and the contemporary experience of the crucified one in the people of God still crying out the ancient psalm: "My God, my God, why have you forsaken me?"

Or, if we look at the poems of mystical love and tenderness of John of the Cross, we often forget that they were written under excruciating circumstances, as John was locked in a closet, starved to death, tortured by his own brethren, and derided for his understanding of the religious community's call to imitate the crucified one in their vows, their way of living, and their prayers. These magnificent love songs, written under awful duress, were filtered through the word of God.

The Word made flesh is the source of spirituality for believers. Our spirituality lies in the Word that is the community of the Trinity, the Word that is justice in practice, the Word that is mercy for sinners, and the Word that is transforming grace in the face of evil and sin. Our heritage is this word of the Lord in the mouths of our ancestors: Moses; Elijah and Elisha; Isaiah and the prophets of exile; John the Baptizer; and, finally, Jesus, the word of God made flesh that dwells among us now and always.

A question students often ask deals with the methodology of the prophet. And, again, the method *is* the message. The clothing that is chosen, the gestures and dramas enacted, the rituals invoked, the words and tone chosen, the appearance and disappearance of the prophet—all are the message and the method. The prophet Elijah is testimony to this reality. Every time the king of Israel catches sight of Elijah approaching, he cringes and cries out: "You disturber of Israel, what do you want now?" The Christian Community Bible's translation reads: "On seeing Elijah, Ahab said to him, 'Is it you, the plague of Israel?'" (1 Kings 18:17). The very sight of the prophet can evoke the consciousness that all is not well in the world and that it is time for a reckoning, according to God's vantage point on history. This constant presence of the prophets as carriers of the message of God is backdrop for a line attributed to Francis of Assisi. "You must preach the gospel insistently, relentlessly, without rest, but only as a last resort use words." Our words must be backed up with our actions, and our flesh and blood must be revealed in what we stand for and against, in our ethical choices and moral decisions.

It seems that prophets are usually best known for what they resist, for what they stand against. They represent God's point of view in stark contrast to all other points of view. In this we share their stance, for our second baptismal promise is phrased: "Do you promise to resist evil and refuse to be mastered by any sin?" What we resist defines us as clearly as what we profess to stand for. The prophets resist evil and sin and their effects on individuals and society—they resist with all their hearts and minds and souls and strength, as creatively and imaginatively as they can, with the inspiration of God's Spirit.

And how they resist with style and panache! In addition to being prophets, they are poets, priests, shamans, actors, clowns and fools, hermits, exiles, and critics. They can hold their own with the best of the politicians, religious leaders, sociologists, anthropologists, psychologists, and economists. They are conscious tongues of fire and sword points aimed at the heart of public and private life, intent on exposing our motivations and the disastrous effects of our lives and insensitivities on others who suffer because of us. They are embodiments of consciousness-raising who often stand against us, resisting what we have become. Their resistance offers us another vision of humanity's destiny and vocation.

The prophets often see us as nearsighted, meaning we can only see what is immediately under our noses, connected to our own lives. We have lost sight of the vision of hope, of the future that God intends, while we have been concentrating with total self-absorption on our own immediate desires. We are like drivers lost in a fog of our own obsessions, unable to see the road clearly. And so we need the prophets, the far-seeing ones, the dreamers in broad daylight, the long-distance high beams that show us glimpses of where we are going and what the outcome of our choices and lifestyles will be. One way to define a prophet is a person who sees so clearly what is happening in the present moment that he or she can tell us what is going to happen if we don't change immediately and radically.

One of the harder aspects of the prophets and their messages is that they are almost always messages in the plural, messages directed to us as members of a people, of a group, of a community, and not as singular individuals. When a prophet seeks out an individual, it is always one who has a great deal of autonomous power such as a king, a priest, or those who hold authority or power in a society, government, or institution. Otherwise, the message is directed to all, with no escape hatch. In our contemporary society this is perhaps the hardest aspect of prophecy to contend with, because we are intent on being seen and being related to primarily as individuals. When the prophet's message comes stinging home, we resist with, "Who are you to tell *me* what I'm doing or not doing? You don't know me at all," or "You don't know what I've done. . . ." And, frankly, the prophet doesn't care because the prophet sees as God sees: the prophet sees us as members of a people, of a community, of a church or organization or class, and contends with us together, not alone. In fact, if the prophet does attack an individual, it's even harder! In that case, the individual will be held accountable for the group and for his or her influence and ability to change or alter the outcome.

The prophet is a truth-teller, using the power of God to shatter the silence that surrounds injustice. Usually the very appearance of a prophet signals the end of Yahweh's patience with people and a judgment that must be brought to bear on those who have done wrong. The prophet's appearance is a signal of fire that the covenant of God has been betrayed and that we, as the people of God, have been or are unfaithful. When the prophet appears, it is time for us to be held responsible for our actions and the state of our society and community.

The Jewish tradition includes prophets of the oral word and those of the written word, many of whom are often referred to as the later prophets. One of them, Habakkuk (ca. 600 B.C.E.), models this kind of prophet:

> ✽ *Then Yahweh answered me and said,*
> *"Write down the vision, inscribe it on tables so it can be easily read, since this is a vision for an appointed time; it will not fail but will be fulfilled in due time. If it delays, wait for it, for it will come and will not be deferred." (Hab. 2:2–3)*

But always, besides the oral and written traditions, a third tradition holds precedence over the others. That is the living tradition, the person that embodies the word of God in flesh, in his or her life, and in the history of the people. These are also the prophets we will study, seeking to honor them, to incorporate them into our belief, and to pray that God sends more such prophets into the world today and that we heed the word of the Lord in their mouths. We will look at those who have gone before us in faith through the eyes and the words of Jesus, the prophet of God, the Word made flesh among us. *And* we will look forward to the vision that is presented to us now in the Word, the vision that must become true, or else all will perish from the earth.

"Would That All Yahweh's People Were Prophets!" (Numbers 11:29)

A Jewish Midrash says that when God spoke and revealed himself on Sinai there was "a miracle of God's word" and that each person who has ever lived or will live heard that voice as it echoed through the universe. But each heard it in the way they could absorb it and integrate it into their lives and world.

Many people today have trouble hearing the voice. There are, however, also many for whom the voice still permeates every fiber of their being and drives them in every season to speak out on behalf of God's glory, on behalf of their neighbors, especially those who suffer injustice at another's hand, and on behalf of the land itself. The roots of this marvelous universality of revelation are found among the stories of Moses as he prepared the people to enter the land they had sought for forty years.

One revealing story is found in the book of Numbers, chapter 11. Moses, it seems, is exhausted. The whining and complaining of the people have worn him out. Throughout the arduous escape from Egypt and the long years in the desert Moses alone has borne the responsibility of being the liaison between the rebellious people and the Holy One. When Yahweh instructs him to choose seventy older men upon whom God will confer shared authority, Moses questions God on how he will provide so many people (six hundred thousand) with meat for a whole month! God's reply is cryptic: "Is Yahweh's arm shortened? Now you will see whether or not my word is true" (Num. 11:23). The text continues:

> ✡   *Moses then went out and told the people what Yahweh had said. He assembled seventy men from among the elders and placed them round about the Tent. Yahweh came down in the cloud and spoke to him. He took some of the Spirit that was upon him and put it on the seventy elders. Now when the Spirit rested upon them, they prophesied. But this they did not do again.*
>
> *Two men had remained in the camp; the name of one was Eldad, the name of the other Medad. However, the Spirit came on them for they were among those who were registered though they had not gone out to the Tent. As they prophesied inside the camp, a young man ran and told Moses, "Eldad and Medad are prophesying in the camp." Joshua, the son of Nun, who ministered to Moses from his youth, said, "My lord Moses, stop them!"*
>
> *But Moses said to him, "Are you jealous on my behalf? Would that all Yahweh's people were prophets and that Yahweh would send his Spirit upon them!" (Num. 11:24–29)*

We are told that Moses was unique among the prophets, having walked with God and seen him face-to-face, that he was beloved by God, and that there would never be another like him. This was Moses' fervent dream for his people and for his God's honor: that all might be prophets and that the Spirit of God would rest on them all, making them zealous for justice, for obedience to the law, and devoted to the word of God.

Only two of the seventy are named, Eldad and Medad, and they did not enter into the Tent of Meeting with the rest. Jewish tradition says that they are remembered by name because they alone of the seventy were humble and asked: Why us? According to the tradition, their prophecy came immediately from God alone and was a permanent gift, while the other elders were able to prophesy only for a short time. And, according to the tradition, they were considered young men, not old ones, and of all the people the Spirit came upon that day, they alone entered the promised land.

From Moses on, there will be people touched by this Spirit of God, which is often described as the Spirit rushing upon them. Just before the people enter the promised land, Yahweh, through Moses, promises that prophets will be with them to give them access to and understanding of the will of God:

> I shall raise up a prophet from their midst, one of their broth-
> ers, who will be like you. I will put my words into his mouth and
> he will tell them all that I command. If someone does not listen
> to my words, when the prophet speaks on my behalf, I myself
> will call him to account for it. But any prophet who says in my
> name anything that I did not command, or speaks in the name
> of other gods, that prophet shall die.
>
> (DEUT. 18:18–20)

And so goes the history of Israel, interpreted through the prophets, through the word of Yahweh their God. Today, thousands of years later, this concept of the prophet can be found on every continent and in nearly every religion. This chapter will look at contemporary prophets who are still single-heartedly concerned with the worship and honor of God, with God's insistent call to justice and the care of the poorest, and now with even the ravaged earth itself. Since the beginning, the prophets have seen these three issues as one—a demanding, holistic ethic and response to the presence of the other.

The stories that follow speak a word of hope, a demand for justice, and a call to see ourselves as one, a community of diversity in which we are all one. And note carefully that the word of hope is closely linked to the warning that if we do not take this imperative to heart we will all die.

Salmon

Back in Idaho, the home of Boise Cascade, near the city of Lewiston, the Selway and Lochsa Rivers eventually merge with the Snake River, one of the largest tributaries of the Columbia River. This area was mentioned in the Lewis and Clark journals as being "crouded with salmon." The rivers are still awesomely beautiful, but they are now utterly empty of salmon. A writer in *Northern Lights,* a regional journal, tells of what we've lost:

> ✼ But the spirits are gone—the great spirits of salmon, whose bodies made this country, whose nutrients form the vascular tissue of the oldest trees in these parts, whose presence in the lives of the people who once lived here—even at this distance from the ocean—was profound beyond the reach of words. . . . [A]lways more than just food, salmon supplied spiritual nourishment as well as nutrients to the body. The regular, cyclical appearance of anadromous species in rivers and streams signaled that these fish were in touch with powers outside of human comprehension. . . . Their miraculous arrival was a mystery that required explanation, and the explanation came in the form of legends, stories and creation myths in which the shape-shifting Salmon interacted with other magical figures: Raven, Coyote, Fog Woman, Eagle, Bear. The natural, as always, possessed supernatural origins.
>
> The great abundance of salmon seemed to have a counterintuitive effect on the people who depended upon them. Rather than taking these life-giving animals for granted, humans adopted an intricate set of rituals whose existence suggested an ongoing fear that if things did not go right, these fish, no matter how numerous, would not return. In fact, it was thought, humans played an important role in bringing salmon back into the spawning country, making salmon feel welcome enough to return home. (Don Snow, "Meditation on the Kooskooske," Northern Lights [spring 2000] 3)

These creatures range over thousands of miles of coastal lands, ocean areas, and inland communities in Korea, Scotland, Ireland, and Norway; their lives are intimately connected with the tribes of the Ainu of Hokkaido Island, Japan; the Ulchi of Siberia; the Tlingit of Alaska; the Makah of Washington State's Olympic Peninsula; and many other peoples. All these ancient peoples believed that the salmon chose to return in abundance or scarcity. The salmon watched humans to see if their lives and rituals demonstrated sufficient reverence toward life and expressed harmony. These ancient groups, thus, considered the salmon "people." These groups still express their reverence for the salmon in various "ways." One of the most important "ways" is called the "First Salmon Ceremony." When the first fish is caught, all fishing stops. The fish is carefully cleaned and cooked and fed in small pieces to all the youngest children. The ceremony is meant to honor the fish and their coming and to hasten their way through the rivers to the spawning grounds. There is singing, dancing, and prayers, and a portion of the first fish is returned to the river. During these days no one is allowed to fish, thus ensuring that the first and largest run of salmon gets through to replenish stocks for the future.

Don Snow writes of what these rituals reveal of the humans involved:

> These careful rituals suggest a profound moral orientation towards the natural world. The first salmon ceremony is an encapsulation of the idea of "right action," and the affirmation of the relationship between moral behavior and good livelihood. The salmon simply would not return unless they were welcomed and treated with proper reverence. Right action involved careful observation, sacrifice, precise behavior, humility, duty, and a sense of shared destiny: as the salmon goes, so go the people. The abundant, life-giving fish were the animal representatives of an endless cycle of living. Humans participate in this cycle; they aid it along; and if they fail in their responsibilities,

then the cycle may fail, too. . . . We are finally ready to see native wisdom evolved into a sophisticated conception of reciprocal stewardship. You take care of us, and we—incompetent humans—will try our best to take care of you.

(IBID.)

But now the salmon are almost gone, not only in the American and Canadian and Alaskan Northwest but also in Scotland and many other parts of the world. We have traded them for farm-raised fish (which must be fed with an enormous amount of other wild fish), for kilowatts and turbines. Wilderness areas dwindle and are replaced by large industrial farms and sprawling developments. Snow ends his article with the question: "Is the restoration of the salmon possible without the restoration of reverence?" That is the core of the issue, the heart of the moral debate.

Salmon are now protected in the United States under the Endangered Species Act in an attempt to save some of these mythic fish. The story of the dwindling supplies of salmon worldwide is symptomatic of a crisis: the seas are running out of fish. As is the case with trees and logging, oil reserves and drilling, and so many other exploitable resources, the issue of food—of fish—is one of globalized arrangements between governments in the First World and Third World. It is usually the local and indigenous communities that are caught in the middle. From Senegal and Mauritania to Australia and Scotland, the story of the salmon is repeated with tuna, shrimp, snapper, whales, sharks, sea bass, swordfish, marlins, and cod.

The World Trade Organization often refuses to acknowledge the depletion of whole species of fish or to encourage precautionary principles to save fish stocks already in dire shortage. Or, as protesters have written on their signs: "Corporations have always relied on governments to conduct their fishy business." Terms of trade, unfortunately, rule even the seas as industries desperately look for more and more fish stocks. Perhaps we must become impolite diners and protest how our fish is caught, where it comes from, and how healthy it is, let alone become more involved with regulation of fishing. The four largest "fishmongers" in the business are Mitsui, Mitsubishi, Marubeni, and Heinz (this last includes StarKist, John West, Petit Navire, and Greenseas). Seventy percent of the planet's marine stocks are fully exploited or overexploited already. (Website: www.newint.org)

Rice

India—along with many other countries, such as Pakistan, Indonesia, Malaysia, Singapore, China, and Japan—lives on rice. "The" rice of rice is the basmati, one among more than a hundred thousand varieties of rice evolved by Indian farmers. It is the women who are the "seedkeepers and seed breeders" and who begin every planting season with prayers and dances. They then offer the diverse seeds to the village deity and share the seeds among their neighbors. It is the annual festival of Akti, which binds together the rice, the land, the water canals, the water buffaloes, and the people. *Akti* means "survival," but it also has the same meaning as "religion"—to bind or tie together.

The rice-consuming parts of the world are very disturbed by a new development in large corporations called seed patenting. Vandana Shiva, of the Research Foundation for Science, Technology, and Ecology in New Delhi, writes:

> *The basmati rice which farmers in my valley have been growing for centuries is today being claimed as "an instant invention of a novel rice line" by a U.S. corporation called RiceTec. The "neem," which our mothers and grandmothers have used for centuries as a pesticide and fungicide, has been patented for these uses by W. R. Grace, another U.S. corporation.*
>
> *. . . Intellectual property rights on seeds are, however, criminalizing this duty to the earth and each other by making seed saving and seed exchange illegal. The attempt to prevent farmers from saving seed is not just being made through new IPR [International Property Rights] laws, it is also being made through the new ge-*

netic engineering technologies. Delta and Pine Land (now owned by Monsanto) and the USDA have established a new partnership through a jointly held patent [for seed] which has been genetically engineered to ensure that it does not germinate on harvest, thus forcing farmers to buy seed at each planting season.

When we sow seed, we pray, "May this seed be exhaustless." Monsanto and the USDA on the other hand are stating, "Let this seed be terminated, that our profits and monopoly be exhaustless."

There can be no partnership between this terminator logic which destroys nature's renewability and regeneration and the commitment to continuity of life held by women farmers of the Third World. (Cited in "Women and Terminator Technology," Witness [March 2000], 28.)

Women and Trees

Another modern-day prophet is Wangari Maatthai of Kenya. The first woman to receive a doctorate in Kenya, she has chosen to walk a remarkably prophetic path:

Invest in the millennium. Plant sequoias.
Say that your main crop is the forest
that you did not plant,
that you will not live to harvest.
Say that the leaves are harvested
when they have rotted into the mold.
Call that profit. Prophesy such returns.
Put your faith in the two inches of humus
that will build under the trees
every thousand years. . . .
Practice resurrection.

(WENDELL BERRY, "MANIFESTO: THE MAD FARMER LIBERATION FRONT," IN *THE COUNTRY OF MARRIAGE* [NEW YORK: HARCOURT BRACE JOVANOVICH1], 1975)

In the end, the last word belongs to God. It appears in the last chapter of Revelation, the last book of the Bible. It is God's intent, God's dream, God's will, and God's design that we are invited, called, and begged to share in making this come true:

✵   *Then he showed me the river of life, clear as crystal, gushing from the throne of God and of the Lamb. In the middle of the city, on both sides of the river, are the trees of life producing fruit twelve times, once each month, the leaves of which are for the healing of the nations.*

No longer will there be a curse; the throne of God and of the Lamb will be in the City and God's servants will live in his presence. They will see his face and his name will be on their foreheads. There will be no more night. They will not need the light of lamp or sun for God himself will be their light and they will reign forever.

Then the angel said to me, "These words are sure and true; the Lord God who inspires the prophets has sent his angel to show his servants what must happen soon."

"I am coming soon! [Blessed] are those who keep the prophetic words of this book." (Rev. 22:1–7)

The words of these contemporary prophets may not sear and burn our souls, but what they say is poetry, promise, and dire warning—whether couched in mystical, theological, even scientific language. They witness to the truth in word, in deed, in association with the poor, and in the call for religion to be practiced with justice and compassion. Their words echo and fall into the rich tradition of the Word made flesh who pitched his tent among us and remained.

We end with the words of a prophet who simply responded to the cries of his own people in their struggle for justice, life, and dignity and who was murdered for speaking that truth in a violent world:

The prophetic mission is the duty of God's people. So when I am told, in a mocking tone, that I think I am a prophet, I reply, "God be praised! You ought to be one too." For every Christian must develop a prophetic awareness of God's mission in the world and bring to that world a divine presence that makes demands and rejections. (Óscar Romero, quoted in *Mary Knoll Magazine*

[NOVEMBER 2000], 27)

And so we pray: O God, whose name is Justice, Truth, and Mercy, raise up truth-tellers, prophets, and voices that resound throughout the earth with your own cry for compassion on behalf of all those who seek to live with human dignity. May your Words sing through the flesh of those you call forth and send out to declare your presence among us— insisting that we live together in peace with justice—or else! For your truth will prevail among us. May that day be soon. Amen. Amen. Amen.

She taught for a while, but then began to focus on the actions of the corrupt government, particularly in its alliance with American industries to clear-cut much of Kenya and overwhelm the people with "cash" crops instead of food crops . . . —all of which caused massive soil erosion and even more hunger and poverty. Wangari is one of the wonderful rare folks who doesn't know you can't do the impossible. She hit upon a plan to encourage Kenyan women to plant trees. By now, she has 80,000 women involved in a very strong organization called the Green Belt Movement and together they have planted 20 million trees throughout the land on private property. They are now taking on the government itself. Wangari was herself a candidate for the Kenyan election in 2000 that re-elected the current president Moi. She is also a nominee for the Nobel Peace Prize.

(E-MAIL REPORT BY WES VEATCH OF

WHIDBEY INSTITUTE, WHIDBEY ISLAND, WASH.)

Kenyan politicians operate on the premise that all public land belongs to the government (rather than the people), and in addition to making it available to foreign industries, they are using it as gifts to buy personal power and prestige. Wangari and her women (and others) oppose such actions. Jailed, beaten, and greatly maligned, Wangari is an extraordinarily strong, gracious, gentle woman with an awesome perspective. (whidbeyinstitute.org)

The long history of alliances between women and trees tells a story that is both dangerous and life-giving. In India in 1730 a young woman, Amrita Devi, founded what was called the Chipko Movement. From a small village in Rajasthan, she and other women tried to prevent the Maharaja of Jodhpur's soldiers from cutting down the trees surrounding her village by wrapping their arms around the tree trunks. The word "Chipko" actually means "tree-hugging." She and 363 women from her village of Bhishnoi were cut to ribbons. A children's book that tells the story does a terrible disservice to her and the movement, which is very strong in India today, because it tells a story that ends "happily ever after." A small note at the end mentions that Amrita Devi and the others were chopped up along with the trees they sought to protect. In a recent visit to India I read and encountered many women's accounts of their participation in this group and their involvement across the entire Himalayan region.

These intertwining issues of trees, water, land, salmon, rice, and other food staples are contemporary moral issues that are being addressed by contemporary prophets. It is striking that these same issues were known and addressed early on in Christianity, even as early as the fourth century, as is shown in this passage from St. Ambrose:

Why do the injuries of nature delight you? The world has been created for all, while you rich are trying to keep it for yourselves. Not merely the possession of the earth, but the very sky, air and the sea are claimed for the use of the rich few. . . . Not from your own do you bestow on the poor man, but you make return

from what is his. For what has been given as common for the
use of all, you appropriate for yourself alone. The earth belongs
to all, not to the rich.

(DE NABUTHE JEZRAELITA 3, 11)

From the beginning, Yahweh, the prophets of old, and early followers of Christianity reiterated the intimate connections between rich and
poor, people and land, faithfulness and freedom, prosperity for all and
reverence and gratitude to the creator. They foretold the ultimate destruction of all when there was no faithful response in rightful living
among people. Today we are even more all of a piece, and the calls to justice today link us all. Earth, air, water, food, and all that is created are
seamlessly bound into one patchwork quilt. Because it is all of a piece,
it will also unravel together. The prophets' cries today are no different
than those in the centuries before Christ. They are perhaps more com-
plex and intricate, delicate and interwoven, but the sin, the injustice, and
the evils are still the same: arrogance, ego, violence, disregard and disdain for creation (including human beings), racism, and nationalism.

The Other Side, a prophetic monthly magazine, usually includes a
short report called "Short Takes." Here are two announcements that
could have come from the prophets of the Hebrew Scriptures: "240,000
people could be fed for a year with the food Americans waste each day,"
and "The U.N. estimates that universal access to basic education,
healthcare, food and clean water would cost an additional 40 billion per
year—less than 4 percent of the combined wealth of the world's 225
richest people." People cause these injustices that befall the victims, including the earth and all its creatures. But, as Thomas Merton writes,
"Courage comes and goes. Hold on for the next supply." The supply
comes in people like those mentioned above and in all who follow in the
footsteps of the prophets.